UNCANNY X-MEN

QUARANTINE

Writers: **MATT FRACTION** & **KIERON GILLEN**
Pencils: **GREG LAND**
with **PAUL RENAUD** (Issue #534)
Inks: **JAY LEISTEN**
with **PAUL RENAUD** (Issue #534)
Colors: **JUSTIN PONSOR**
Letterer: **VIRTUAL CALLIGRAPHY'S JOE CARAMAGNA**
Cover Art: **GREG LAND** & **JUSTIN PONSOR**
Assistant Editors: **JAKE THOMAS** & **JORDAN D. WHITE**
Associate Editor: **DANIEL KETCHUM**
Editor: **NICK LOWE**

Collection Editor: Jennifer Grünwald • Editorial Assistants: James Emmett & Joe Hochstein
Assistant Editors: Alex Starbuck & Nelson Ribeiro • Editor, Special Projects: Mark D. Beazley
Senior Editor, Special Projects: Jeff Youngquist • Senior Vice President of Sales: David Gabriel
SVP of Brand Planning & Communications: Michael Pasciullo

Editor in Chief: Axel Alonso • Chief Creative Officer: Joe Quesada
Publisher: Dan Buckley • Executive Producer: Alan Fine

CANNY X-MEN: QUARANTINE. Contains material originally published in magazine form as UNCANNY X-MEN #530-534. First printing 2011. ISBN# 978-0-7851-5225-5. Published by MARVEL WORLDWIDE, INC., a
ɔsidiary of MARVEL ENTERTAINMENT, LLC. OFFICE OF PUBLICATION: 135 West 50th Street, New York, NY 10020. Copyright © 2010 and 2011 Marvel Characters, Inc. All rights reserved. $16.99 per copy in the U.S. and
8.50 in Canada (GST #R127032852); Canadian Agreement #40668537. All characters featured in this issue and the distinctive names and likenesses thereof, and all related indicia are trademarks of Marvel Characters,
. No similarity between any of the names, characters, persons, and/or institutions in this magazine with those of any living or dead person or institution is intended, and any such similarity which may exist is purely
ncidental. **Printed in the U.S.A.** ALAN FINE, EVP - Office of the President, Marvel Worldwide, Inc. and EVP & CMO Marvel Characters B.V.; DAN BUCKLEY, Publisher & President - Print, Animation & Digital Divisions;
E QUESADA, Chief Creative Officer; JIM SOKOLOWSKI, Chief Operating Officer; DAVID BOGART, SVP of Business Affairs & Talent Management; TOM BREVOORT, SVP of Publishing; C.B. CEBULSKI, SVP of Creator &
ntent Development; DAVID GABRIEL, SVP of Publishing Sales & Circulation; MICHAEL PASCIULLO, SVP of Brand Planning & Communications; JIM O'KEEFE, VP of Operations & Logistics; DAN CARR, Executive Director
Publishing Technology; JUSTIN F. GABRIE, Director of Publishing & Editorial Operations; SUSAN CRESPI, Editorial Operations Manager; ALEX MORALES, Publishing Operations Manager; STAN LEE, Chairman Emeritus.
information regarding advertising in Marvel Comics or on Marvel.com, please contact John Dokes, SVP Integrated Sales and Marketing, at jdokes@marvel.com. For Marvel subscription inquiries, please call 800-217-
58. **Manufactured between 5/12/2011 and 5/31/2011 by QUAD/GRAPHICS, DUBUQUE, IA, USA.**

9 8 7 6 5 4 3 2 1

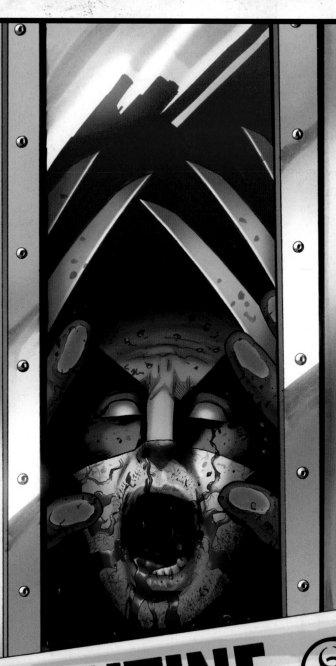

#530

DANGER

KEEP OUT

QUARANTINE

LAND
J-PO

PREVIOUSLY...

HAVING RECENTLY DEFEATED AN ARMY OF NIMROD SENTINELS, THE X-MEN ARE ONLY JUST RECOVERING FROM ONE OF THE LARGEST ATTACKS THEY'VE EVER FACED WHEN THEY ARE BOMBARDED BY ONE OF THE SMALLEST — A DANGEROUS FLU VIRUS THAT IS RUNNING RAMPANT THROUGH THE MUTANT POPULATION OF UTOPIA. AS THOSE ON UTOPIA FIGHT THE VIRUS, A SELF-REPLICATING MUTANT ARRIVES IN SAN FRANCISCO WITH DESIGNS ON THE CITY BY THE BAY.

MEANWHILE, EMMA FROST HEADS TOWARDS PARTS UNKNOWN IN E.V.A., HAVING BROUGHT KITTY PRYDE AND FANTOMEX IN ON A SCHEME OF HER OWN — TO GET RID OF SEBASTIAN SHAW, ONCE AND FOR ALL.

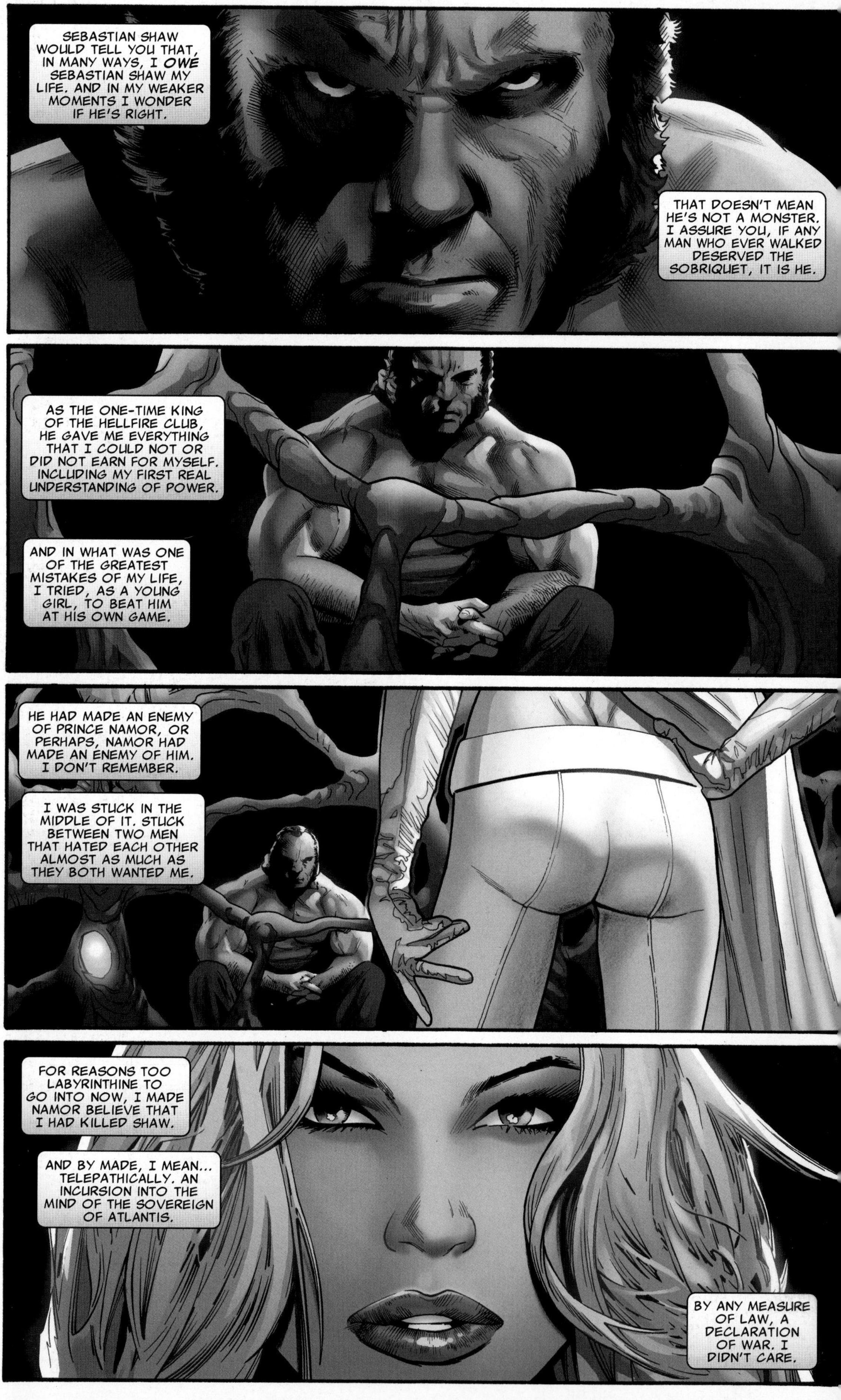
SEBASTIAN SHAW WOULD TELL YOU THAT, IN MANY WAYS, I *OWE* SEBASTIAN SHAW MY LIFE. AND IN MY WEAKER MOMENTS I WONDER IF HE'S RIGHT.
THAT DOESN'T MEAN HE'S NOT A MONSTER. I ASSURE YOU, IF ANY MAN WHO EVER WALKED DESERVED THE SOBRIQUET, IT IS HE.
AS THE ONE-TIME KING OF THE HELLFIRE CLUB, HE GAVE ME EVERYTHING THAT I COULD NOT OR DID NOT EARN FOR MYSELF. INCLUDING MY FIRST REAL UNDERSTANDING OF POWER.
AND IN WHAT WAS ONE OF THE GREATEST MISTAKES OF MY LIFE, I TRIED, AS A YOUNG GIRL, TO BEAT HIM AT HIS OWN GAME.
HE HAD MADE AN ENEMY OF PRINCE NAMOR, OR PERHAPS, NAMOR HAD MADE AN ENEMY OF HIM. I DON'T REMEMBER.
I WAS STUCK IN THE MIDDLE OF IT. STUCK BETWEEN TWO MEN THAT HATED EACH OTHER ALMOST AS MUCH AS THEY BOTH WANTED ME.
FOR REASONS TOO LABYRINTHINE TO GO INTO NOW, I MADE NAMOR BELIEVE THAT I HAD KILLED SHAW.
AND BY MADE, I MEAN... TELEPATHICALLY. AN INCURSION INTO THE MIND OF THE SOVEREIGN OF ATLANTIS.
BY ANY MEASURE OF LAW, A DECLARATION OF WAR. I DIDN'T CARE.

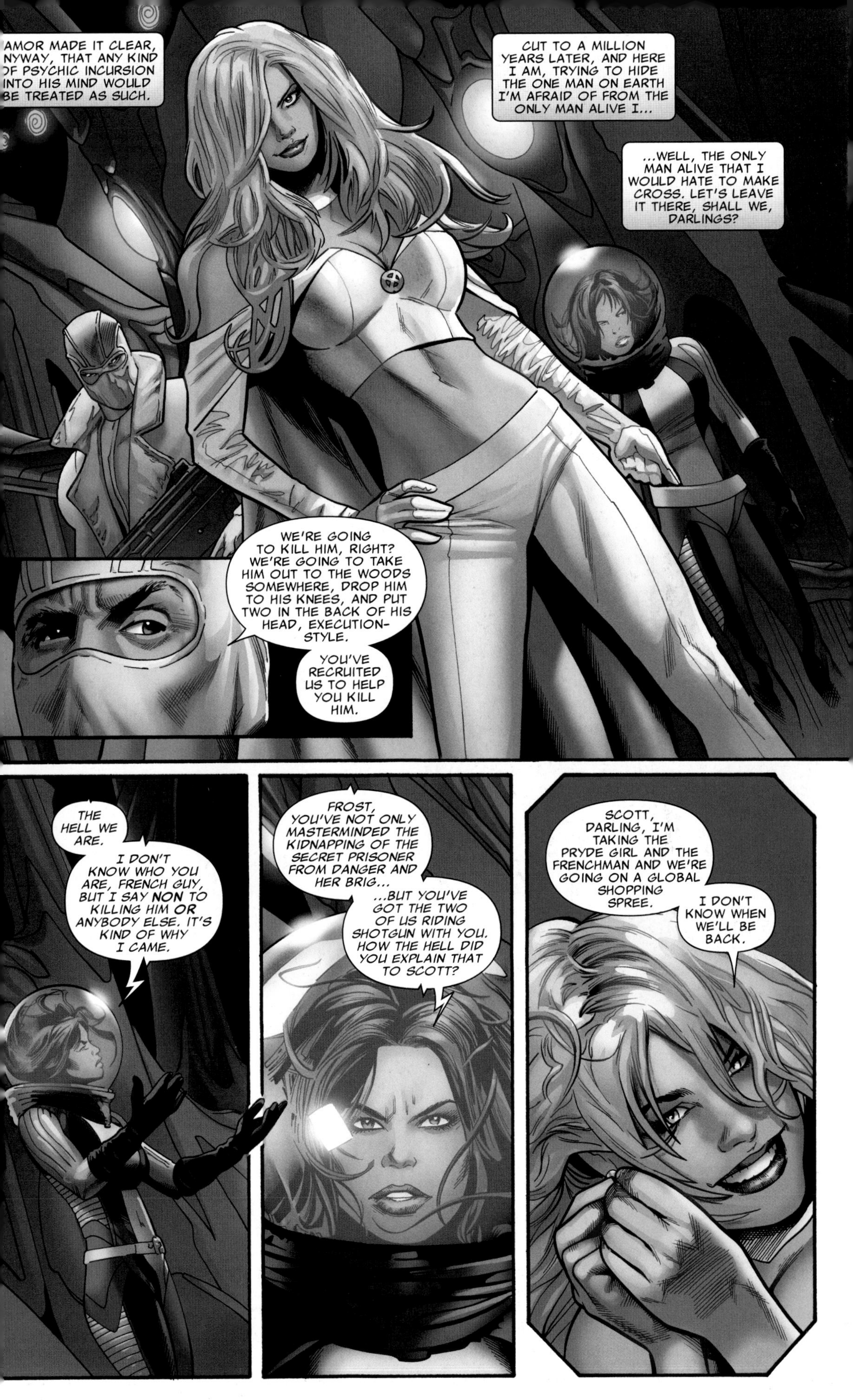

AMOR MADE IT CLEAR, NYWAY, THAT ANY KIND OF PSYCHIC INCURSION INTO HIS MIND WOULD BE TREATED AS SUCH.
CUT TO A MILLION YEARS LATER, AND HERE I AM, TRYING TO HIDE THE ONE MAN ON EARTH I'M AFRAID OF FROM THE ONLY MAN ALIVE I...
...WELL, THE ONLY MAN ALIVE THAT I WOULD HATE TO MAKE CROSS. LET'S LEAVE IT THERE, SHALL WE, DARLINGS?
WE'RE GOING TO KILL HIM, RIGHT? WE'RE GOING TO TAKE HIM OUT TO THE WOODS SOMEWHERE, DROP HIM TO HIS KNEES, AND PUT TWO IN THE BACK OF HIS HEAD, EXECUTION-STYLE.
YOU'VE RECRUITED US TO HELP YOU KILL HIM.
THE HELL WE ARE.
I DON'T KNOW WHO YOU ARE, FRENCH GUY, BUT I SAY NON TO KILLING HIM OR ANYBODY ELSE. IT'S KIND OF WHY I CAME.
FROST, YOU'VE NOT ONLY MASTERMINDED THE KIDNAPPING OF THE SECRET PRISONER FROM DANGER AND HER BRIG...
...BUT YOU'VE GOT THE TWO OF US RIDING SHOTGUN WITH YOU. HOW THE HELL DID YOU EXPLAIN THAT TO SCOTT?
SCOTT, DARLING, I'M TAKING THE PRYDE GIRL AND THE FRENCHMAN AND WE'RE GOING ON A GLOBAL SHOPPING SPREE.
I DON'T KNOW WHEN WE'LL BE BACK.

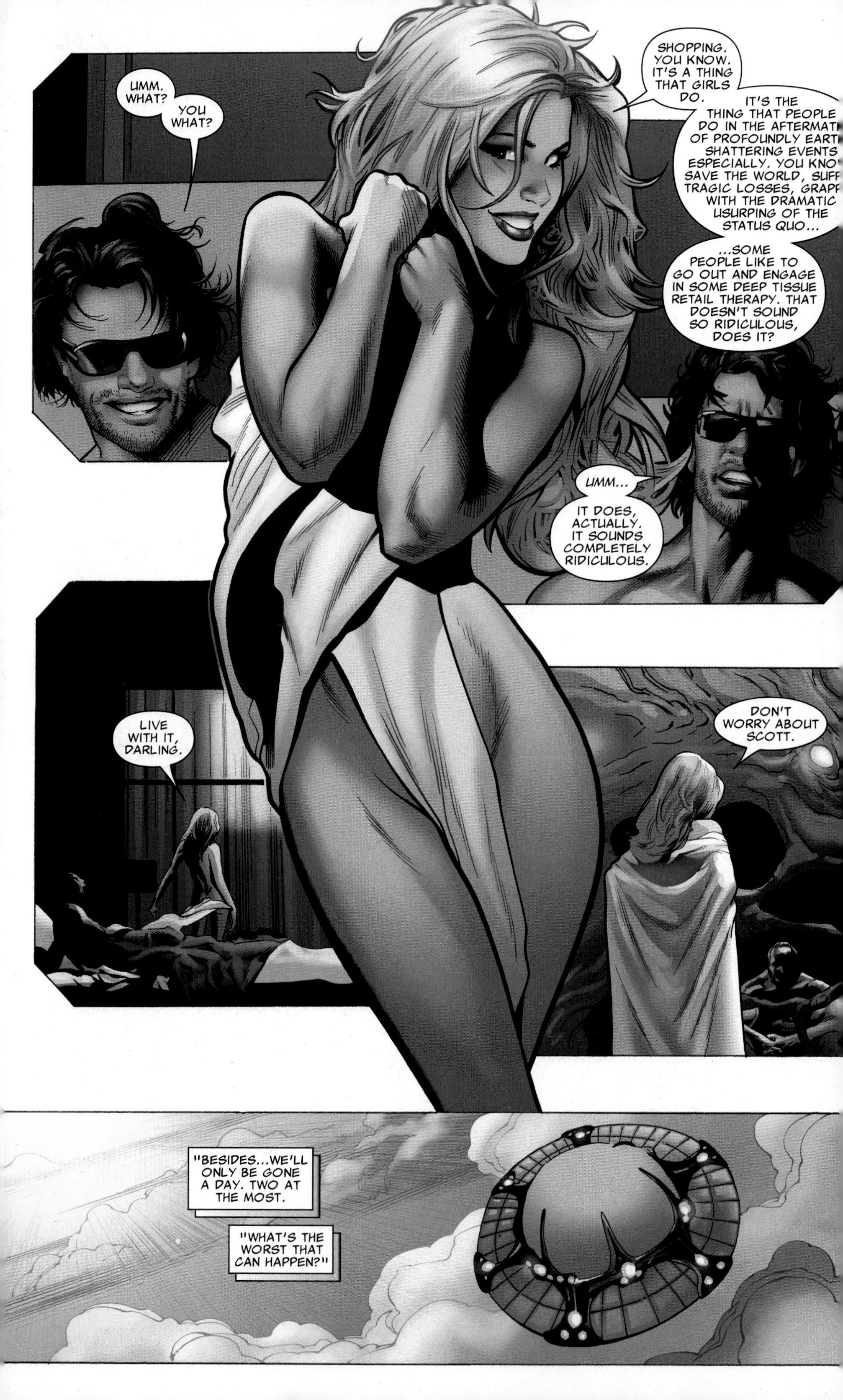
UMM. WHAT?
YOU WHAT?
SHOPPING. YOU KNOW. IT'S A THING THAT GIRLS DO.
IT'S THE THING THAT PEOPLE DO IN THE AFTERMAT OF PROFOUNDLY EART SHATTERING EVENTS ESPECIALLY. YOU KNO SAVE THE WORLD, SUFF TRAGIC LOSSES, GRAPP WITH THE DRAMATIC USURPING OF THE STATUS QUO...
...SOME PEOPLE LIKE TO GO OUT AND ENGAGE IN SOME DEEP TISSUE RETAIL THERAPY. THAT DOESN'T SOUND SO RIDICULOUS, DOES IT?
UMM...
IT DOES, ACTUALLY. IT SOUNDS COMPLETELY RIDICULOUS.
LIVE WITH IT, DARLING.
DON'T WORRY ABOUT SCOTT.
"BESIDES...WE'LL ONLY BE GONE A DAY. TWO AT THE MOST.
"WHAT'S THE WORST THAT CAN HAPPEN?"

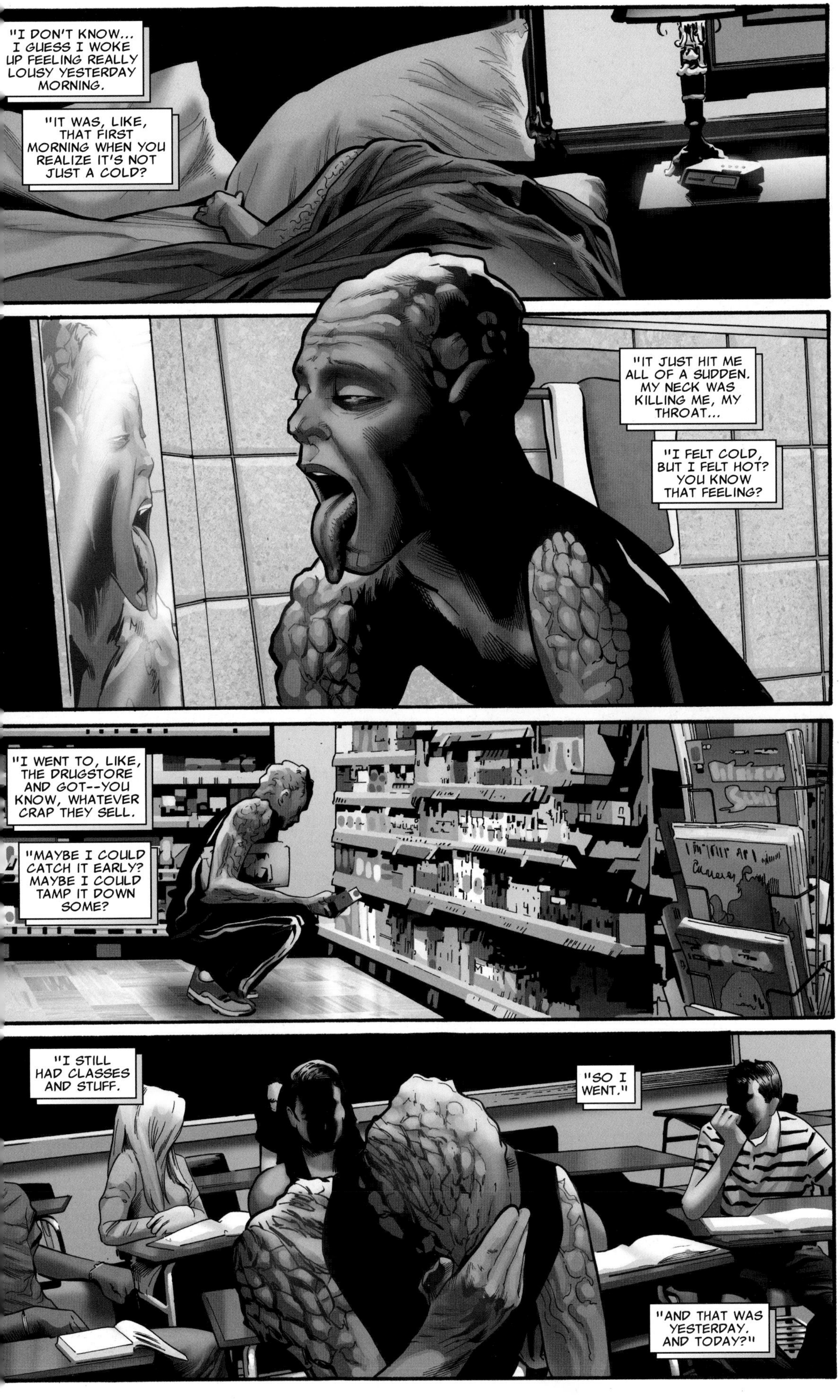
"I DON'T KNOW... I GUESS I WOKE UP FEELING REALLY LOUSY YESTERDAY MORNING.
"IT WAS, LIKE, THAT FIRST MORNING WHEN YOU REALIZE IT'S NOT JUST A COLD?
"IT JUST HIT ME ALL OF A SUDDEN. MY NECK WAS KILLING ME, MY THROAT...
"I FELT COLD, BUT I FELT HOT? YOU KNOW THAT FEELING?
"I WENT TO, LIKE, THE DRUGSTORE AND GOT--YOU KNOW, WHATEVER CRAP THEY SELL.
"MAYBE I COULD CATCH IT EARLY? MAYBE I COULD TAMP IT DOWN SOME?
"I STILL HAD CLASSES AND STUFF.
"SO I WENT."
"AND THAT WAS YESTERDAY. AND TODAY?"

"I DIDN'T EVEN MAKE IT TO SCHOOL TODAY.

"GOT ACROSS THE BAY AND GOT HERE BUT...IT'S TOO MUCH. I CAN'T EVEN SWALLOW RIGHT NOW. MY HEAD IS KILLING ME.

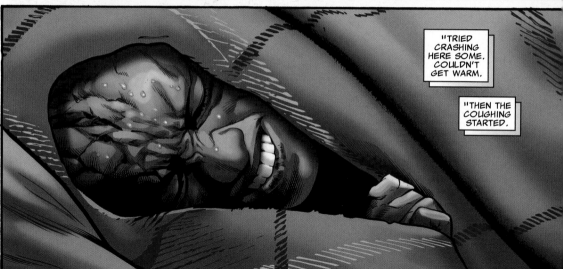

"TRIED CRASHING HERE SOME. COULDN'T GET WARM.

"THEN THE COUGHING STARTED.

"AND I COULDN'T STOP.

"...

"THAT'S WHEN I KNEW OVER-THE-COUNTER WASN'T GOING TO HELP ME."

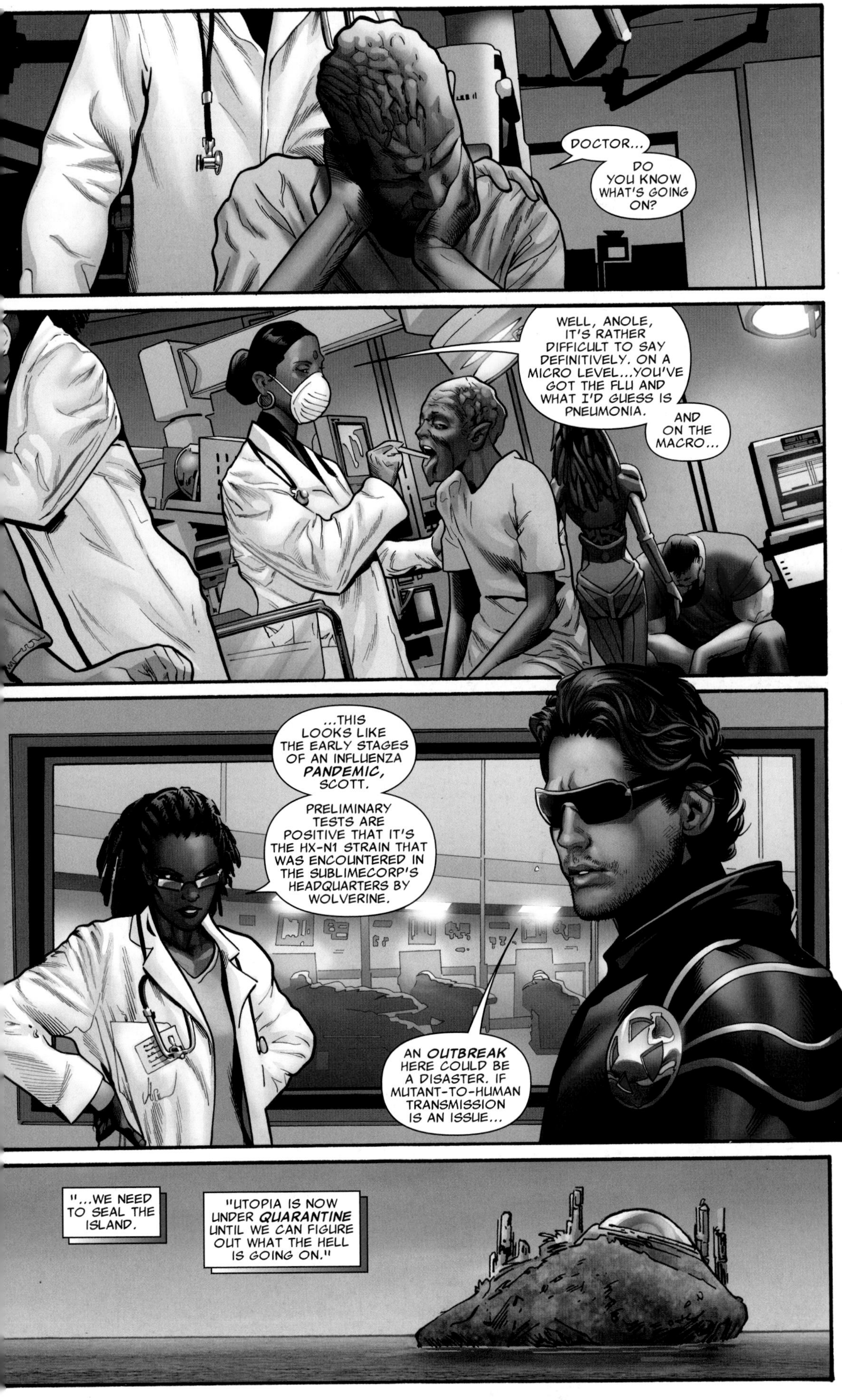
DOCTOR...
DO YOU KNOW WHAT'S GOING ON?
WELL, ANOLE, IT'S RATHER DIFFICULT TO SAY DEFINITIVELY. ON A MICRO LEVEL...YOU'VE GOT THE FLU AND WHAT I'D GUESS IS PNEUMONIA.
AND ON THE MACRO...
...THIS LOOKS LIKE THE EARLY STAGES OF AN INFLUENZA *PANDEMIC,* SCOTT.
PRELIMINARY TESTS ARE POSITIVE THAT IT'S THE HX-N1 STRAIN THAT WAS ENCOUNTERED IN THE SUBLIMECORP'S HEADQUARTERS BY WOLVERINE.
AN *OUTBREAK* HERE COULD BE A DISASTER. IF MUTANT-TO-HUMAN TRANSMISSION IS AN ISSUE...
"...WE NEED TO SEAL THE ISLAND.
"UTOPIA IS NOW UNDER *QUARANTINE* UNTIL WE CAN FIGURE OUT WHAT THE HELL IS GOING ON."

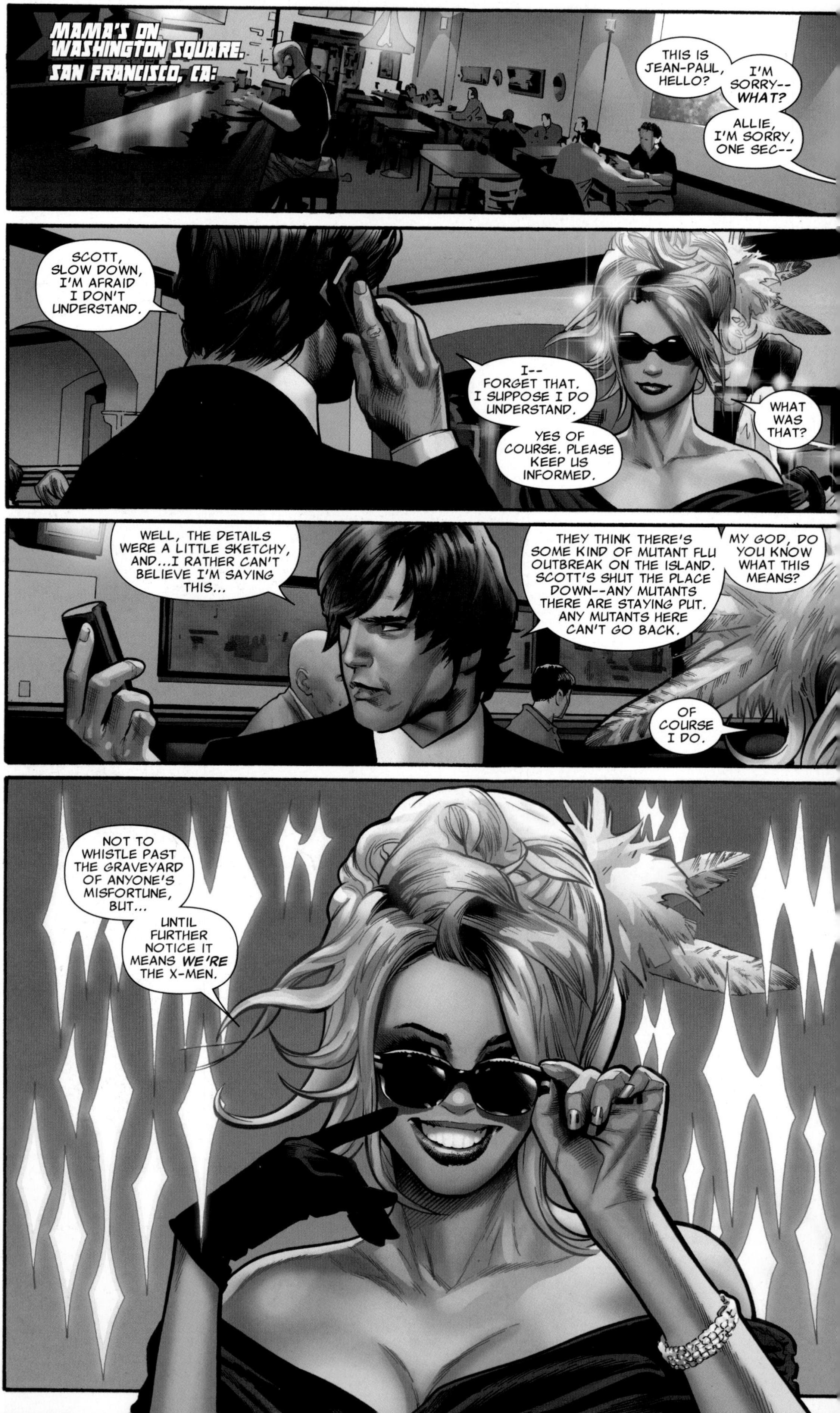
MAMA'S ON WASHINGTON SQUARE. SAN FRANCISCO, CA:
THIS IS JEAN-PAUL, HELLO?
I'M SORRY-- WHAT?
ALLIE, I'M SORRY, ONE SEC--
SCOTT, SLOW DOWN, I'M AFRAID I DON'T UNDERSTAND.
I-- FORGET THAT. I SUPPOSE I DO UNDERSTAND.
YES OF COURSE. PLEASE KEEP US INFORMED.
WHAT WAS THAT?
WELL, THE DETAILS WERE A LITTLE SKETCHY, AND...I RATHER CAN'T BELIEVE I'M SAYING THIS...
THEY THINK THERE'S SOME KIND OF MUTANT FLU OUTBREAK ON THE ISLAND. SCOTT'S SHUT THE PLACE DOWN--ANY MUTANTS THERE ARE STAYING PUT. ANY MUTANTS HERE CAN'T GO BACK.
MY GOD, DO YOU KNOW WHAT THIS MEANS?
OF COURSE I DO.
NOT TO WHISTLE PAST THE GRAVEYARD OF ANYONE'S MISFORTUNE, BUT...
UNTIL FURTHER NOTICE IT MEANS WE'RE THE X-MEN.

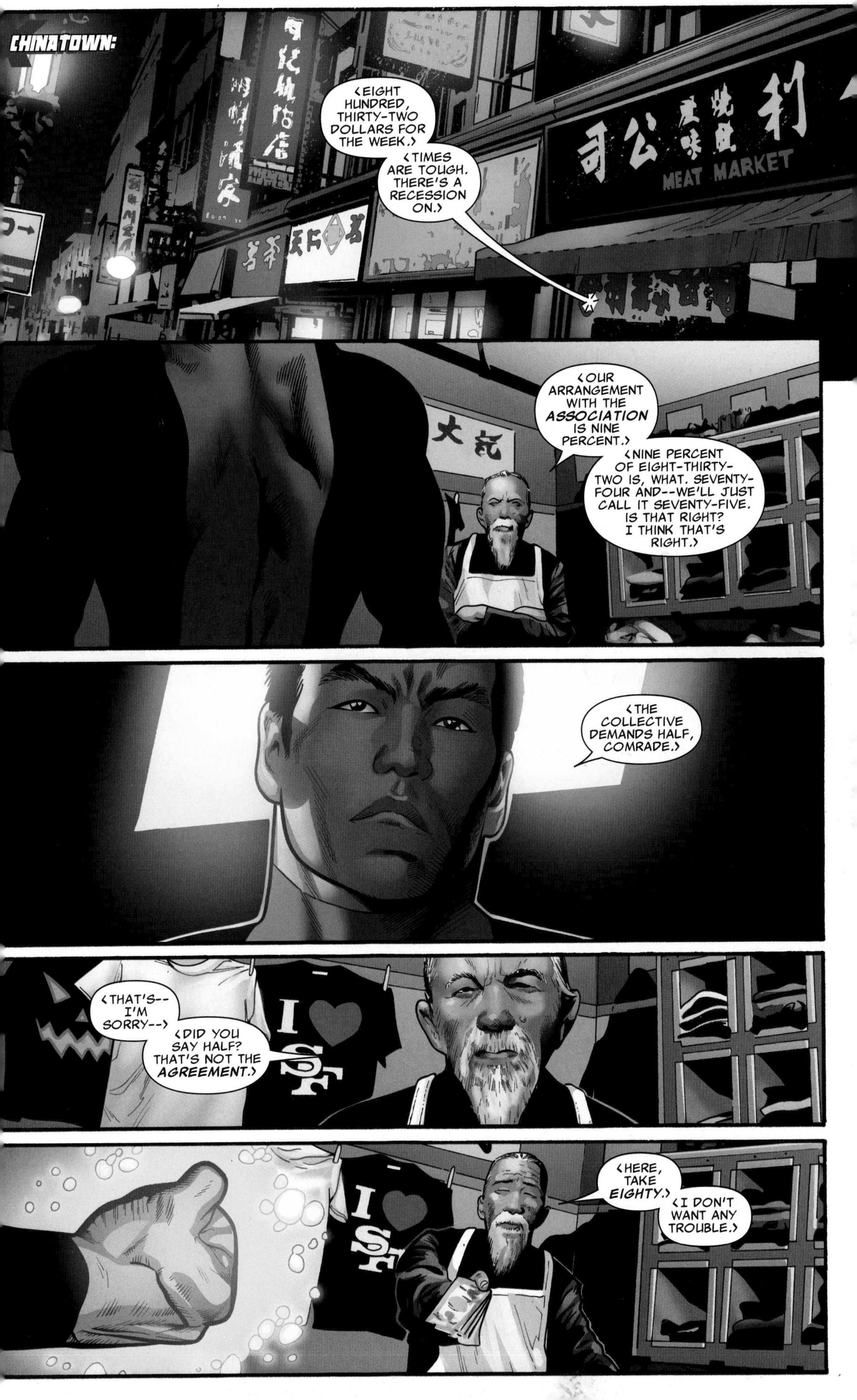
CHINATOWN:
‹EIGHT HUNDRED, THIRTY-TWO DOLLARS FOR THE WEEK.›
‹TIMES ARE TOUGH. THERE'S A RECESSION ON.›
MEAT MARKET
‹OUR ARRANGEMENT WITH THE ASSOCIATION IS NINE PERCENT.›
‹NINE PERCENT OF EIGHT-THIRTY-TWO IS, WHAT. SEVENTY-FOUR AND--WE'LL JUST CALL IT SEVENTY-FIVE. IS THAT RIGHT? I THINK THAT'S RIGHT.›
‹THE COLLECTIVE DEMANDS HALF, COMRADE.›
‹THAT'S--I'M SORRY--›
‹DID YOU SAY HALF? THAT'S NOT THE AGREEMENT.›
‹HERE, TAKE EIGHTY.›
‹I DON'T WANT ANY TROUBLE.›

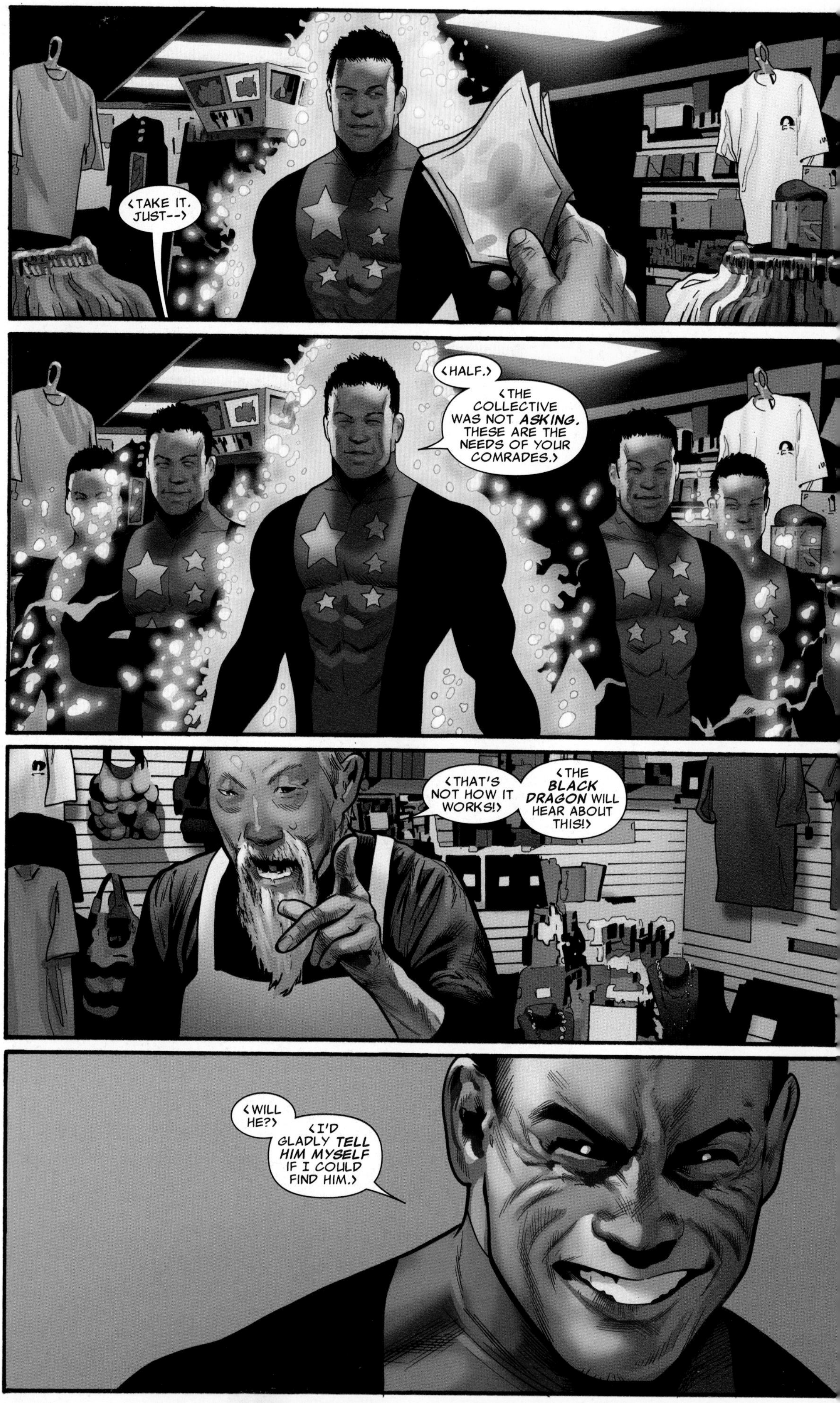
‹TAKE IT. JUST--›
‹HALF.›
‹THE COLLECTIVE WAS NOT ASKING. THESE ARE THE NEEDS OF YOUR COMRADES.›
‹THAT'S NOT HOW IT WORKS!›
‹THE BLACK DRAGON WILL HEAR ABOUT THIS!›
‹WILL HE?›
‹I'D GLADLY TELL HIM MYSELF IF I COULD FIND HIM.›

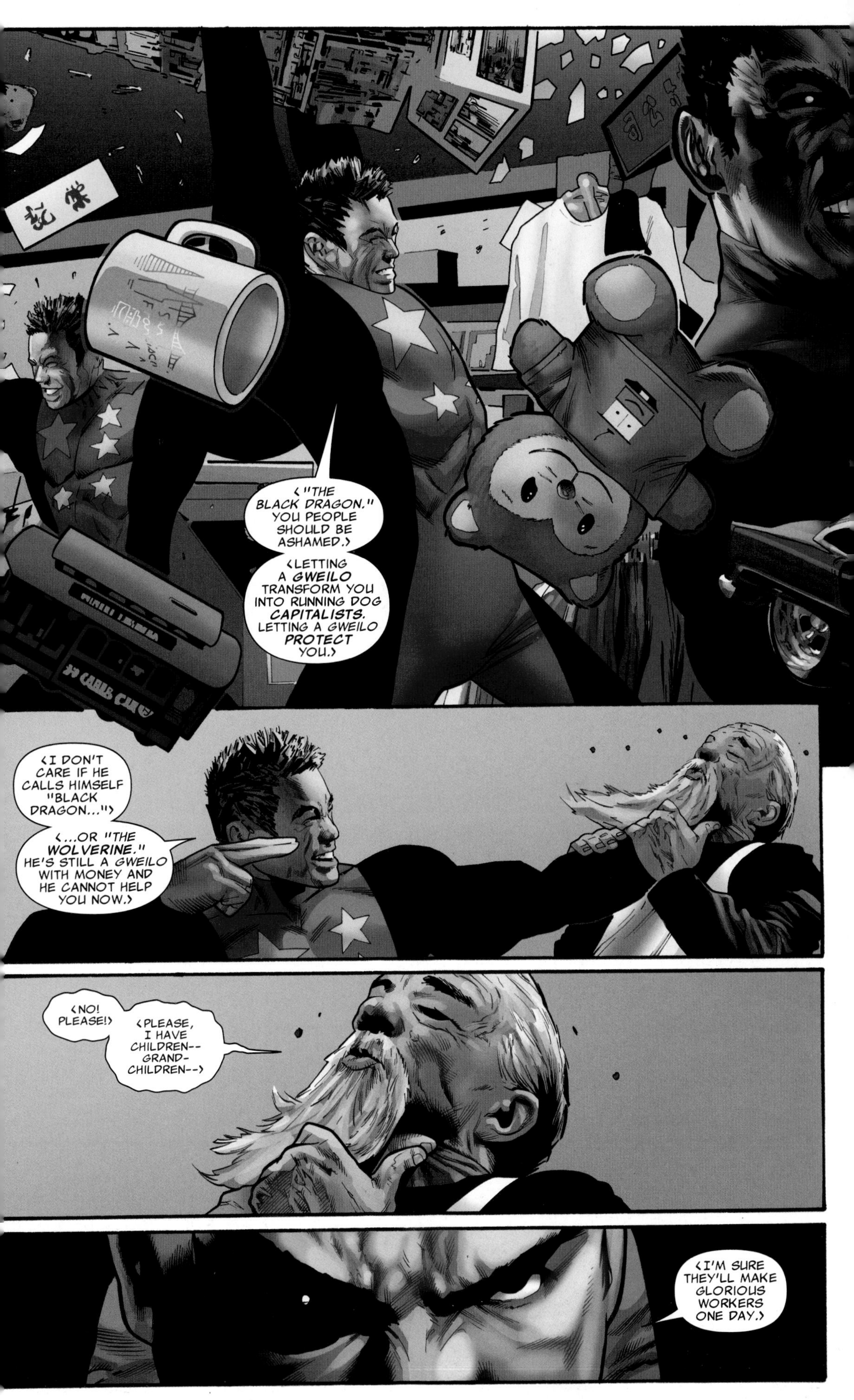
‹"THE BLACK DRAGON." YOU PEOPLE SHOULD BE ASHAMED.›
‹LETTING A GWEILO TRANSFORM YOU INTO RUNNING DOG CAPITALISTS. LETTING A GWEILO PROTECT YOU.›
‹I DON'T CARE IF HE CALLS HIMSELF "BLACK DRAGON..."›
‹...OR "THE WOLVERINE." HE'S STILL A GWEILO WITH MONEY AND HE CANNOT HELP YOU NOW.›
‹NO! PLEASE!›
‹PLEASE, I HAVE CHILDREN-- GRAND-CHILDREN--›
‹I'M SURE THEY'LL MAKE GLORIOUS WORKERS ONE DAY.›

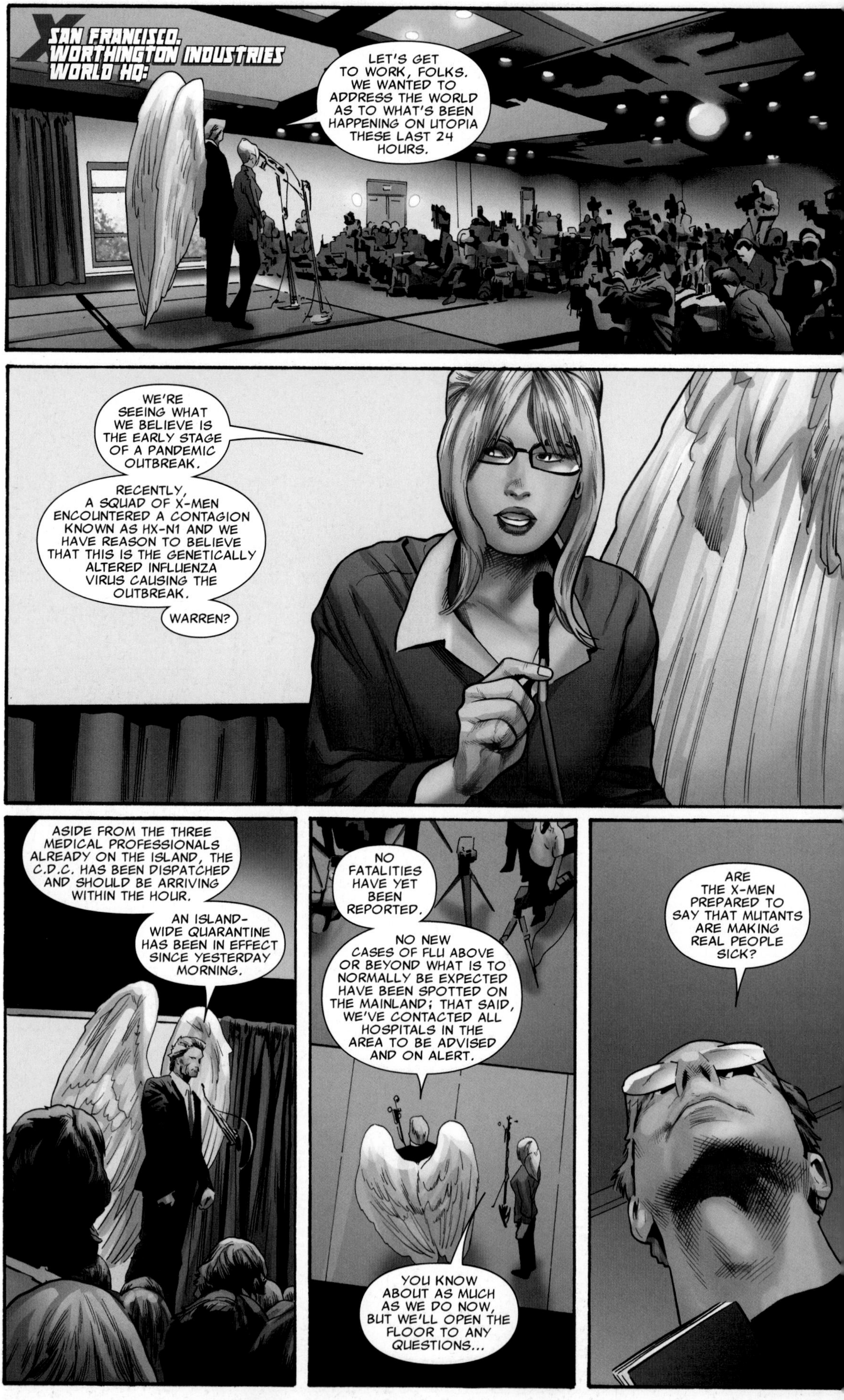
SAN FRANCISCO. WORTHINGTON INDUSTRIES WORLD HQ:
LET'S GET TO WORK, FOLKS. WE WANTED TO ADDRESS THE WORLD AS TO WHAT'S BEEN HAPPENING ON UTOPIA THESE LAST 24 HOURS.
WE'RE SEEING WHAT WE BELIEVE IS THE EARLY STAGE OF A PANDEMIC OUTBREAK.
RECENTLY, A SQUAD OF X-MEN ENCOUNTERED A CONTAGION KNOWN AS HX-N1 AND WE HAVE REASON TO BELIEVE THAT THIS IS THE GENETICALLY ALTERED INFLUENZA VIRUS CAUSING THE OUTBREAK.
WARREN?
ASIDE FROM THE THREE MEDICAL PROFESSIONALS ALREADY ON THE ISLAND, THE C.D.C. HAS BEEN DISPATCHED AND SHOULD BE ARRIVING WITHIN THE HOUR.
AN ISLAND-WIDE QUARANTINE HAS BEEN IN EFFECT SINCE YESTERDAY MORNING.
NO FATALITIES HAVE YET BEEN REPORTED.
NO NEW CASES OF FLU ABOVE OR BEYOND WHAT IS TO NORMALLY BE EXPECTED HAVE BEEN SPOTTED ON THE MAINLAND; THAT SAID, WE'VE CONTACTED ALL HOSPITALS IN THE AREA TO BE ADVISED AND ON ALERT.
YOU KNOW ABOUT AS MUCH AS WE DO NOW, BUT WE'LL OPEN THE FLOOR TO ANY QUESTIONS...
ARE THE X-MEN PREPARED TO SAY THAT MUTANTS ARE MAKING REAL PEOPLE SICK?

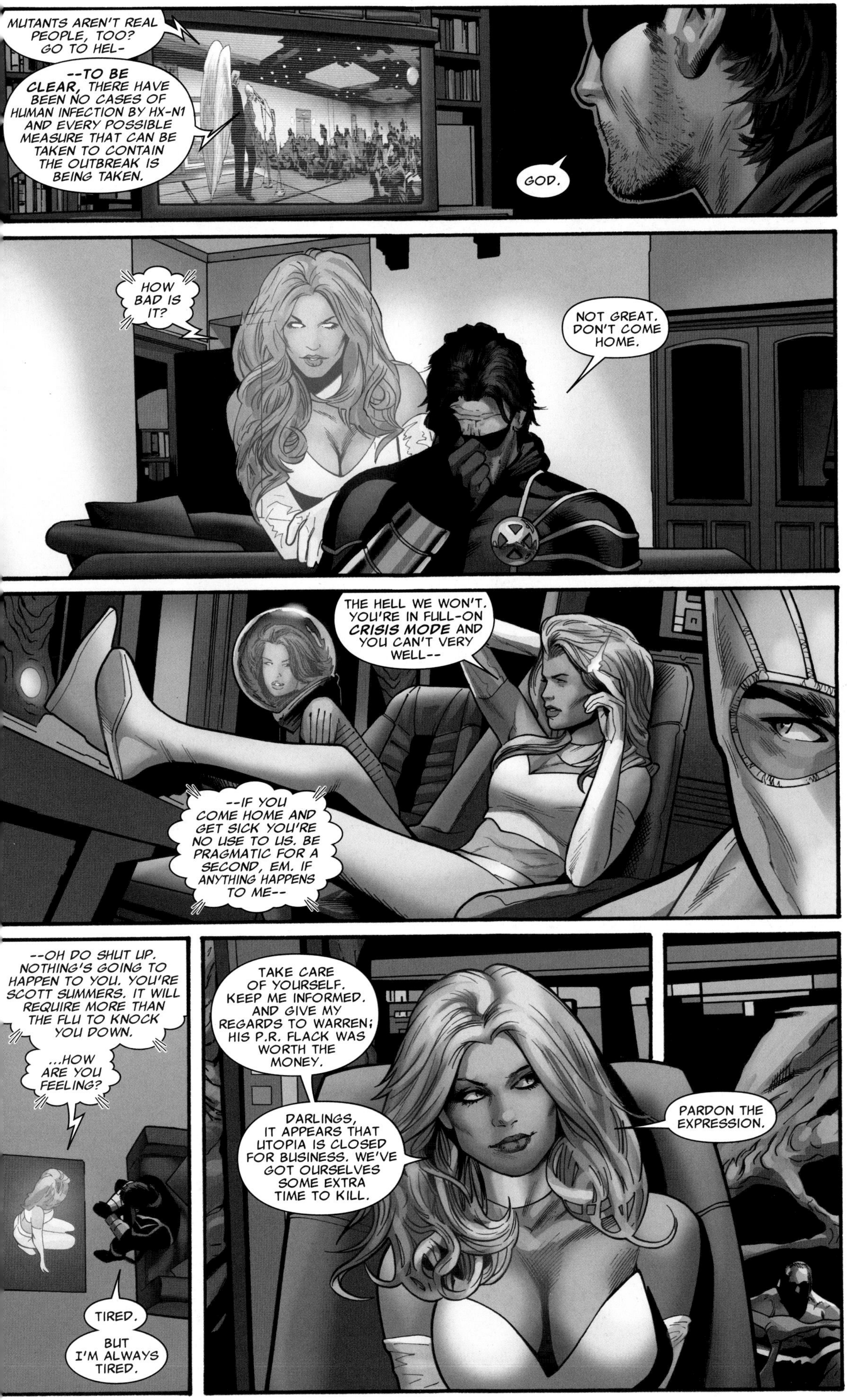

MUTANTS AREN'T REAL PEOPLE, TOO? GO TO HEL-
--TO BE CLEAR, THERE HAVE BEEN NO CASES OF HUMAN INFECTION BY HX-N1 AND EVERY POSSIBLE MEASURE THAT CAN BE TAKEN TO CONTAIN THE OUTBREAK IS BEING TAKEN.
GOD.
HOW BAD IS IT?
NOT GREAT. DON'T COME HOME.
THE HELL WE WON'T. YOU'RE IN FULL-ON CRISIS MODE AND YOU CAN'T VERY WELL--
--IF YOU COME HOME AND GET SICK YOU'RE NO USE TO US. BE PRAGMATIC FOR A SECOND, EM. IF ANYTHING HAPPENS TO ME--
--OH DO SHUT UP. NOTHING'S GOING TO HAPPEN TO YOU. YOU'RE SCOTT SUMMERS. IT WILL REQUIRE MORE THAN THE FLU TO KNOCK YOU DOWN.
...HOW ARE YOU FEELING?
TIRED.
BUT I'M ALWAYS TIRED.
TAKE CARE OF YOURSELF. KEEP ME INFORMED. AND GIVE MY REGARDS TO WARREN; HIS P.R. FLACK WAS WORTH THE MONEY.
DARLINGS, IT APPEARS THAT UTOPIA IS CLOSED FOR BUSINESS. WE'VE GOT OURSELVES SOME EXTRA TIME TO KILL.
PARDON THE EXPRESSION.

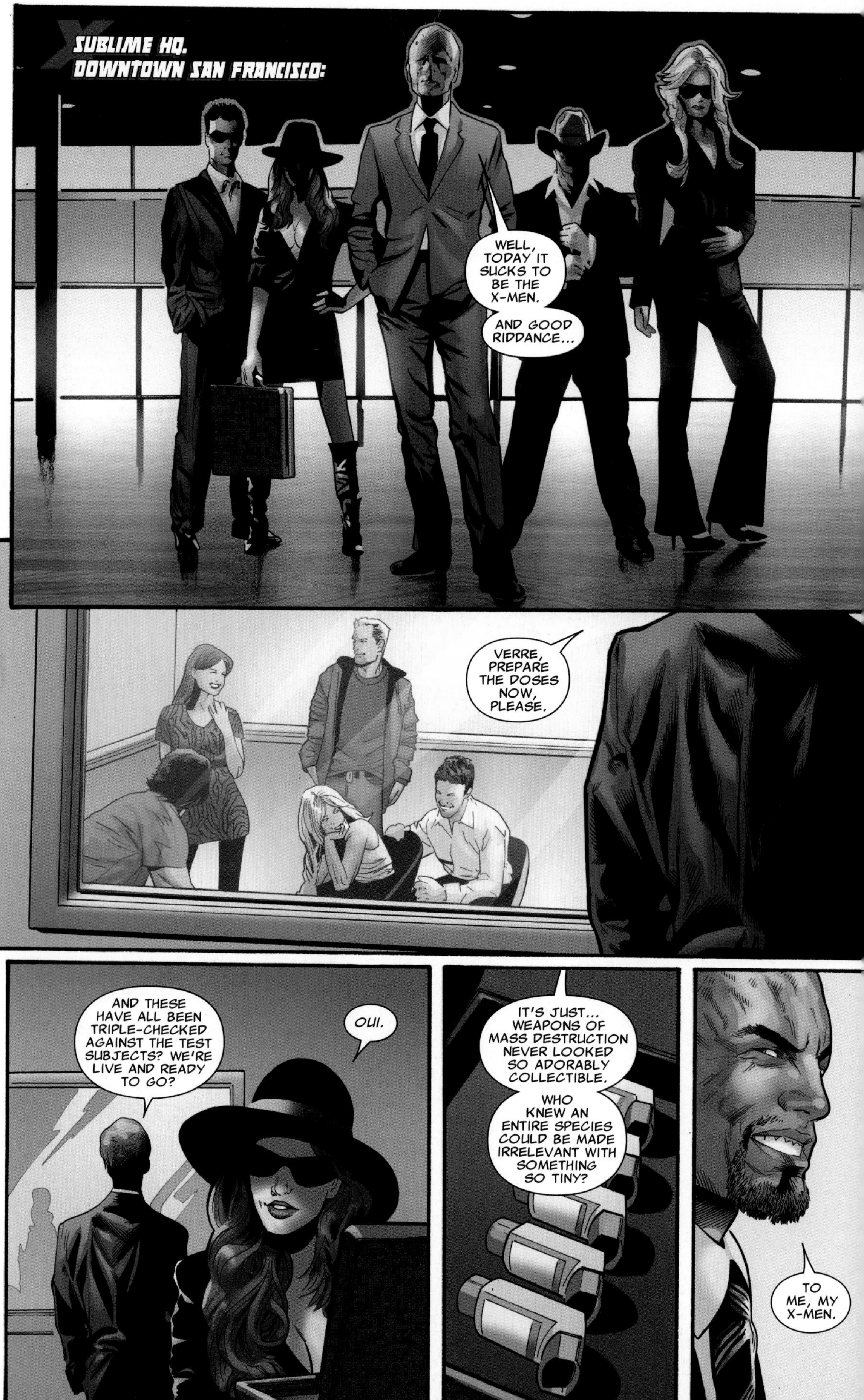
SUBLIME HQ.
DOWNTOWN SAN FRANCISCO:
WELL, TODAY IT SUCKS TO BE THE X-MEN.
AND GOOD RIDDANCE...
VERRE, PREPARE THE DOSES NOW, PLEASE.
AND THESE HAVE ALL BEEN TRIPLE-CHECKED AGAINST THE TEST SUBJECTS? WE'RE LIVE AND READY TO GO?
OUI.
IT'S JUST... WEAPONS OF MASS DESTRUCTION NEVER LOOKED SO ADORABLY COLLECTIBLE.
WHO KNEW AN ENTIRE SPECIES COULD BE MADE IRRELEVANT WITH SOMETHING SO TINY?
TO ME, MY X-MEN.

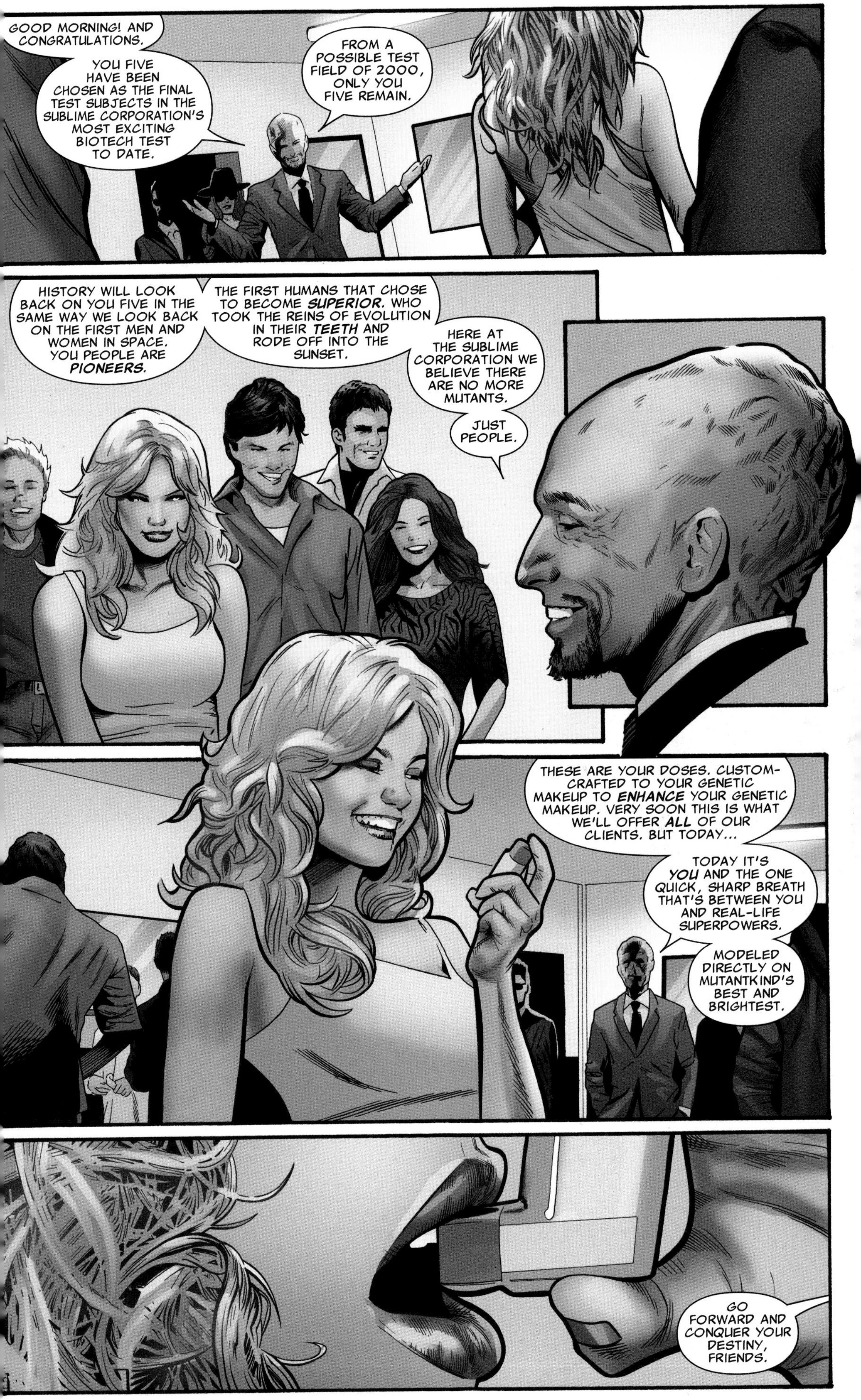
GOOD MORNING! AND CONGRATULATIONS.
YOU FIVE HAVE BEEN CHOSEN AS THE FINAL TEST SUBJECTS IN THE SUBLIME CORPORATION'S MOST EXCITING BIOTECH TEST TO DATE.
FROM A POSSIBLE TEST FIELD OF 2000, ONLY YOU FIVE REMAIN.
HISTORY WILL LOOK BACK ON YOU FIVE IN THE SAME WAY WE LOOK BACK ON THE FIRST MEN AND WOMEN IN SPACE. YOU PEOPLE ARE PIONEERS.
THE FIRST HUMANS THAT CHOSE TO BECOME SUPERIOR. WHO TOOK THE REINS OF EVOLUTION IN THEIR TEETH AND RODE OFF INTO THE SUNSET.
HERE AT THE SUBLIME CORPORATION WE BELIEVE THERE ARE NO MORE MUTANTS.
JUST PEOPLE.
THESE ARE YOUR DOSES. CUSTOM-CRAFTED TO YOUR GENETIC MAKEUP TO ENHANCE YOUR GENETIC MAKEUP. VERY SOON THIS IS WHAT WE'LL OFFER ALL OF OUR CLIENTS. BUT TODAY...
TODAY IT'S YOU AND THE ONE QUICK, SHARP BREATH THAT'S BETWEEN YOU AND REAL-LIFE SUPERPOWERS.
MODELED DIRECTLY ON MUTANTKIND'S BEST AND BRIGHTEST.
GO FORWARD AND CONQUER YOUR DESTINY, FRIENDS.

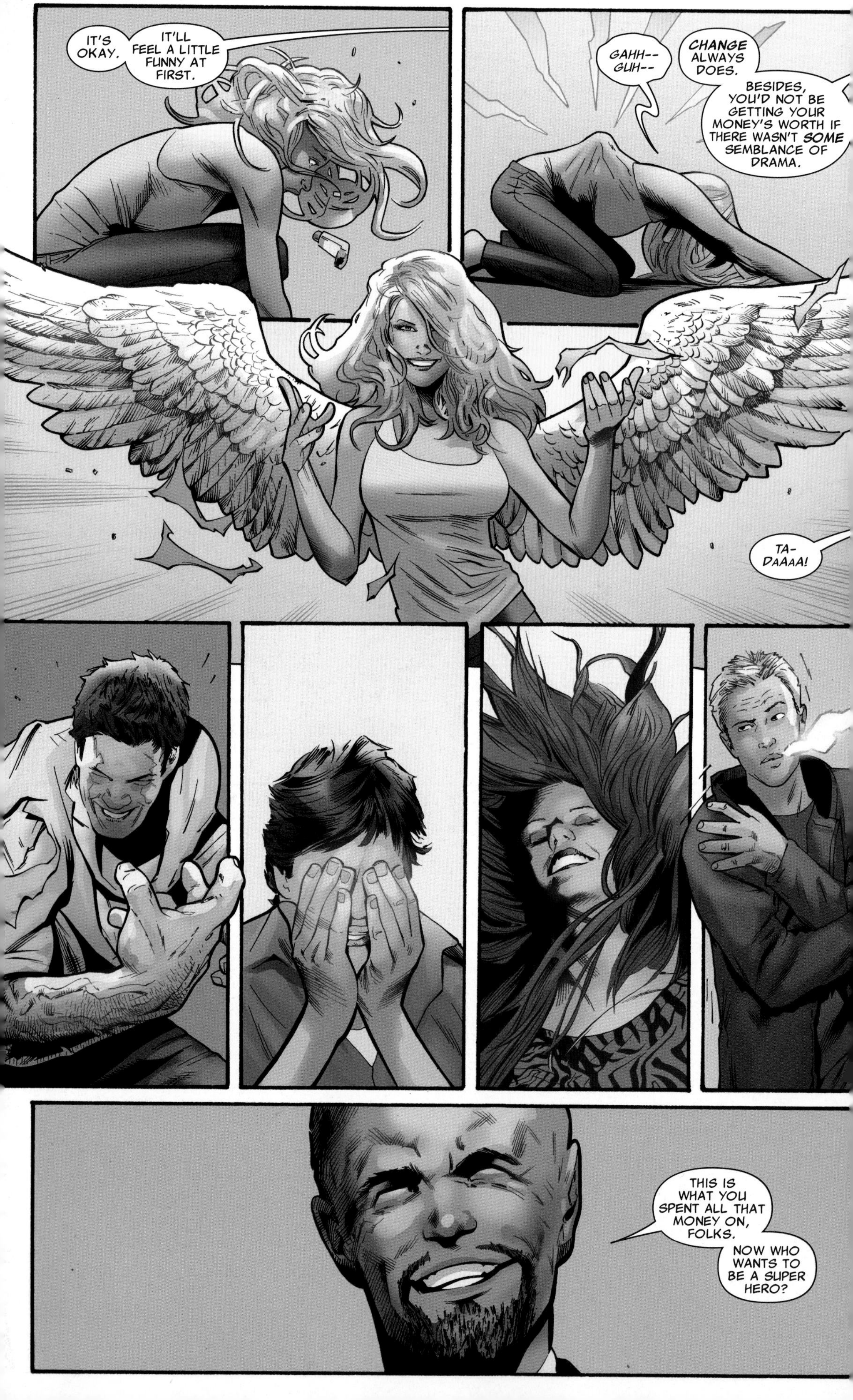
IT'S OKAY.
IT'LL FEEL A LITTLE FUNNY AT FIRST.
GAHH-- GUH--
CHANGE ALWAYS DOES.
BESIDES, YOU'D NOT BE GETTING YOUR MONEY'S WORTH IF THERE WASN'T SOME SEMBLANCE OF DRAMA.
TA-DAAAA!
THIS IS WHAT YOU SPENT ALL THAT MONEY ON, FOLKS.
NOW WHO WANTS TO BE A SUPER HERO?

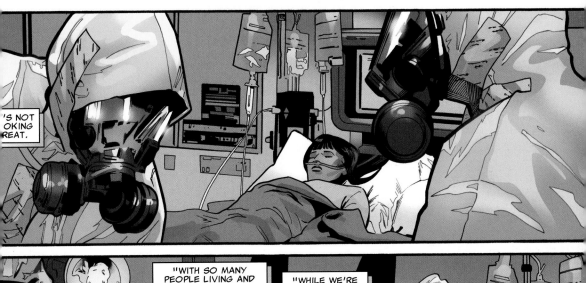

'S NOT
OKING
REAT.

"WITH SO MANY PEOPLE LIVING AND WORKING IN SUCH CLOSE QUARTERS, THIS KIND OF VELOCITY IS TO BE EXPECTED IN AN OUTBREAK."

"WHILE WE'RE WAITING ON THE X-CLUB'S FULL WORKUP ON THE VIRUS STRAIN, HERE'S WHAT WE KNOW:"

THE BEST POSSIBLE NEWS IS THAT SO FAR, 72 HOURS INTO THE OUTBREAK, WE HAVE ZERO CASES OF HUMAN CONTAMINATION ON THE ISLAND. THAT IS THE BEGINNING AND THE END OF THE GOOD NEWS.

ON TOP OF TYPICAL SEVERE FLU SYMPTOMS, THE MOST CONCERNING EFFECT OF INFECTION SEEMS TO BE POWER DAMPENING.

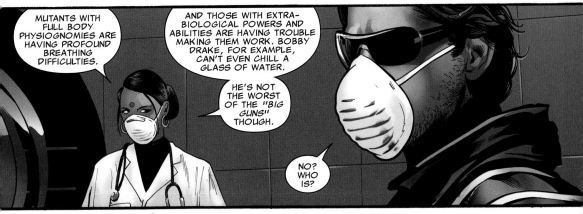

MUTANTS WITH FULL BODY PHYSIOGNOMIES ARE HAVING PROFOUND BREATHING DIFFICULTIES.

AND THOSE WITH EXTRA-BIOLOGICAL POWERS AND ABILITIES ARE HAVING TROUBLE MAKING THEM WORK. BOBBY DRAKE, FOR EXAMPLE, CAN'T EVEN CHILL A GLASS OF WATER.

HE'S NOT THE WORST OF THE "BIG GUNS" THOUGH.

NO? WHO IS?

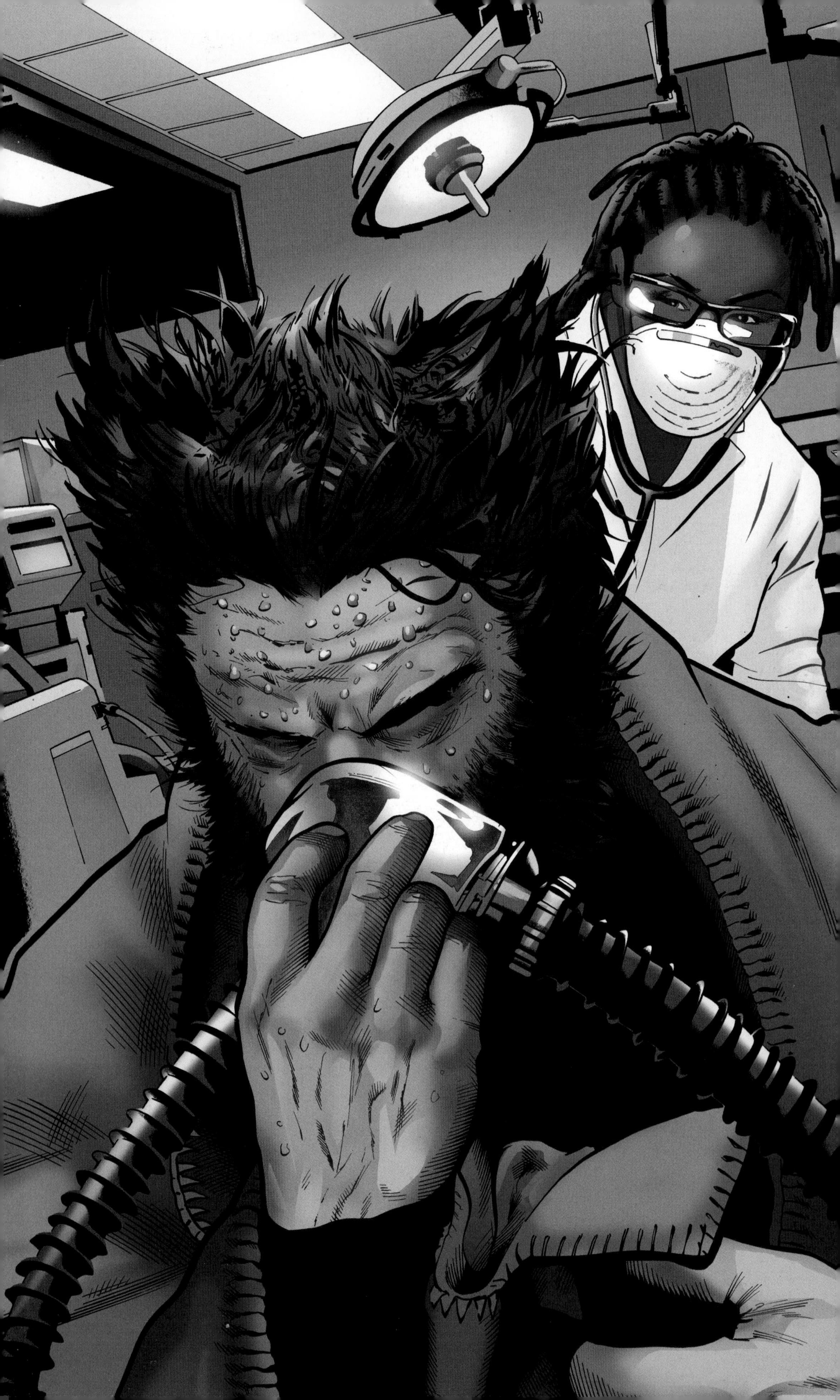

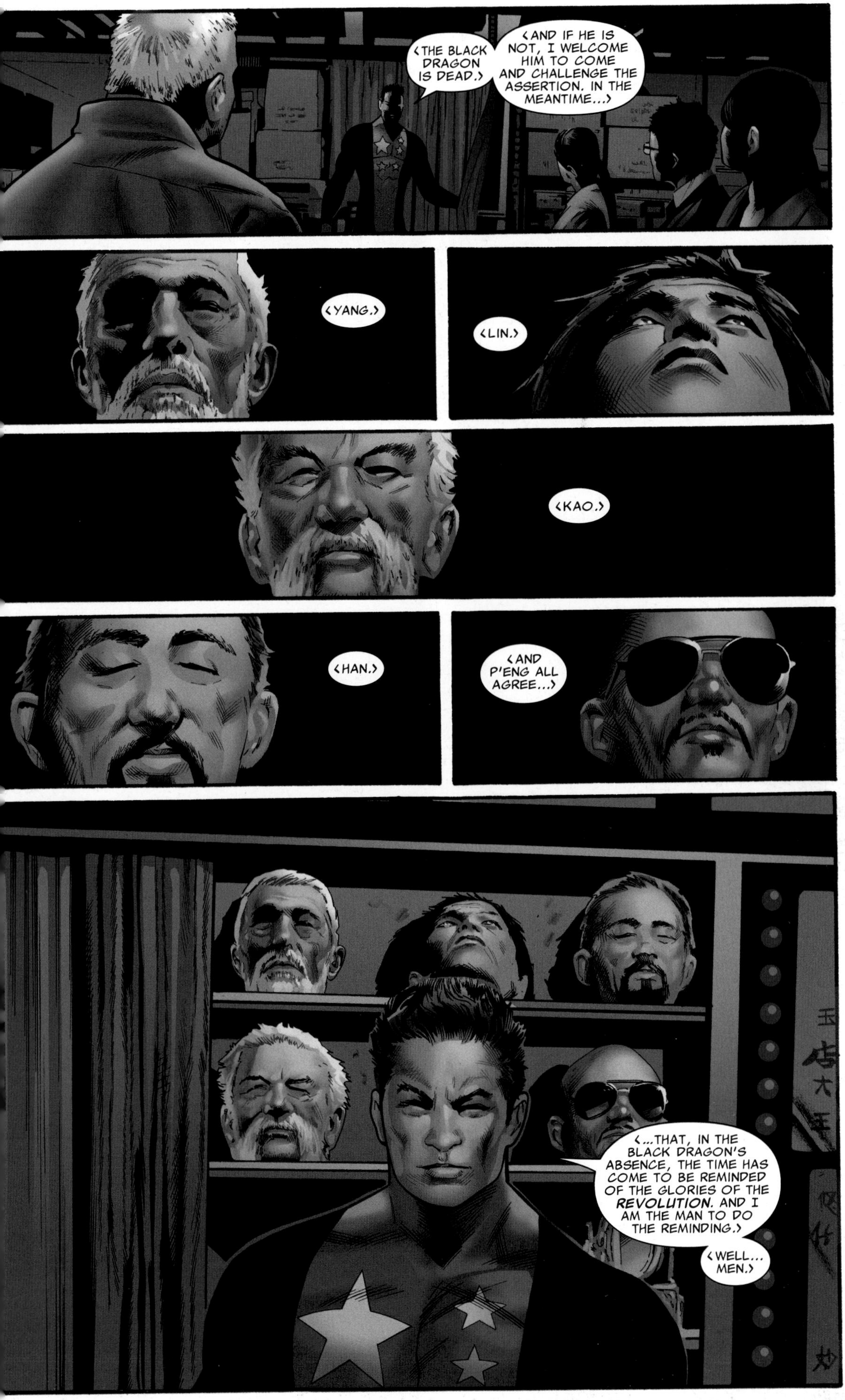

‹THE BLACK DRAGON IS DEAD.›
‹AND IF HE IS NOT, I WELCOME HIM TO COME AND CHALLENGE THE ASSERTION. IN THE MEANTIME...›
‹YANG.›
‹LIN.›
‹KAO.›
‹HAN.›
‹AND P'ENG ALL AGREE...›
‹...THAT, IN THE BLACK DRAGON'S ABSENCE, THE TIME HAS COME TO BE REMINDED OF THE GLORIES OF THE REVOLUTION. AND I AM THE MAN TO DO THE REMINDING.›
‹WELL... MEN.›

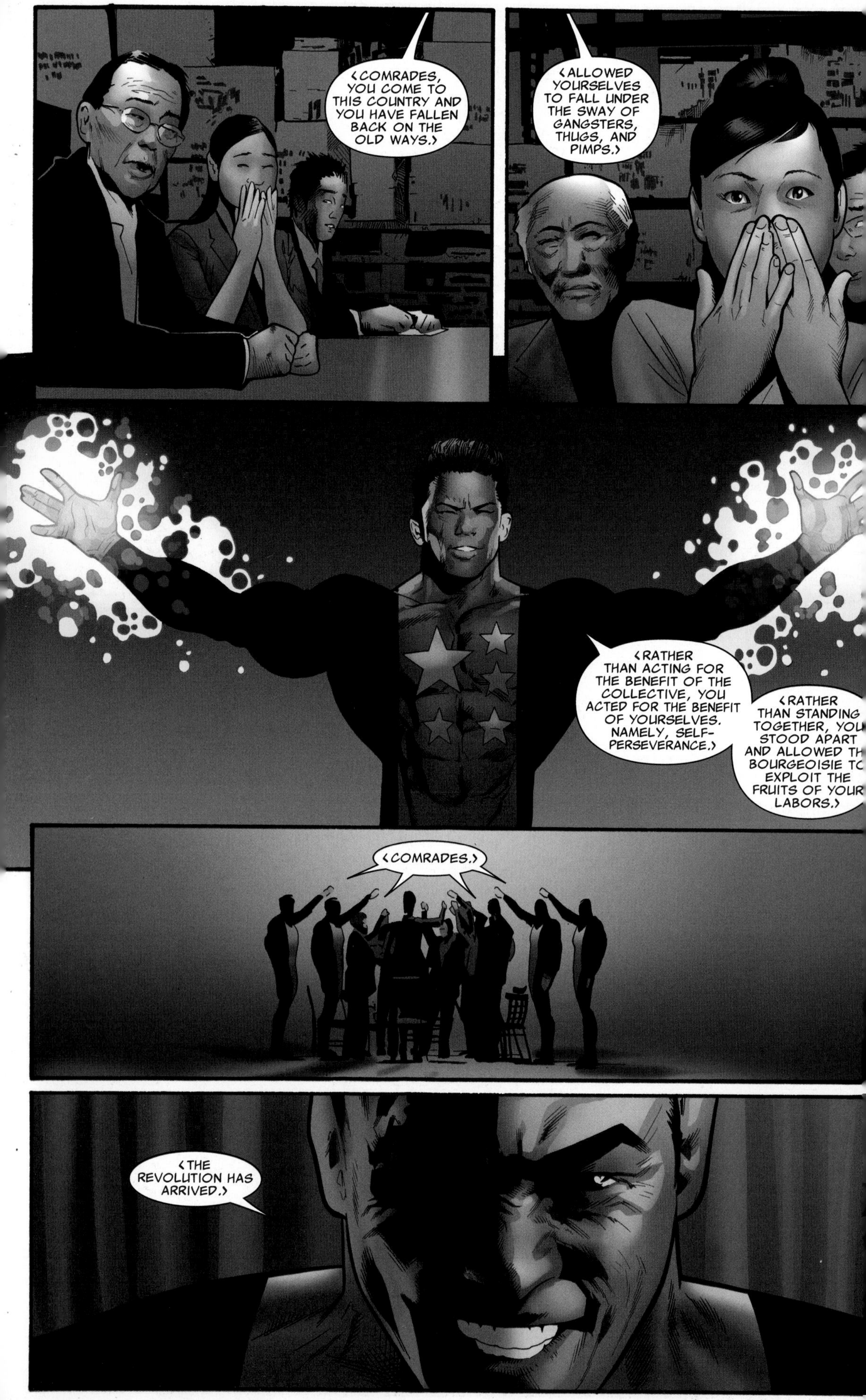
‹COMRADES, YOU COME TO THIS COUNTRY AND YOU HAVE FALLEN BACK ON THE OLD WAYS.›
‹ALLOWED YOURSELVES TO FALL UNDER THE SWAY OF GANGSTERS, THUGS, AND PIMPS.›
‹RATHER THAN ACTING FOR THE BENEFIT OF THE COLLECTIVE, YOU ACTED FOR THE BENEFIT OF YOURSELVES. NAMELY, SELF-PERSEVERANCE.›
‹RATHER THAN STANDING TOGETHER, YOU STOOD APART AND ALLOWED THE BOURGEOISIE TO EXPLOIT THE FRUITS OF YOUR LABORS.›
‹COMRADES.›
‹THE REVOLUTION HAS ARRIVED.›

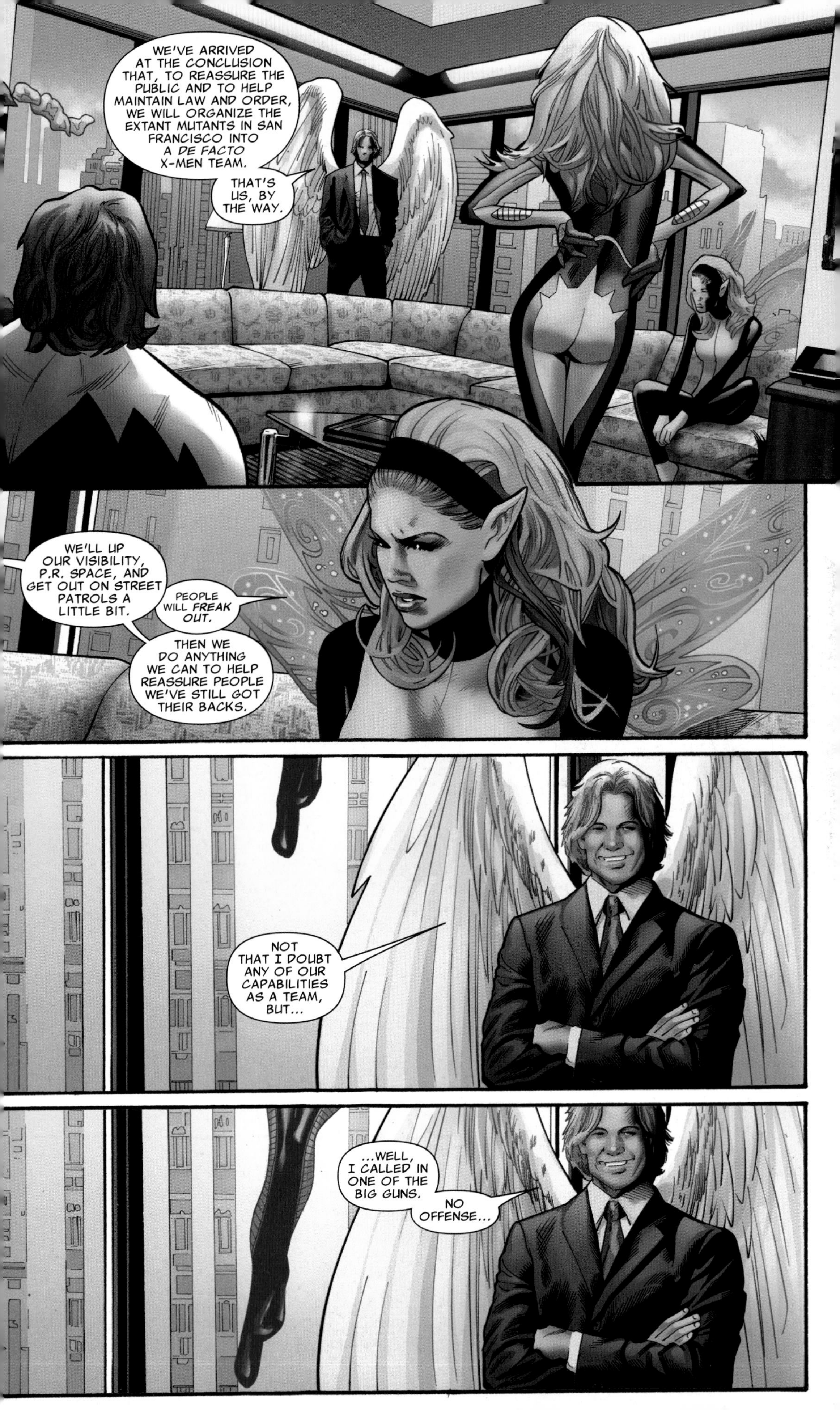

WE'VE ARRIVED AT THE CONCLUSION THAT, TO REASSURE THE PUBLIC AND TO HELP MAINTAIN LAW AND ORDER, WE WILL ORGANIZE THE EXTANT MUTANTS IN SAN FRANCISCO INTO A *DE FACTO* X-MEN TEAM.
THAT'S US, BY THE WAY.
WE'LL UP OUR VISIBILITY, P.R. SPACE, AND GET OUT ON STREET PATROLS A LITTLE BIT.
PEOPLE WILL *FREAK OUT.*
THEN WE DO ANYTHING WE CAN TO HELP REASSURE PEOPLE WE'VE STILL GOT THEIR BACKS.
NOT THAT I DOUBT ANY OF OUR CAPABILITIES AS A TEAM, BUT...
...WELL, I CALLED IN ONE OF THE BIG GUNS.
NO OFFENSE...

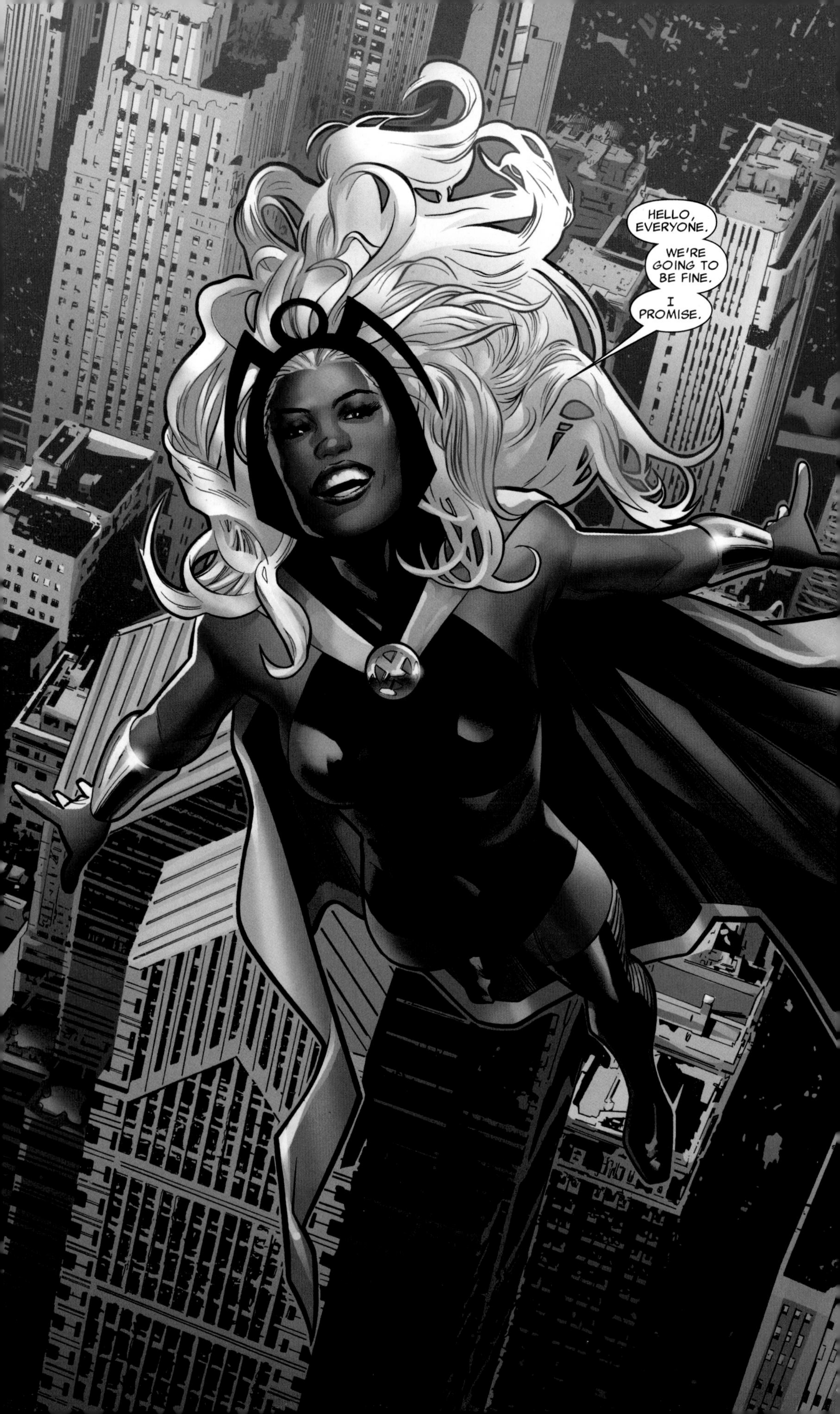
HELLO, EVERYONE.
WE'RE GOING TO BE FINE.
I PROMISE.

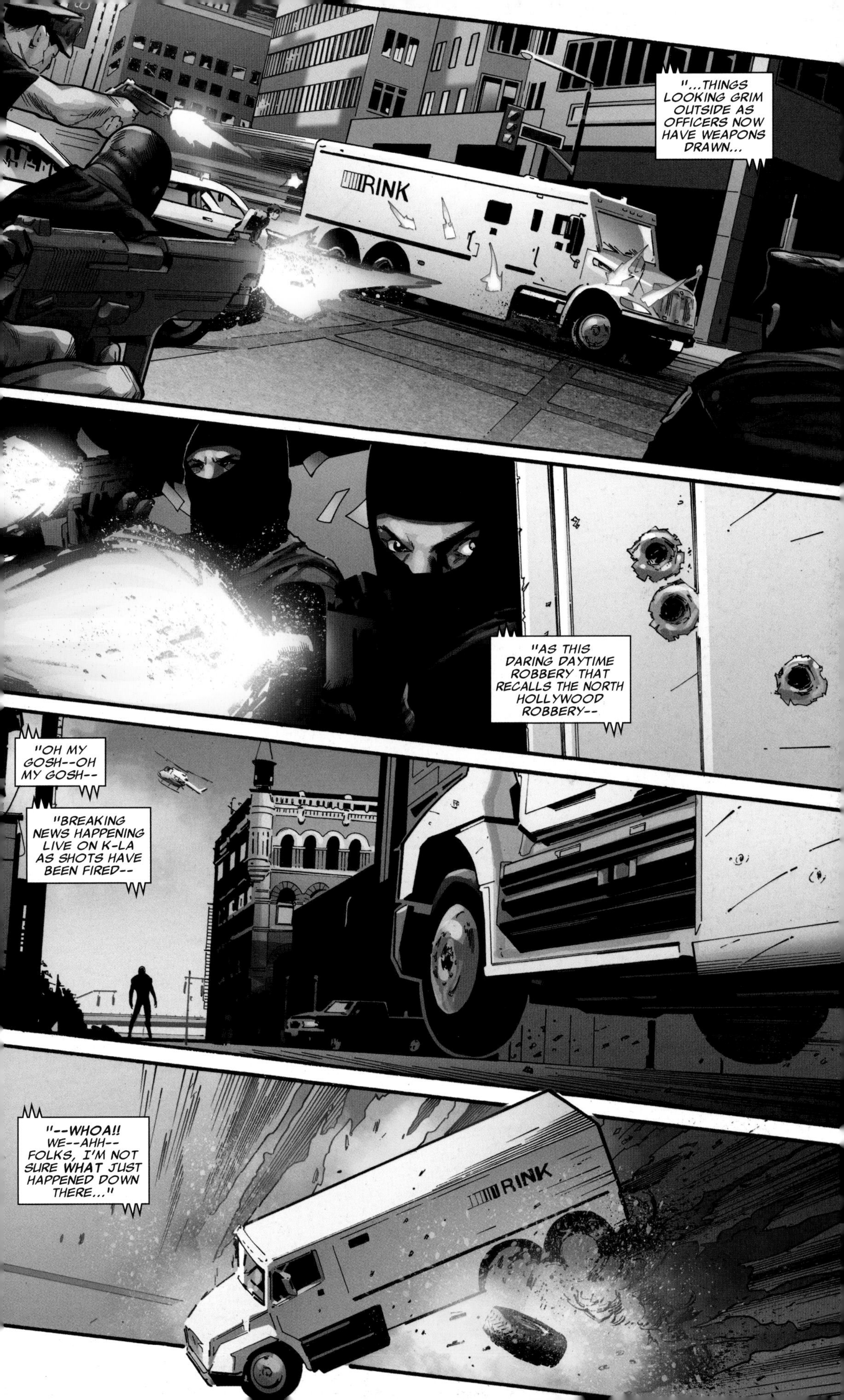
"...THINGS LOOKING GRIM OUTSIDE AS OFFICERS NOW HAVE WEAPONS DRAWN...
RINK
"AS THIS DARING DAYTIME ROBBERY THAT RECALLS THE NORTH HOLLYWOOD ROBBERY--
"OH MY GOSH--OH MY GOSH--
"BREAKING NEWS HAPPENING LIVE ON K-LA AS SHOTS HAVE BEEN FIRED--
"--WHOA!! WE--AHH-- FOLKS, I'M NOT SURE WHAT JUST HAPPENED DOWN THERE..."
RINK

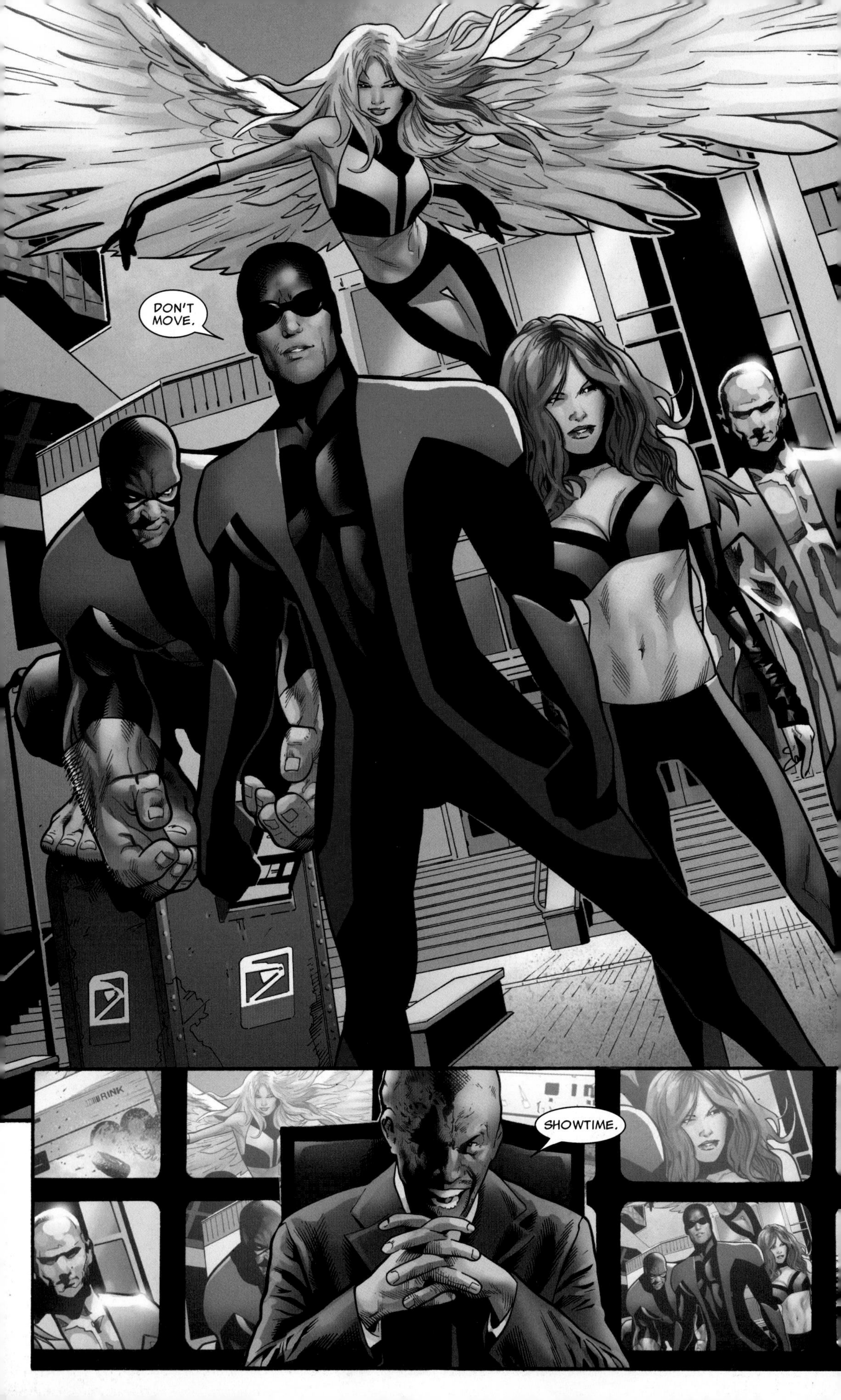
DON'T MOVE.
SHOWTIME.

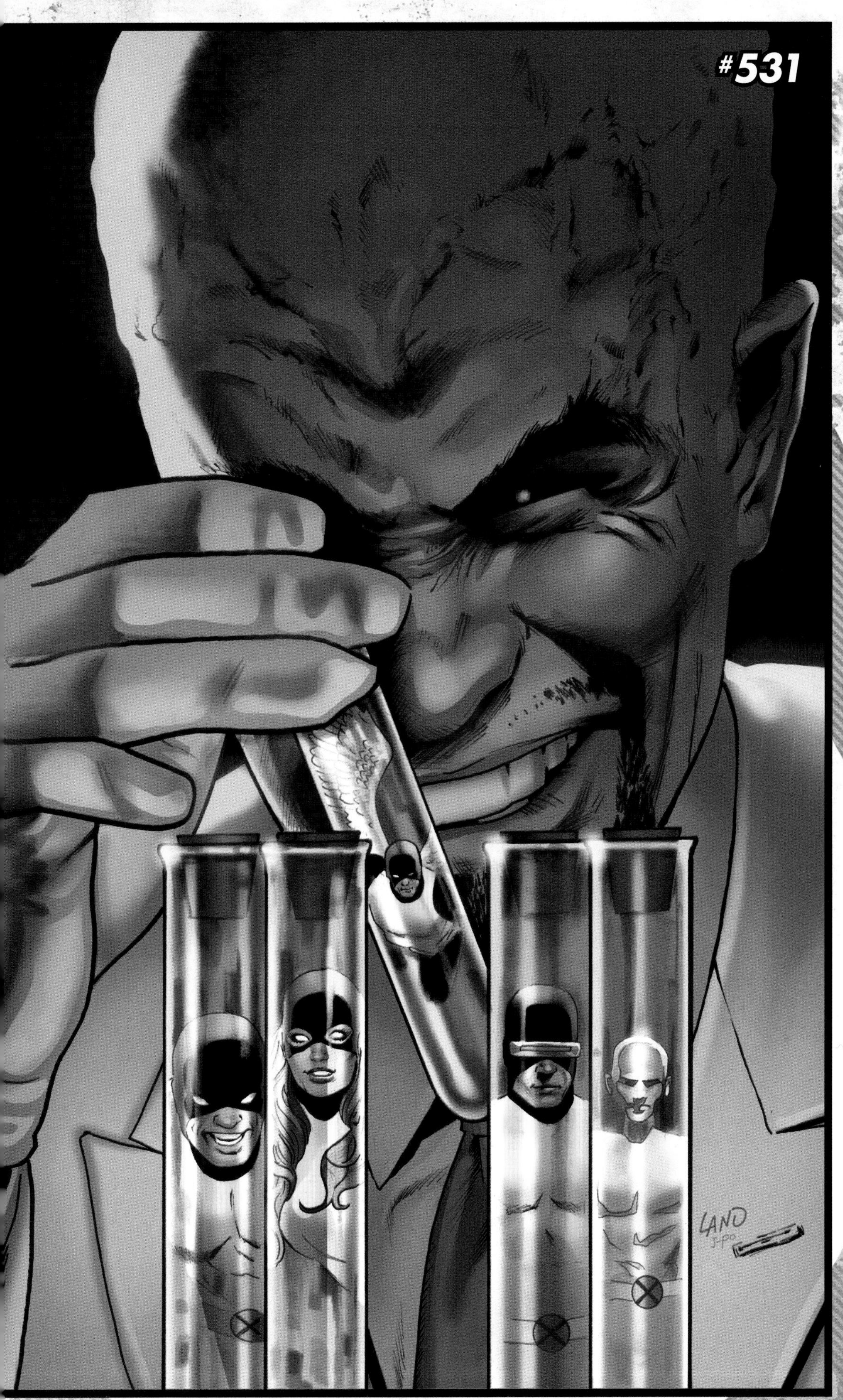
#531
LAND
J-PO

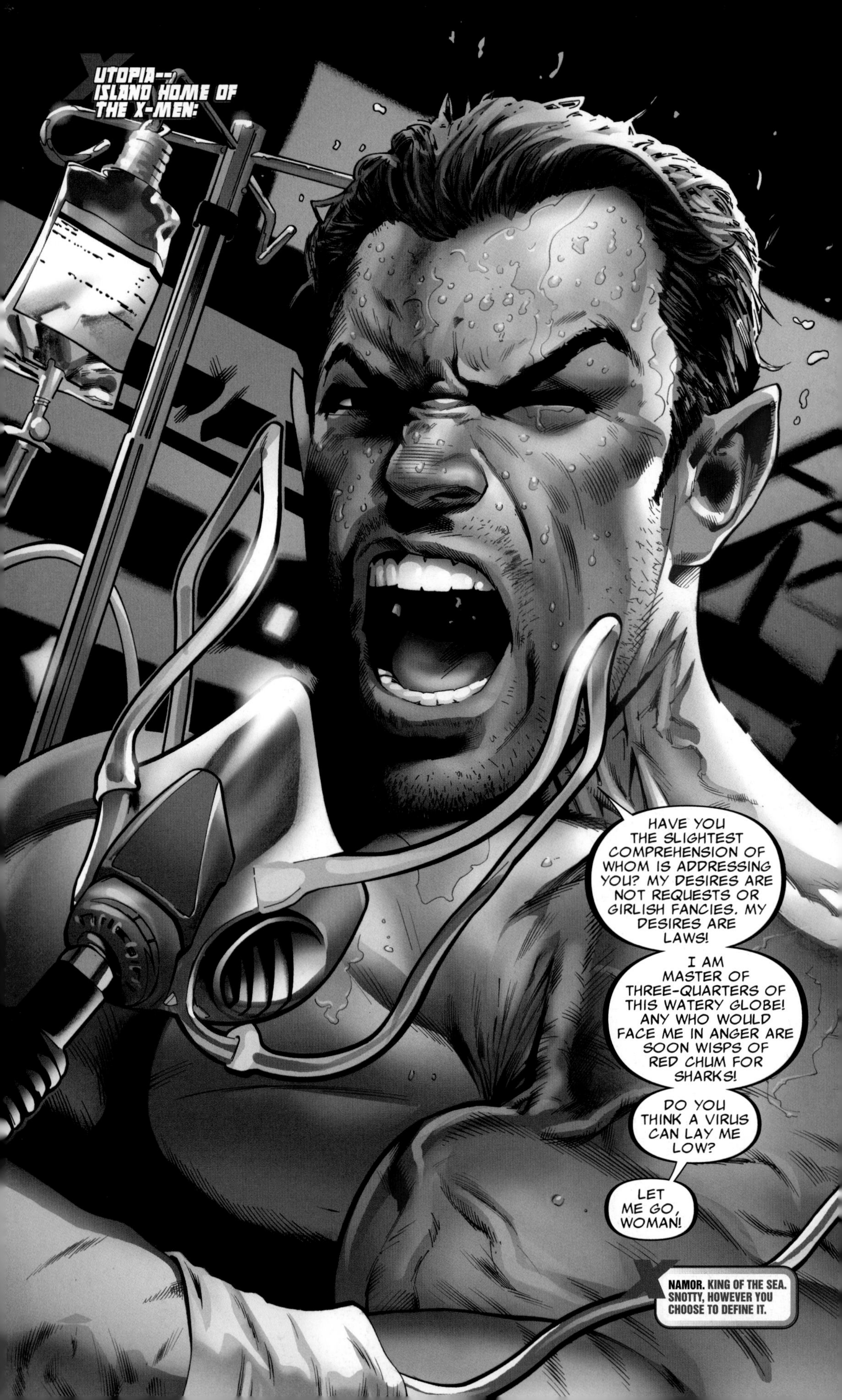
UTOPIA-- ISLAND HOME OF THE X-MEN:
HAVE YOU THE SLIGHTEST COMPREHENSION OF WHOM IS ADDRESSING YOU? MY DESIRES ARE NOT REQUESTS OR GIRLISH FANCIES. MY DESIRES ARE LAWS!
I AM MASTER OF THREE-QUARTERS OF THIS WATERY GLOBE! ANY WHO WOULD FACE ME IN ANGER ARE SOON WISPS OF RED CHUM FOR SHARKS!
DO YOU THINK A VIRUS CAN LAY ME LOW?
LET ME GO, WOMAN!
NAMOR. KING OF THE SEA. SNOTTY, HOWEVER YOU CHOOSE TO DEFINE IT.

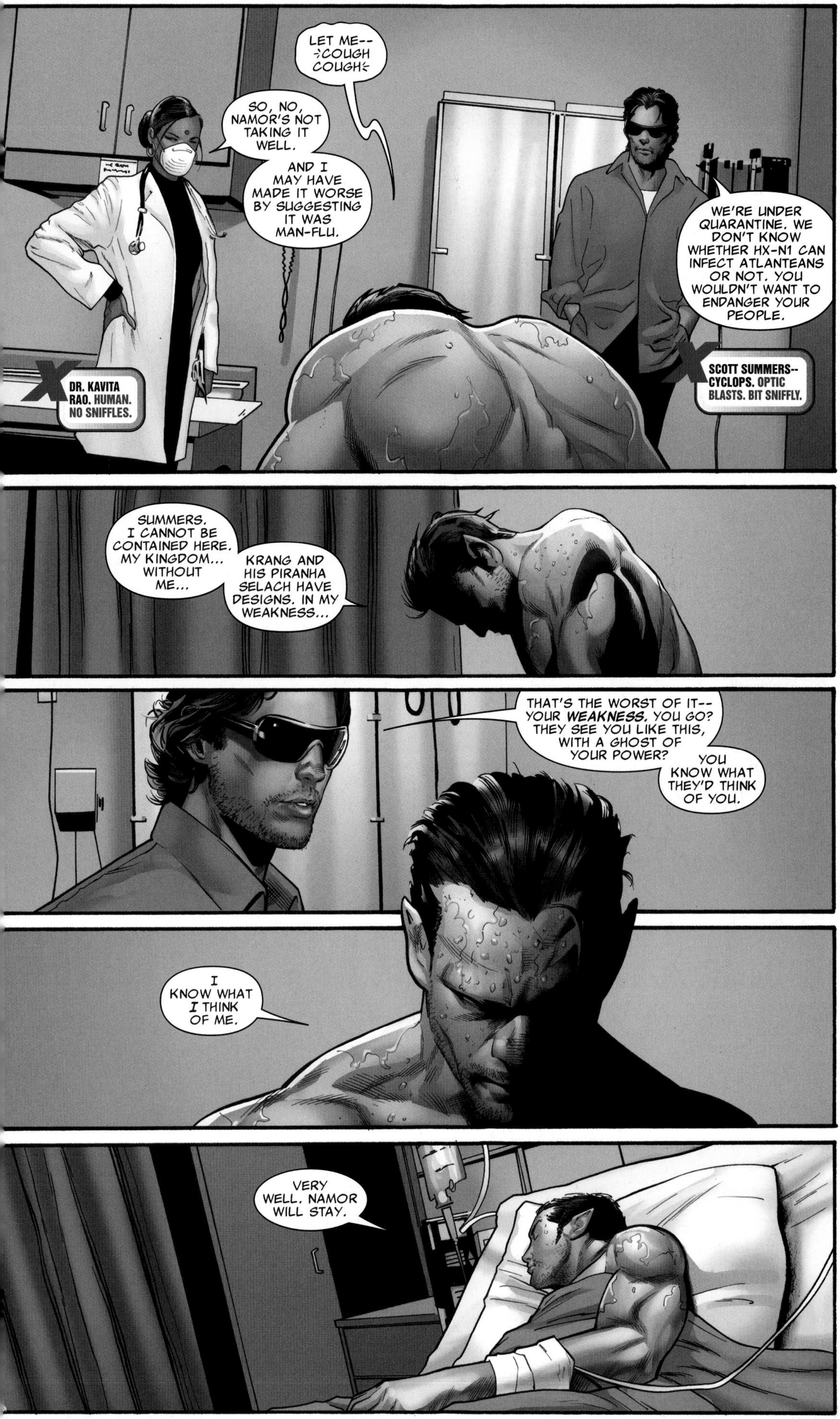

SO, NO, NAMOR'S NOT TAKING IT WELL.
AND I MAY HAVE MADE IT WORSE BY SUGGESTING IT WAS MAN-FLU.
LET ME-- COUGH COUGH
WE'RE UNDER QUARANTINE. WE DON'T KNOW WHETHER HX-N1 CAN INFECT ATLANTEANS OR NOT. YOU WOULDN'T WANT TO ENDANGER YOUR PEOPLE.
DR. KAVITA RAO. HUMAN. NO SNIFFLES.
SCOTT SUMMERS-- CYCLOPS. OPTIC BLASTS. BIT SNIFFLY.
SUMMERS. I CANNOT BE CONTAINED HERE. MY KINGDOM... WITHOUT ME...
KRANG AND HIS PIRANHA SELACH HAVE DESIGNS. IN MY WEAKNESS...
THAT'S THE WORST OF IT-- YOUR WEAKNESS. YOU GO? THEY SEE YOU LIKE THIS, WITH A GHOST OF YOUR POWER?
YOU KNOW WHAT THEY'D THINK OF YOU.
I KNOW WHAT I THINK OF ME.
VERY WELL. NAMOR WILL STAY.

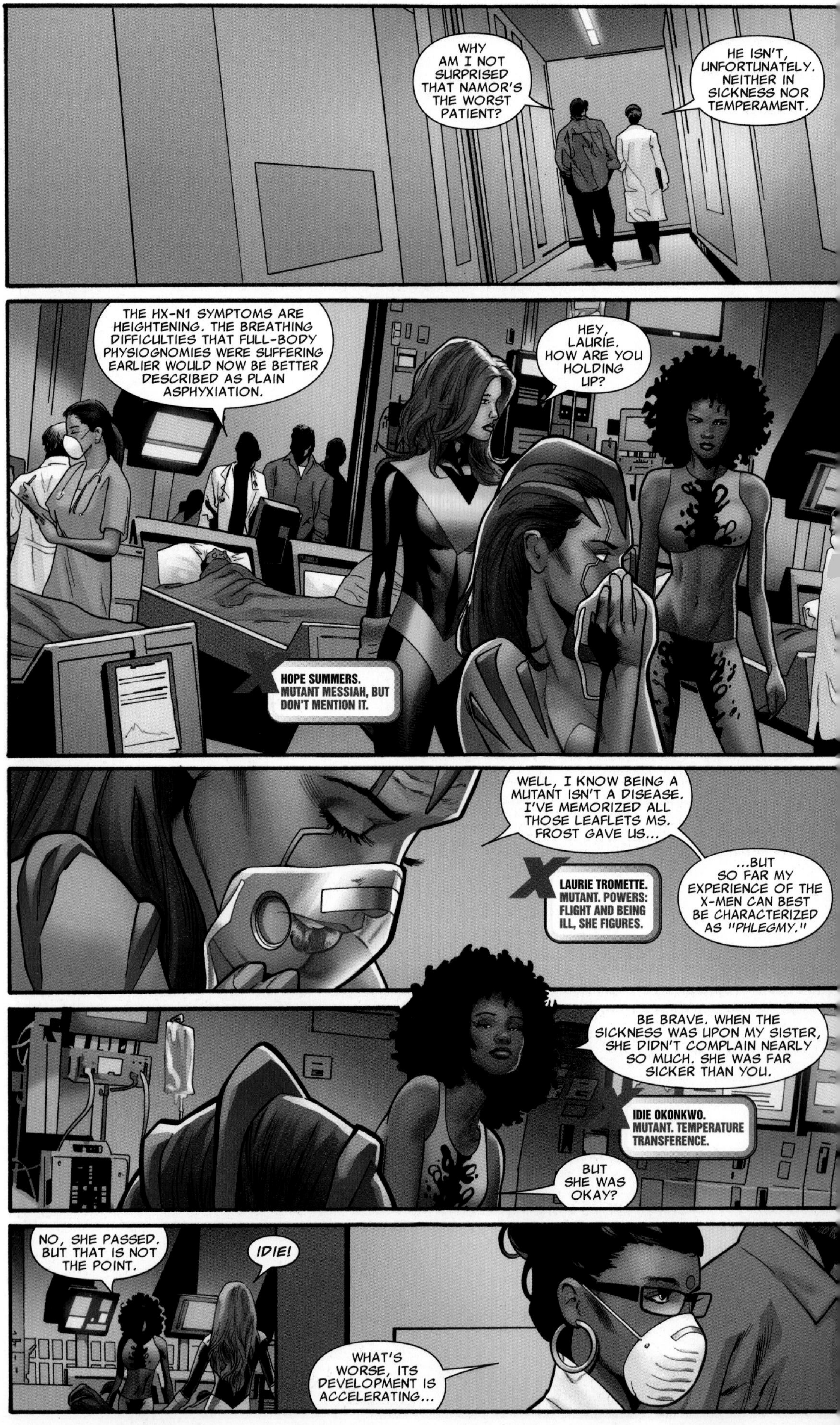
WHY AM I NOT SURPRISED THAT NAMOR'S THE WORST PATIENT?
HE ISN'T, UNFORTUNATELY. NEITHER IN SICKNESS NOR TEMPERAMENT.
THE HX-N1 SYMPTOMS ARE HEIGHTENING. THE BREATHING DIFFICULTIES THAT FULL-BODY PHYSIOGNOMIES WERE SUFFERING EARLIER WOULD NOW BE BETTER DESCRIBED AS PLAIN ASPHYXIATION.
HEY, LAURIE. HOW ARE YOU HOLDING UP?
HOPE SUMMERS. MUTANT MESSIAH, BUT DON'T MENTION IT.
WELL, I KNOW BEING A MUTANT ISN'T A DISEASE. I'VE MEMORIZED ALL THOSE LEAFLETS MS. FROST GAVE US...
LAURIE TROMETTE. MUTANT. POWERS: FLIGHT AND BEING ILL, SHE FIGURES.
...BUT SO FAR MY EXPERIENCE OF THE X-MEN CAN BEST BE CHARACTERIZED AS "PHLEGMY."
BE BRAVE. WHEN THE SICKNESS WAS UPON MY SISTER, SHE DIDN'T COMPLAIN NEARLY SO MUCH. SHE WAS FAR SICKER THAN YOU.
IDIE OKONKWO. MUTANT. TEMPERATURE TRANSFERENCE.
BUT SHE WAS OKAY?
NO, SHE PASSED. BUT THAT IS NOT THE POINT.
IDIE!
WHAT'S WORSE, ITS DEVELOPMENT IS ACCELERATING...

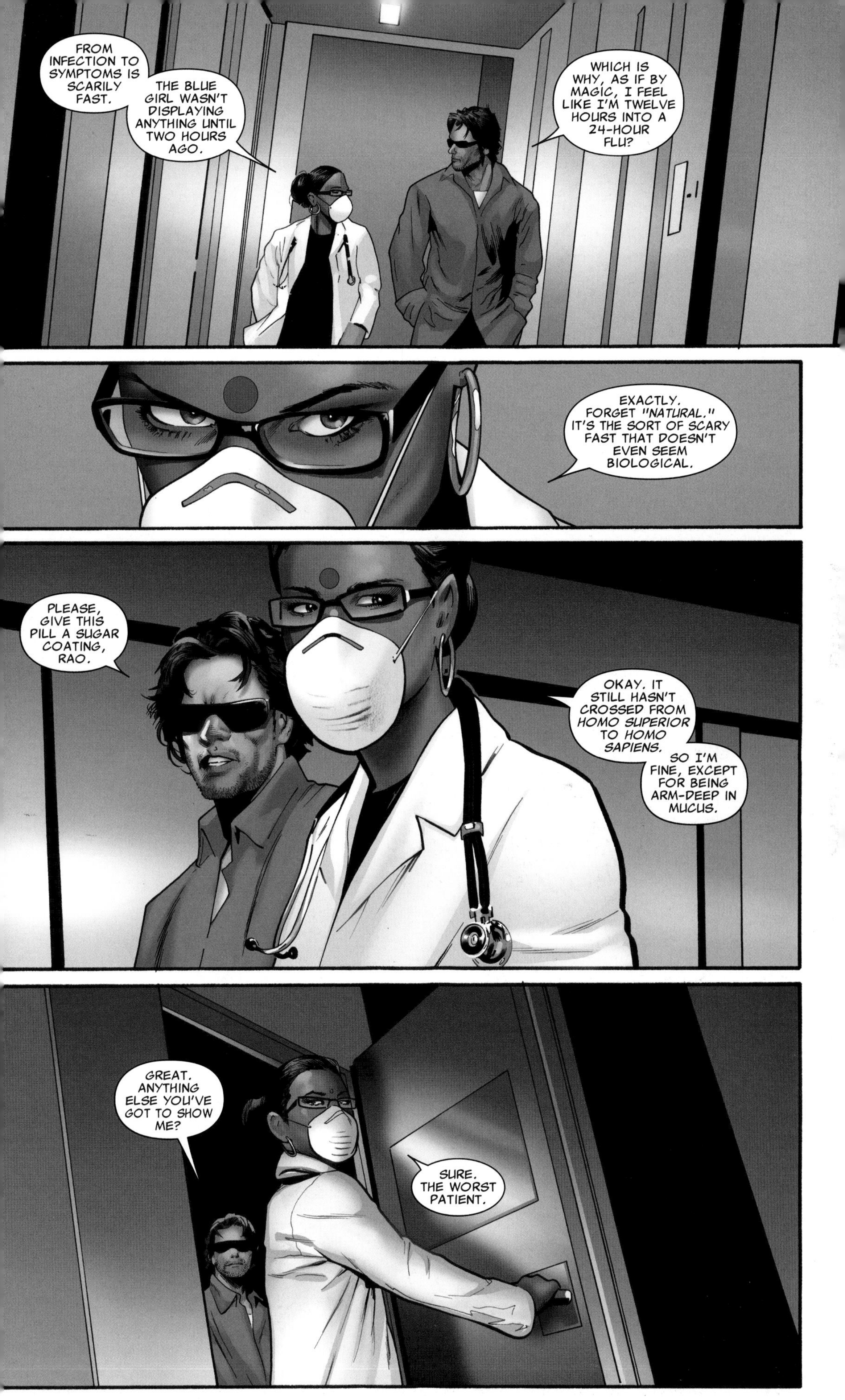
FROM INFECTION TO SYMPTOMS IS SCARILY FAST.
THE BLUE GIRL WASN'T DISPLAYING ANYTHING UNTIL TWO HOURS AGO.
WHICH IS WHY, AS IF BY MAGIC, I FEEL LIKE I'M TWELVE HOURS INTO A 24-HOUR FLU?
EXACTLY. FORGET "NATURAL." IT'S THE SORT OF SCARY FAST THAT DOESN'T EVEN SEEM BIOLOGICAL.
PLEASE, GIVE THIS PILL A SUGAR COATING, RAO.
OKAY. IT STILL HASN'T CROSSED FROM HOMO SUPERIOR TO HOMO SAPIENS.
SO I'M FINE, EXCEPT FOR BEING ARM-DEEP IN MUCUS.
GREAT. ANYTHING ELSE YOU'VE GOT TO SHOW ME?
SURE. THE WORST PATIENT.

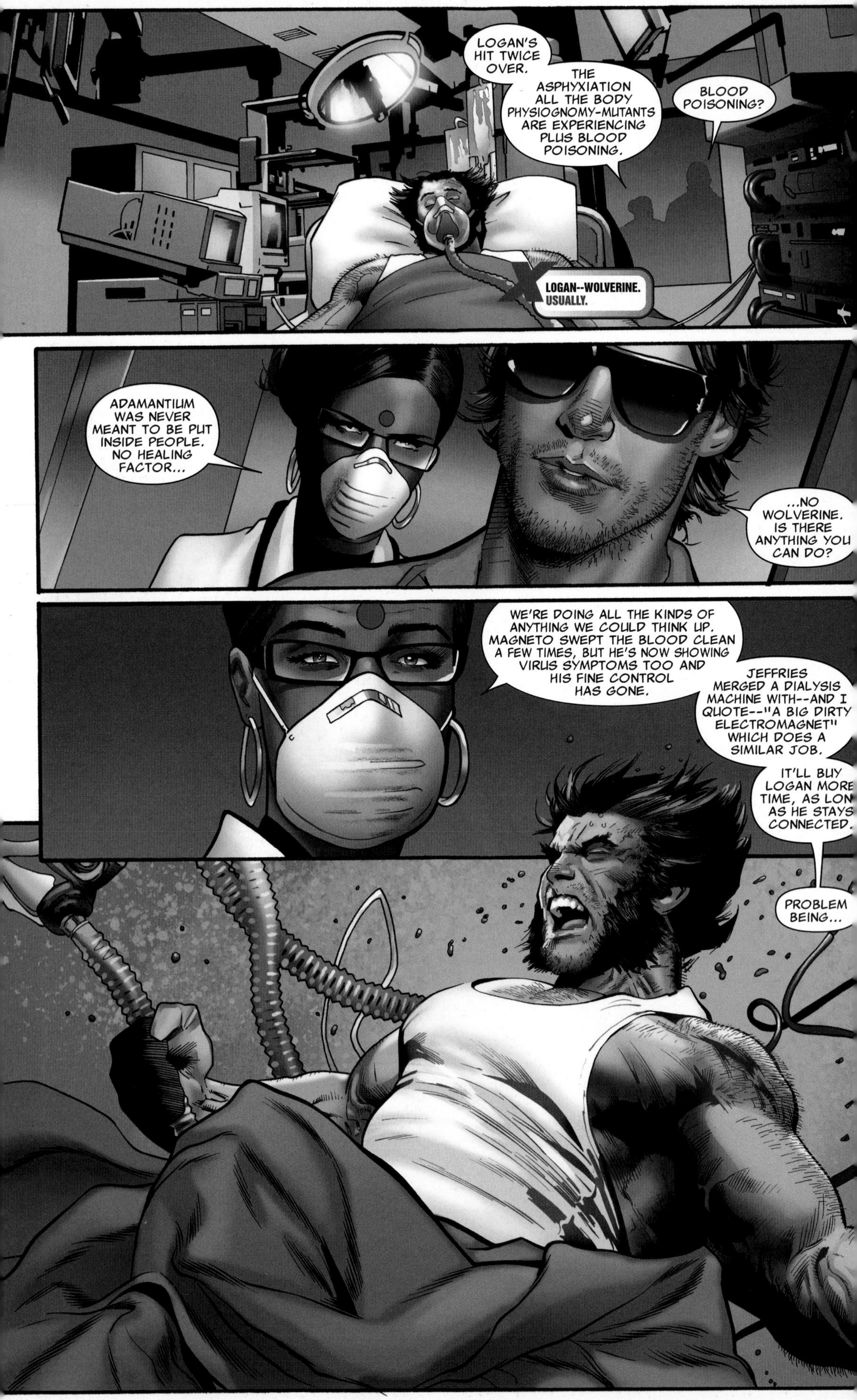
LOGAN'S HIT TWICE OVER.
THE ASPHYXIATION ALL THE BODY PHYSIOGNOMY-MUTANTS ARE EXPERIENCING PLUS BLOOD POISONING.
BLOOD POISONING?
LOGAN--WOLVERINE. USUALLY.
ADAMANTIUM WAS NEVER MEANT TO BE PUT INSIDE PEOPLE. NO HEALING FACTOR...
...NO WOLVERINE. IS THERE ANYTHING YOU CAN DO?
WE'RE DOING ALL THE KINDS OF ANYTHING WE COULD THINK UP. MAGNETO SWEPT THE BLOOD CLEAN A FEW TIMES, BUT HE'S NOW SHOWING VIRUS SYMPTOMS TOO AND HIS FINE CONTROL HAS GONE.
JEFFRIES MERGED A DIALYSIS MACHINE WITH--AND I QUOTE--"A BIG DIRTY ELECTROMAGNET" WHICH DOES A SIMILAR JOB.
IT'LL BUY LOGAN MORE TIME, AS LON AS HE STAYS CONNECTED.
PROBLEM BEING...

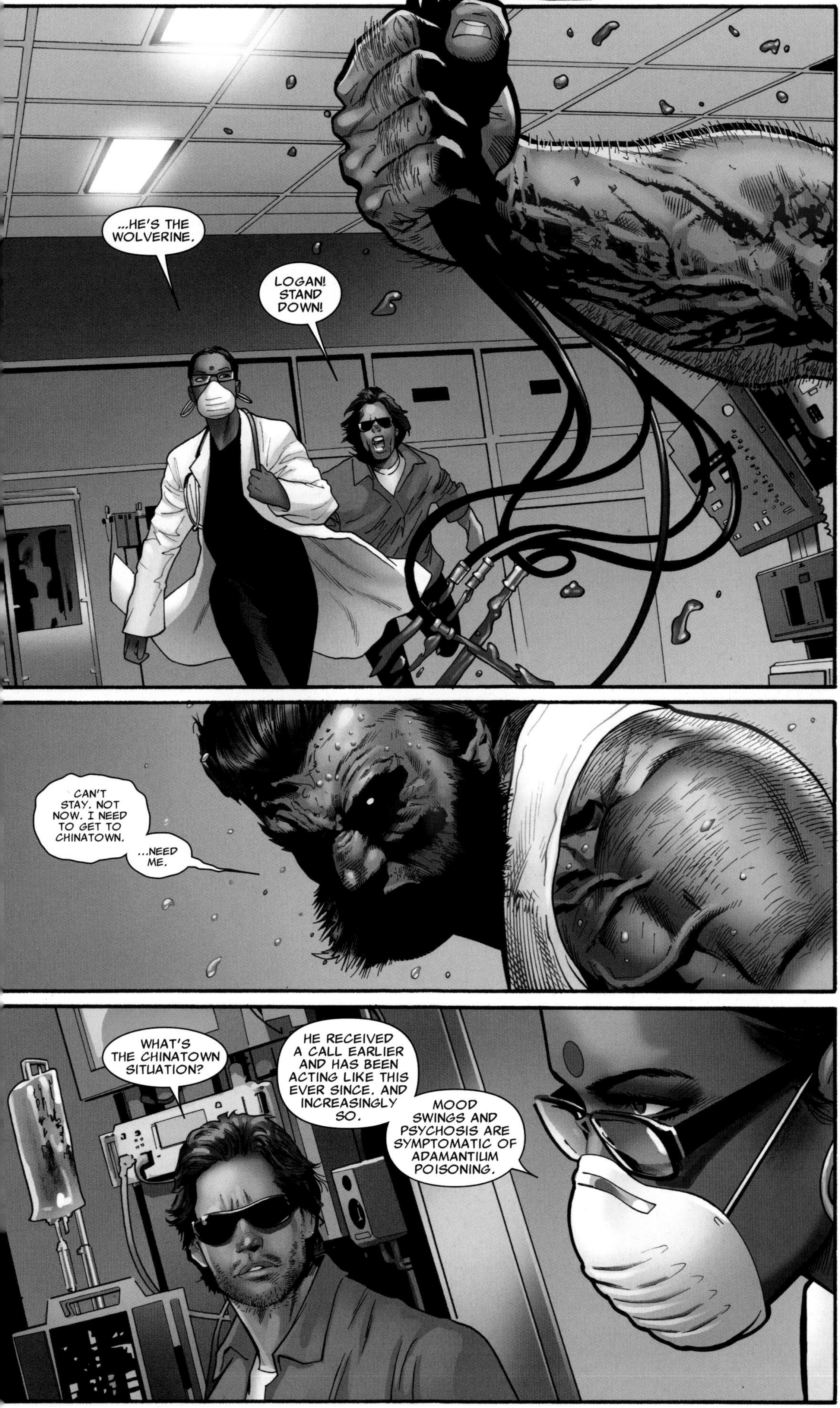

...HE'S THE WOLVERINE.
LOGAN! STAND DOWN!
CAN'T STAY. NOT NOW. I NEED TO GET TO CHINATOWN.
...NEED ME.
WHAT'S THE CHINATOWN SITUATION?
HE RECEIVED A CALL EARLIER AND HAS BEEN ACTING LIKE THIS EVER SINCE, AND INCREASINGLY SO.
MOOD SWINGS AND PSYCHOSIS ARE SYMPTOMATIC OF ADAMANTIUM POISONING.

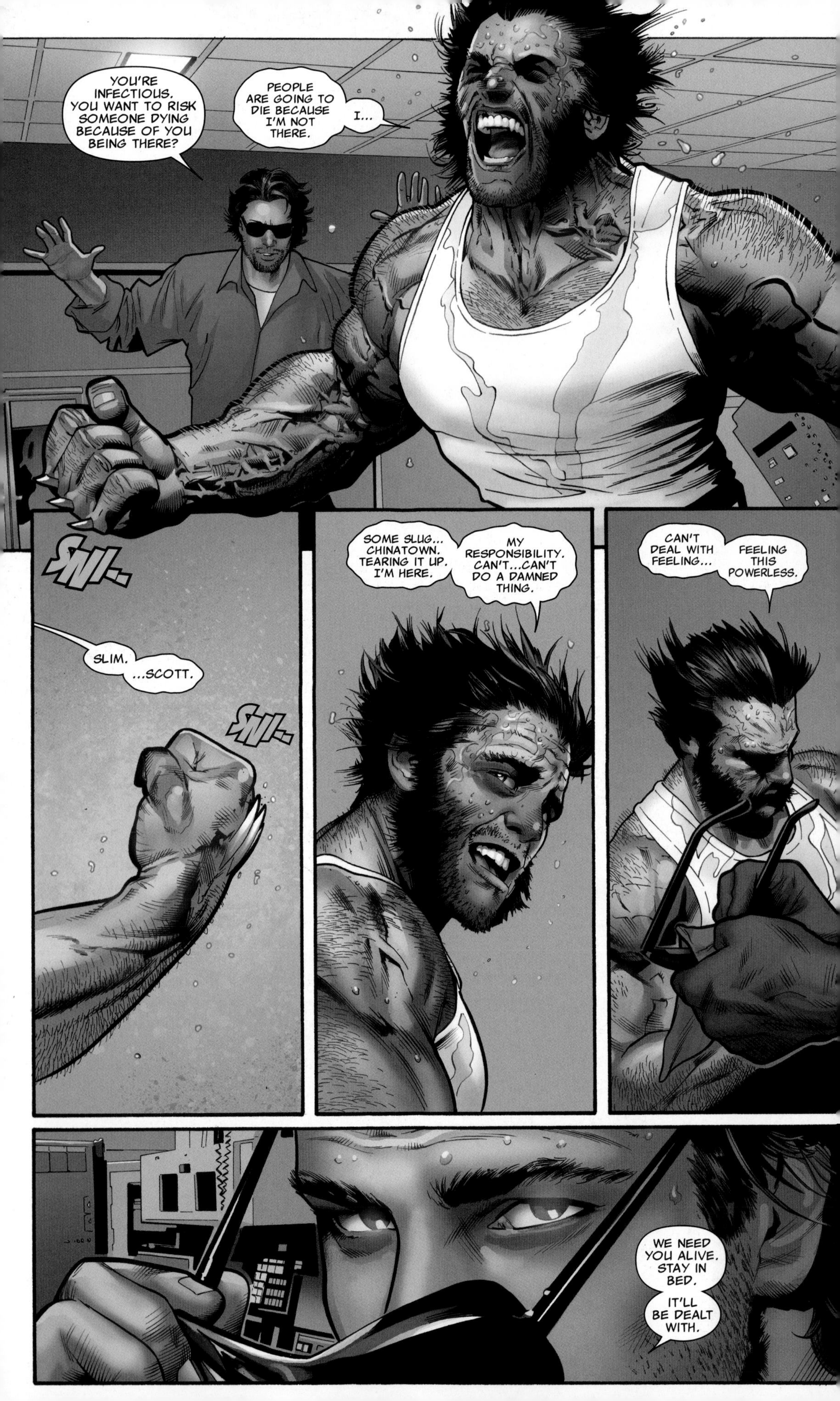
YOU'RE INFECTIOUS. YOU WANT TO RISK SOMEONE DYING BECAUSE OF YOU BEING THERE?
PEOPLE ARE GOING TO DIE BECAUSE I'M NOT THERE.
I...
SNI--
SLIM.
...SCOTT.
SNI--
SOME SLUG... CHINATOWN. TEARING IT UP. I'M HERE.
MY RESPONSIBILITY. CAN'T...CAN'T DO A DAMNED THING.
CAN'T DEAL WITH FEELING...
FEELING THIS POWERLESS.
WE NEED YOU ALIVE. STAY IN BED.
IT'LL BE DEALT WITH.

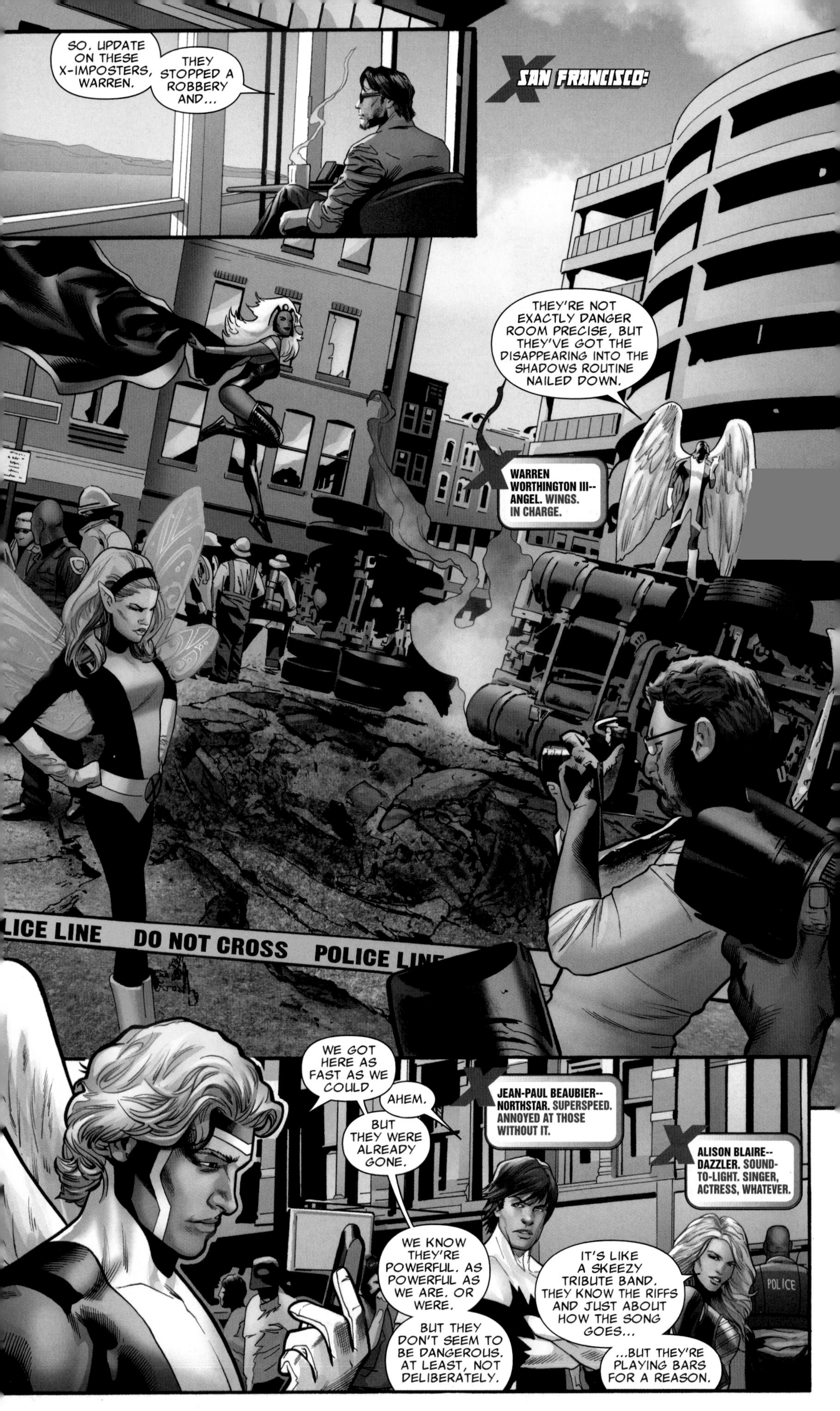

SO. UPDATE ON THESE X-IMPOSTERS, WARREN.
THEY STOPPED A ROBBERY AND...
SAN FRANCISCO:
THEY'RE NOT EXACTLY DANGER ROOM PRECISE, BUT THEY'VE GOT THE DISAPPEARING INTO THE SHADOWS ROUTINE NAILED DOWN.
WARREN WORTHINGTON III-- ANGEL. WINGS. IN CHARGE.
POLICE LINE DO NOT CROSS POLICE LINE
WE GOT HERE AS FAST AS WE COULD.
AHEM.
BUT THEY WERE ALREADY GONE.
JEAN-PAUL BEAUBIER-- NORTHSTAR. SUPERSPEED. ANNOYED AT THOSE WITHOUT IT.
ALISON BLAIRE-- DAZZLER. SOUND-TO-LIGHT. SINGER, ACTRESS, WHATEVER.
WE KNOW THEY'RE POWERFUL. AS POWERFUL AS WE ARE. OR WERE.
BUT THEY DON'T SEEM TO BE DANGEROUS. AT LEAST, NOT DELIBERATELY.
IT'S LIKE A SKEEZY TRIBUTE BAND. THEY KNOW THE RIFFS AND JUST ABOUT HOW THE SONG GOES...
...BUT THEY'RE PLAYING BARS FOR A REASON.
POLICE

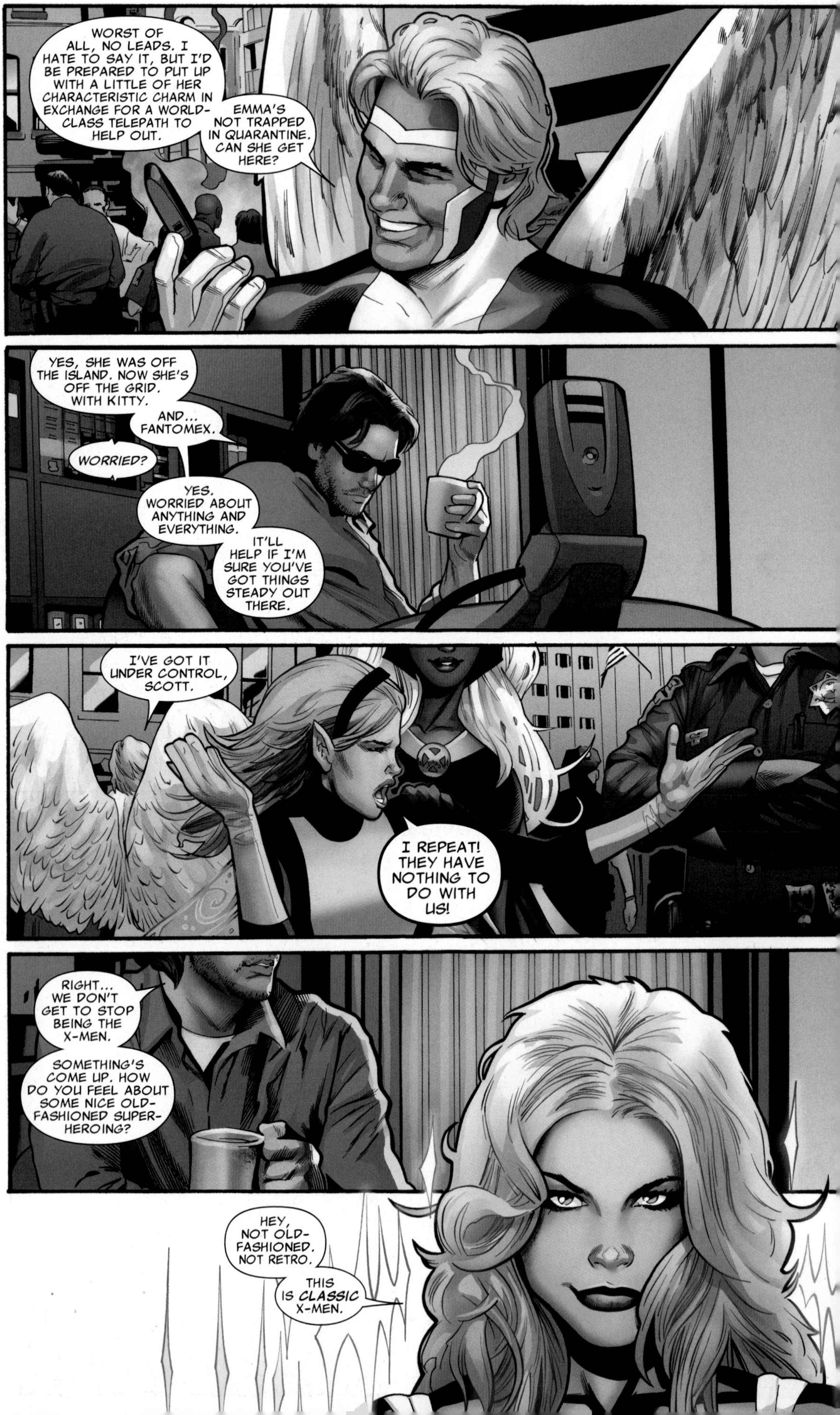
WORST OF ALL, NO LEADS. I HATE TO SAY IT, BUT I'D BE PREPARED TO PUT UP WITH A LITTLE OF HER CHARACTERISTIC CHARM IN EXCHANGE FOR A WORLD-CLASS TELEPATH TO HELP OUT.
EMMA'S NOT TRAPPED IN QUARANTINE. CAN SHE GET HERE?
YES, SHE WAS OFF THE ISLAND. NOW SHE'S OFF THE GRID. WITH KITTY.
AND... FANTOMEX.
WORRIED?
YES. WORRIED ABOUT ANYTHING AND EVERYTHING.
IT'LL HELP IF I'M SURE YOU'VE GOT THINGS STEADY OUT THERE.
I'VE GOT IT UNDER CONTROL, SCOTT.
I REPEAT! THEY HAVE NOTHING TO DO WITH US!
RIGHT... WE DON'T GET TO STOP BEING THE X-MEN.
SOMETHING'S COME UP. HOW DO YOU FEEL ABOUT SOME NICE OLD-FASHIONED SUPER-HEROING?
HEY, NOT OLD-FASHIONED. NOT RETRO.
THIS IS *CLASSIC* X-MEN.

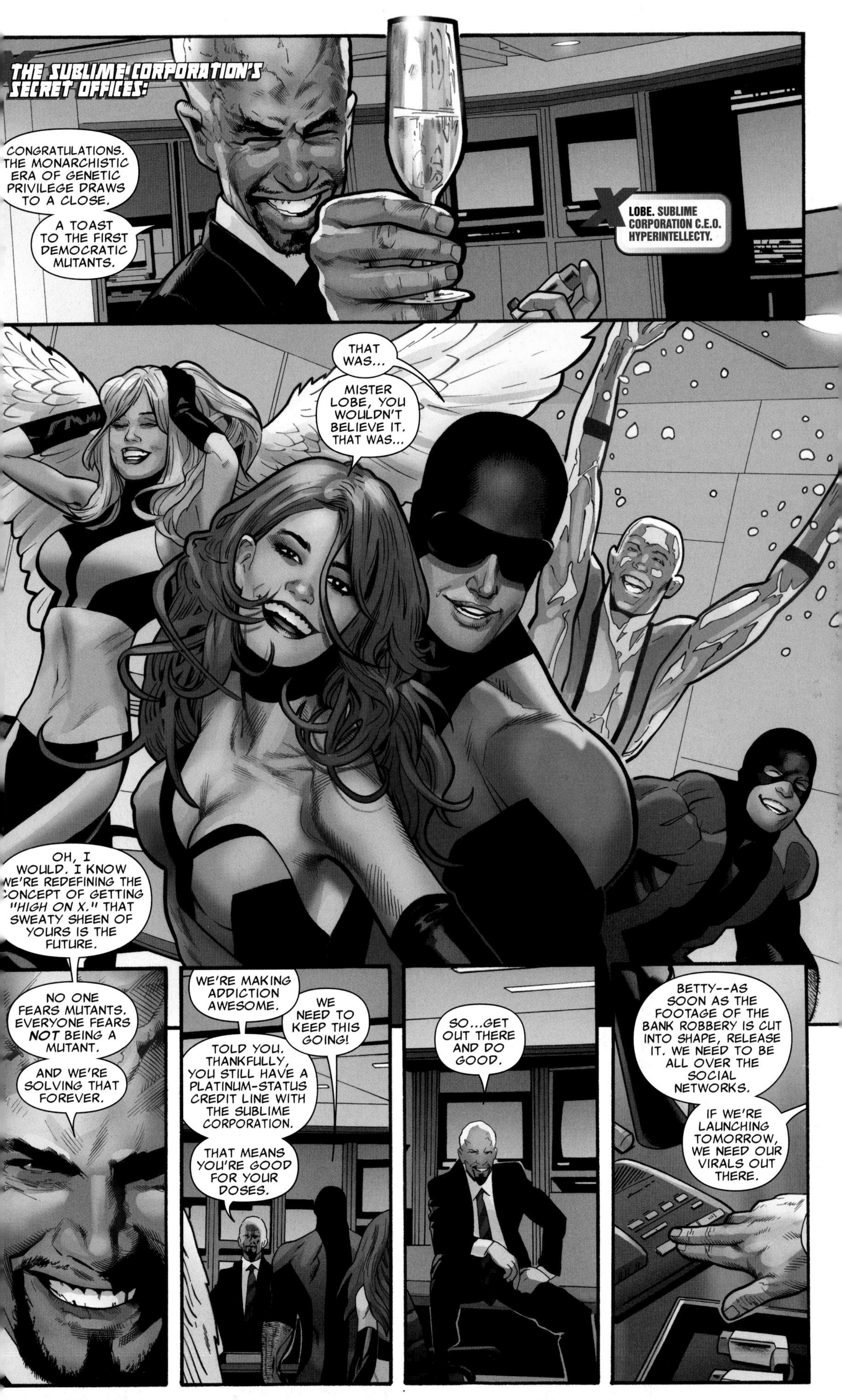
THE SUBLIME CORPORATION'S SECRET OFFICES:
CONGRATULATIONS. THE MONARCHISTIC ERA OF GENETIC PRIVILEGE DRAWS TO A CLOSE.
A TOAST TO THE FIRST DEMOCRATIC MUTANTS.
LOBE. SUBLIME CORPORATION C.E.O. HYPERINTELLECTY.
THAT WAS...
MISTER LOBE, YOU WOULDN'T BELIEVE IT. THAT WAS...
OH, I WOULD. I KNOW WE'RE REDEFINING THE CONCEPT OF GETTING "HIGH ON X." THAT SWEATY SHEEN OF YOURS IS THE FUTURE.
NO ONE FEARS MUTANTS. EVERYONE FEARS NOT BEING A MUTANT.
AND WE'RE SOLVING THAT FOREVER.
WE'RE MAKING ADDICTION AWESOME.
WE NEED TO KEEP THIS GOING!
TOLD YOU. THANKFULLY, YOU STILL HAVE A PLATINUM-STATUS CREDIT LINE WITH THE SUBLIME CORPORATION.
THAT MEANS YOU'RE GOOD FOR YOUR DOSES.
SO...GET OUT THERE AND DO GOOD.
BETTY--AS SOON AS THE FOOTAGE OF THE BANK ROBBERY IS CUT INTO SHAPE, RELEASE IT. WE NEED TO BE ALL OVER THE SOCIAL NETWORKS.
IF WE'RE LAUNCHING TOMORROW, WE NEED OUR VIRALS OUT THERE.

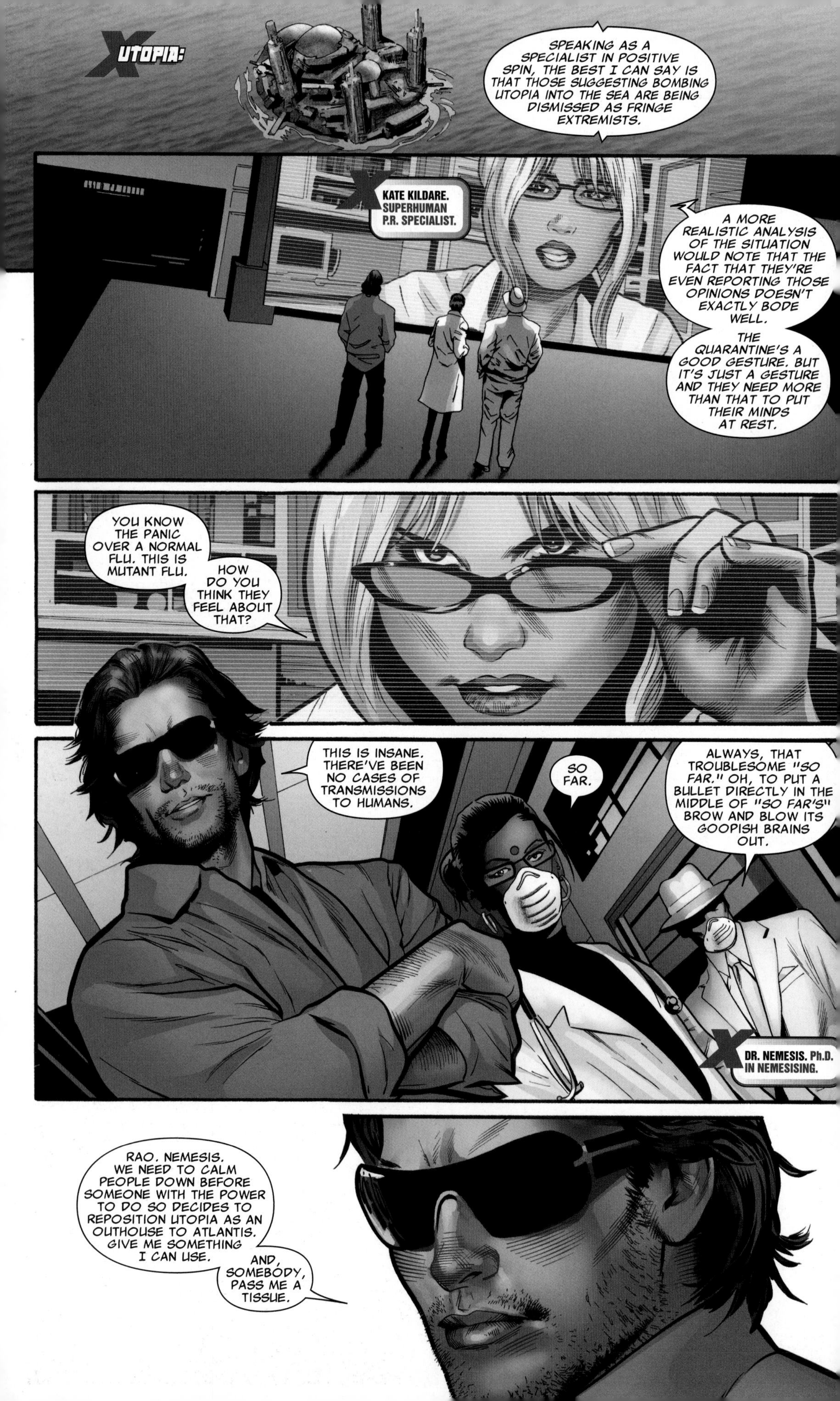
UTOPIA:
SPEAKING AS A SPECIALIST IN POSITIVE SPIN, THE BEST I CAN SAY IS THAT THOSE SUGGESTING BOMBING UTOPIA INTO THE SEA ARE BEING DISMISSED AS FRINGE EXTREMISTS.
KATE KILDARE. SUPERHUMAN P.R. SPECIALIST.
A MORE REALISTIC ANALYSIS OF THE SITUATION WOULD NOTE THAT THE FACT THAT THEY'RE EVEN REPORTING THOSE OPINIONS DOESN'T EXACTLY BODE WELL.
THE QUARANTINE'S A GOOD GESTURE. BUT IT'S JUST A GESTURE AND THEY NEED MORE THAN THAT TO PUT THEIR MINDS AT REST.
YOU KNOW THE PANIC OVER A NORMAL FLU. THIS IS MUTANT FLU.
HOW DO YOU THINK THEY FEEL ABOUT THAT?
THIS IS INSANE. THERE'VE BEEN NO CASES OF TRANSMISSIONS TO HUMANS.
SO FAR.
ALWAYS, THAT TROUBLESOME "SO FAR." OH, TO PUT A BULLET DIRECTLY IN THE MIDDLE OF "SO FAR'S" BROW AND BLOW ITS GOOPISH BRAINS OUT.
DR. NEMESIS. Ph.D. IN NEMESISING.
RAO. NEMESIS. WE NEED TO CALM PEOPLE DOWN BEFORE SOMEONE WITH THE POWER TO DO SO DECIDES TO REPOSITION UTOPIA AS AN OUTHOUSE TO ATLANTIS. GIVE ME SOMETHING I CAN USE.
AND, SOMEBODY, PASS ME A TISSUE.

HX-N1 NOTES ADDENDUM. MEETING WITH SUMMERS WENT AS WELL AS COULD BE EXPECTED.

STILL-- *BREAKTHROUGH.* THEY'RE NANO-MACHINES, DESIGNED TO MIMIC A VIRUS STRUCTURE. VERY CLEVER. WOULD ADMIRE IT, IF I HAD THE TIME.

MADISON'S MANAGED TO SYNTHESIZE THE VIRUS. WE CAN MAKE IT, BUT NOT CURE IT. NON-METALLIC, SO THE MAGNETO OPTION'S OFF THE TABLE. VERY ANNOYING.

NORMAL INFECTION [TE]STS ARE EITHER TOO [S]LOW OR NOT SURE [E]NOUGH. A DISTINCT [LA]CK OF HOMO SAPIEN [TE]ST SUBJECTS ON [U]TOPIA DOESN'T HELP.

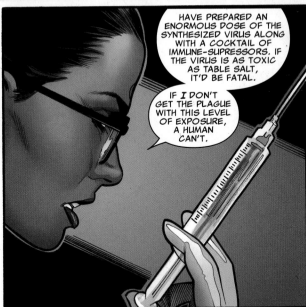

HAVE PREPARED AN ENORMOUS DOSE OF THE SYNTHESIZED VIRUS ALONG WITH A COCKTAIL OF IMMUNE-SUPRESSORS. IF THE VIRUS IS AS TOXIC AS TABLE SALT, IT'D BE FATAL.

IF *I* DON'T GET THE PLAGUE WITH THIS LEVEL OF EXPOSURE, A HUMAN CAN'T.

WE'LL KNOW ONE WAY OR ANOTHER SOON ENOUGH.

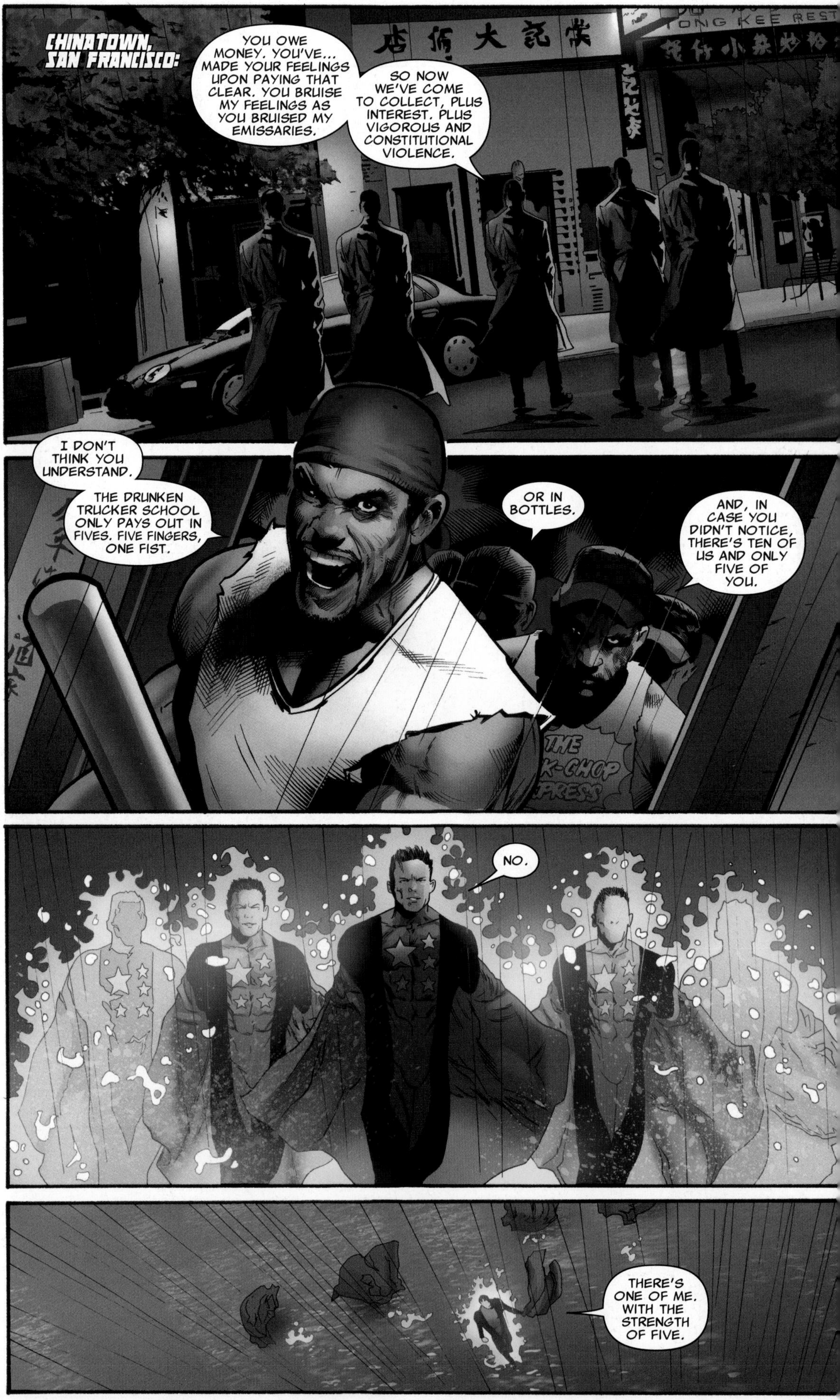

CHINATOWN, SAN FRANCISCO:
YOU OWE MONEY. YOU'VE... MADE YOUR FEELINGS UPON PAYING THAT CLEAR. YOU BRUISE MY FEELINGS AS YOU BRUISED MY EMISSARIES.
SO NOW WE'VE COME TO COLLECT, PLUS INTEREST. PLUS VIGOROUS AND CONSTITUTIONAL VIOLENCE.
TONG KEE REST
I DON'T THINK YOU UNDERSTAND.
THE DRUNKEN TRUCKER SCHOOL ONLY PAYS OUT IN FIVES. FIVE FINGERS, ONE FIST.
OR IN BOTTLES.
AND, IN CASE YOU DIDN'T NOTICE, THERE'S TEN OF US AND ONLY FIVE OF YOU.
NO.
THERE'S ONE OF ME. WITH THE STRENGTH OF FIVE.

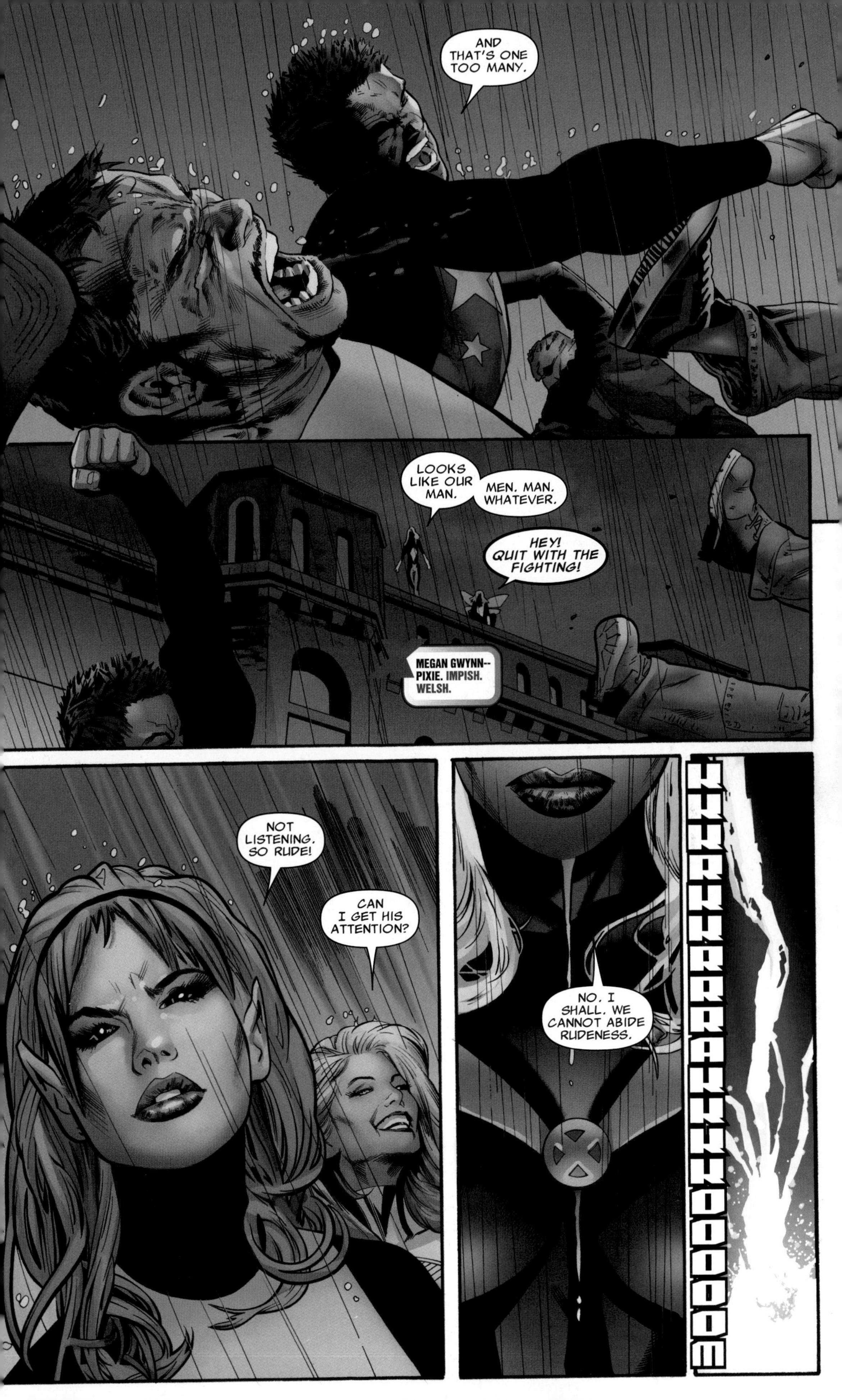
AND THAT'S ONE TOO MANY.
LOOKS LIKE OUR MAN.
MEN. MAN. WHATEVER.
HEY! QUIT WITH THE FIGHTING!
MEGAN GWYNN-- PIXIE. IMPISH. WELSH.
NOT LISTENING. SO RUDE!
CAN I GET HIS ATTENTION?
NO, I SHALL. WE CANNOT ABIDE RUDENESS.
KKRRRRRAKKKOOOOOOM

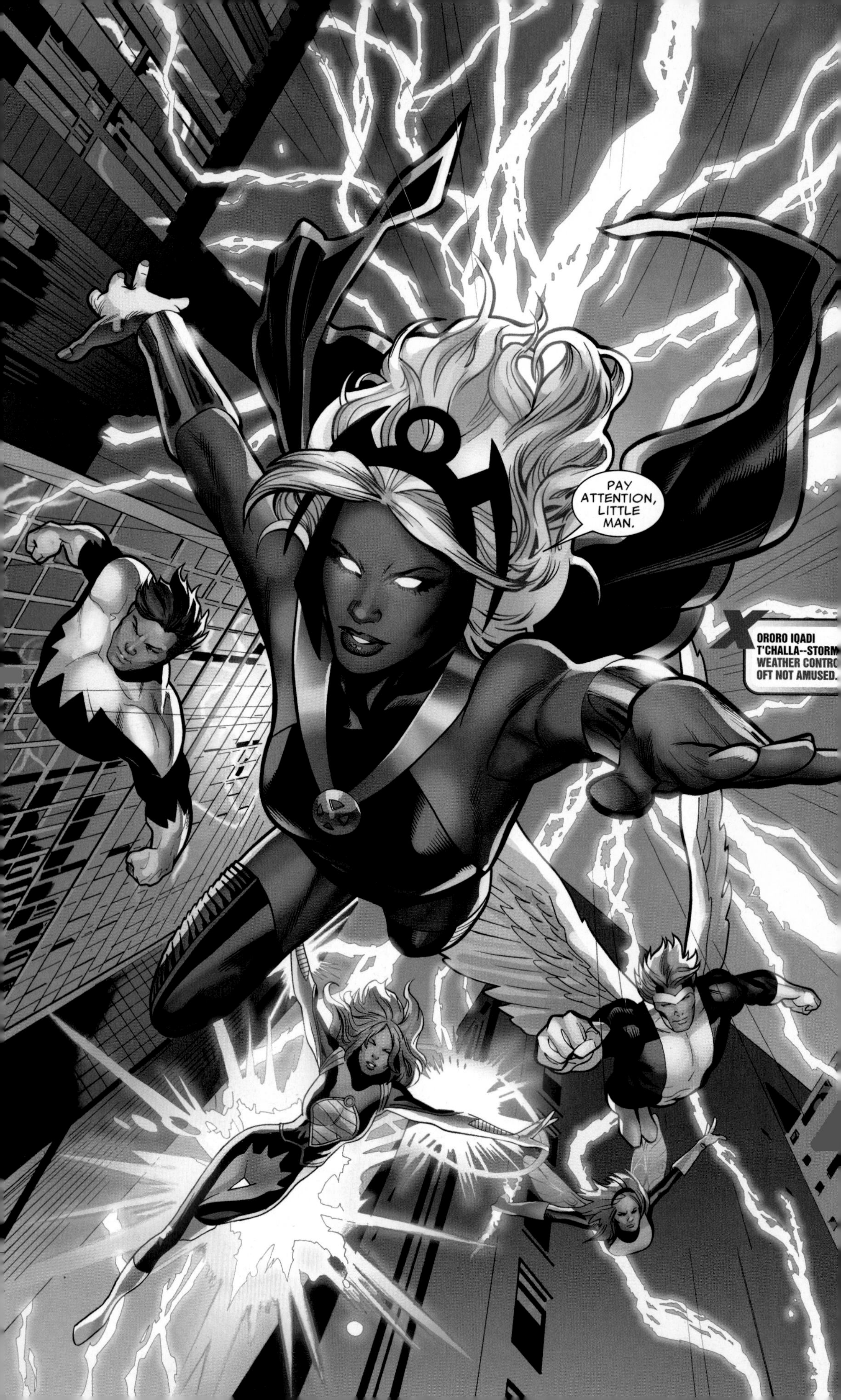
PAY ATTENTION, LITTLE MAN.
ORORO IQADI T'CHALLA--STORM WEATHER CONTRO OFT NOT AMUSED.

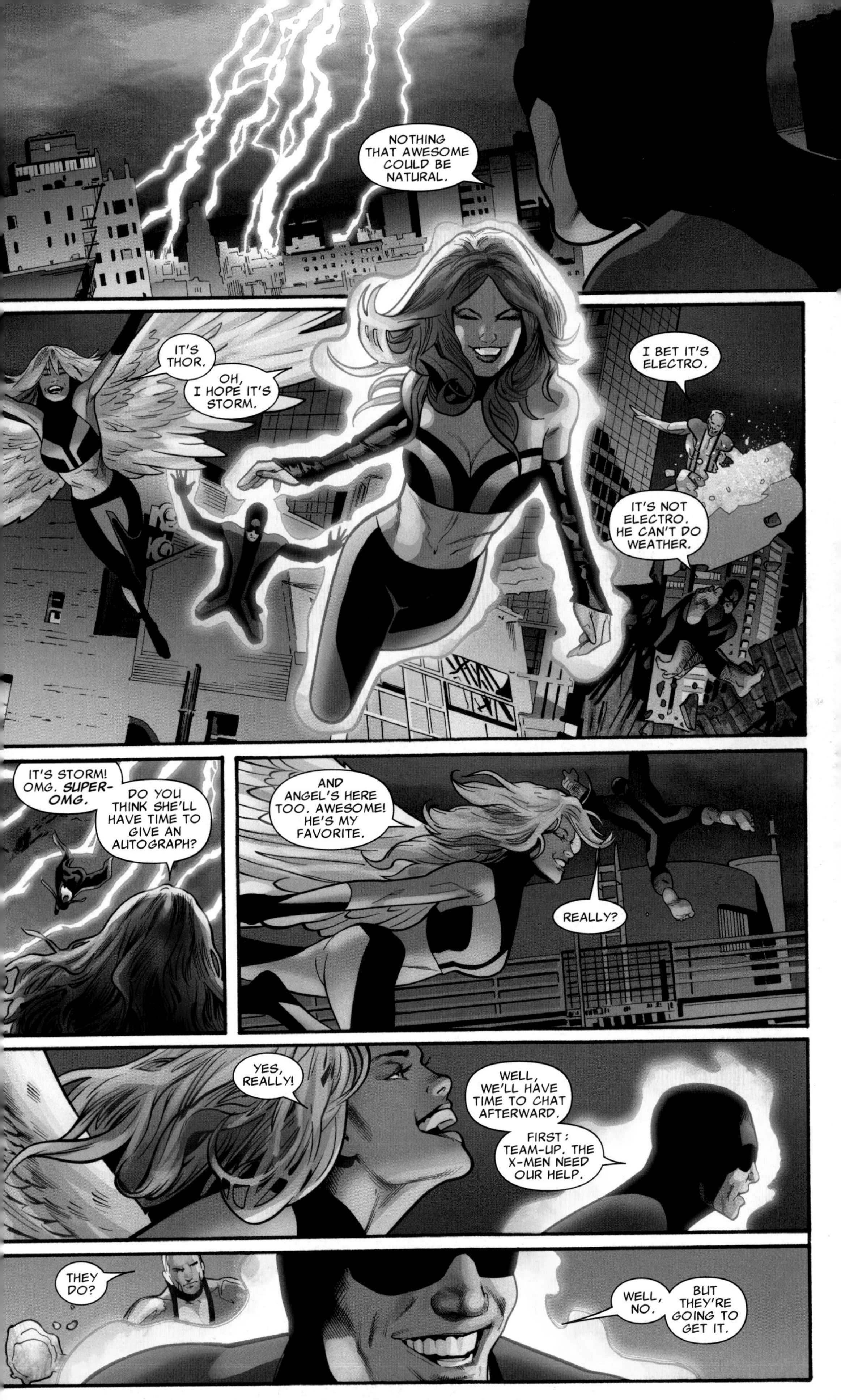
NOTHING THAT AWESOME COULD BE NATURAL.
IT'S THOR.
OH, I HOPE IT'S STORM.
I BET IT'S ELECTRO.
IT'S NOT ELECTRO. HE CAN'T DO WEATHER.
IT'S STORM! OMG. SUPER-OMG.
DO YOU THINK SHE'LL HAVE TIME TO GIVE AN AUTOGRAPH?
AND ANGEL'S HERE TOO. AWESOME! HE'S MY FAVORITE.
REALLY?
YES, REALLY!
WELL, WE'LL HAVE TIME TO CHAT AFTERWARD.
FIRST: TEAM-UP. THE X-MEN NEED OUR HELP.
THEY DO?
WELL, NO.
BUT THEY'RE GOING TO GET IT.

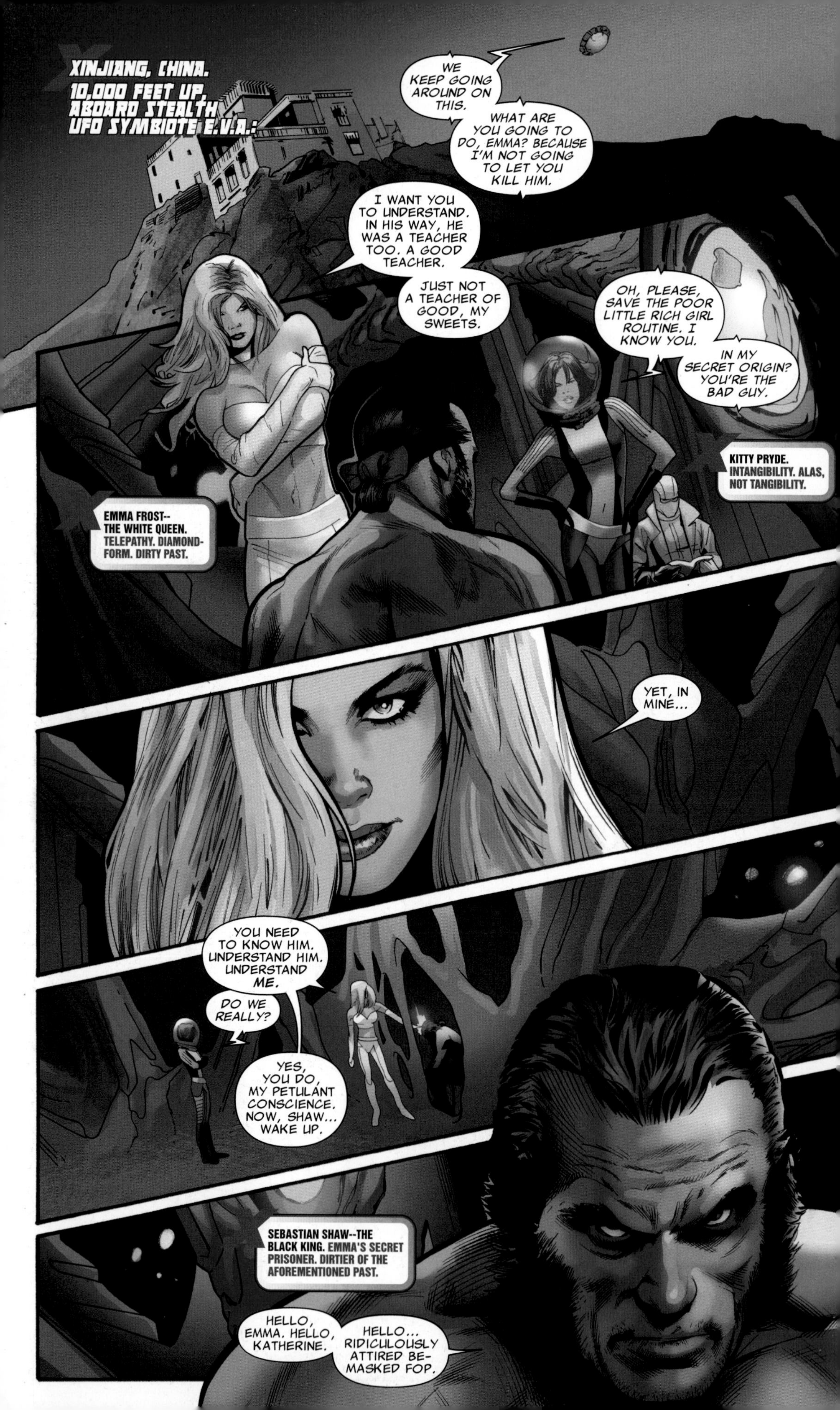
XINJIANG, CHINA.
10,000 FEET UP, ABOARD STEALTH UFO SYMBIOTE E.V.A.:
WE KEEP GOING AROUND ON THIS.
WHAT ARE YOU GOING TO DO, EMMA? BECAUSE I'M NOT GOING TO LET YOU KILL HIM.
I WANT YOU TO UNDERSTAND. IN HIS WAY, HE WAS A TEACHER TOO. A GOOD TEACHER.
JUST NOT A TEACHER OF GOOD, MY SWEETS.
OH, PLEASE, SAVE THE POOR LITTLE RICH GIRL ROUTINE. I KNOW YOU.
IN MY SECRET ORIGIN? YOU'RE THE BAD GUY.
KITTY PRYDE. INTANGIBILITY. ALAS, NOT TANGIBILITY.
EMMA FROST-- THE WHITE QUEEN. TELEPATHY. DIAMOND-FORM. DIRTY PAST.
YET, IN MINE...
YOU NEED TO KNOW HIM. UNDERSTAND HIM. UNDERSTAND ME.
DO WE REALLY?
YES, YOU DO, MY PETULANT CONSCIENCE. NOW, SHAW... WAKE UP.
SEBASTIAN SHAW--THE BLACK KING. EMMA'S SECRET PRISONER. DIRTIER OF THE AFOREMENTIONED PAST.
HELLO, EMMA. HELLO, KATHERINE.
HELLO... RIDICULOUSLY ATTIRED BE-MASKED FOP.

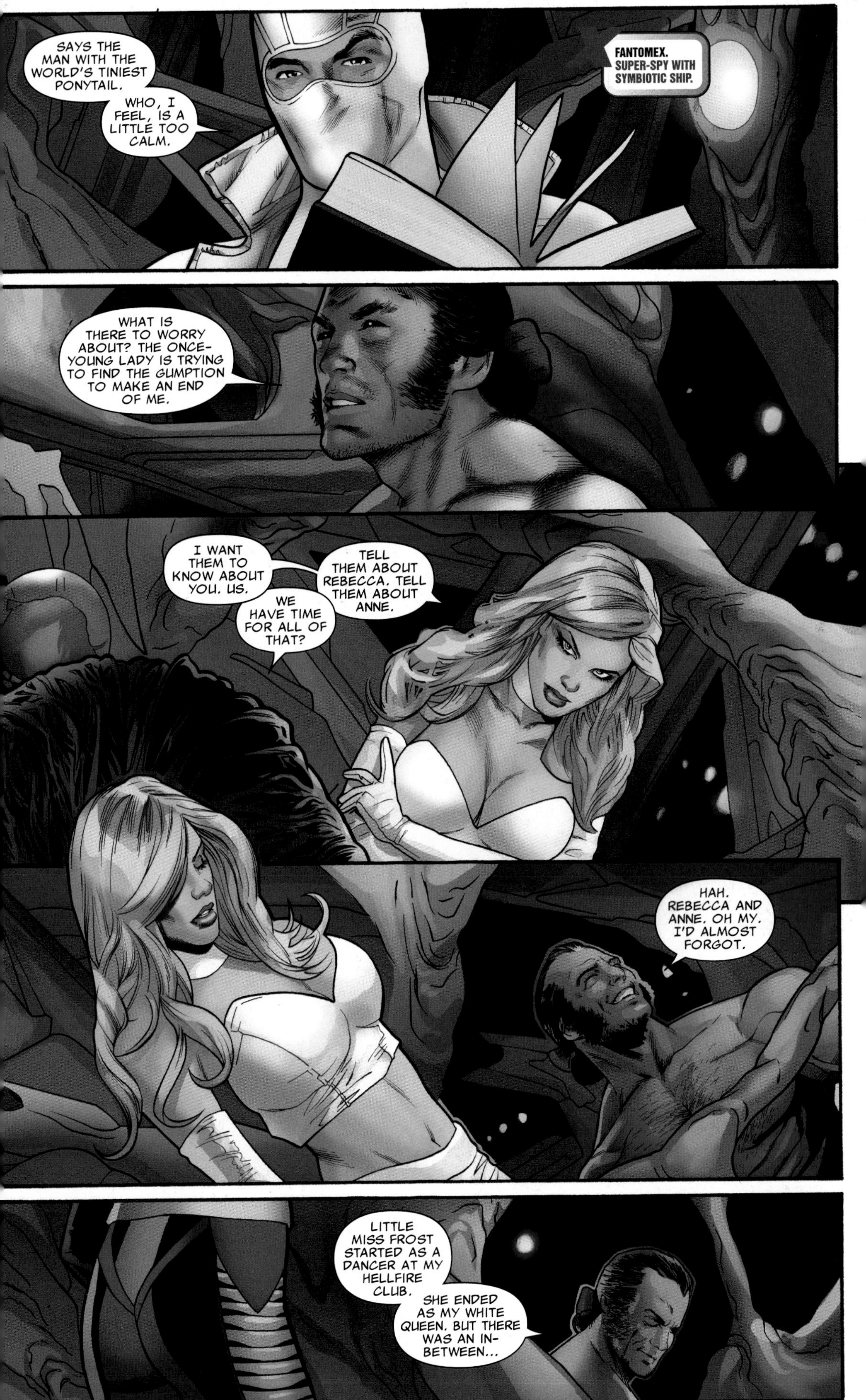
SAYS THE MAN WITH THE WORLD'S TINIEST PONYTAIL.
WHO, I FEEL, IS A LITTLE TOO CALM.
FANTOMEX. SUPER-SPY WITH SYMBIOTIC SHIP.
WHAT IS THERE TO WORRY ABOUT? THE ONCE-YOUNG LADY IS TRYING TO FIND THE GUMPTION TO MAKE AN END OF ME.
I WANT THEM TO KNOW ABOUT YOU. US.
TELL THEM ABOUT REBECCA. TELL THEM ABOUT ANNE.
WE HAVE TIME FOR ALL OF THAT?
HAH. REBECCA AND ANNE. OH MY. I'D ALMOST FORGOT.
LITTLE MISS FROST STARTED AS A DANCER AT MY HELLFIRE CLUB.
SHE ENDED AS MY WHITE QUEEN. BUT THERE WAS AN IN-BETWEEN...

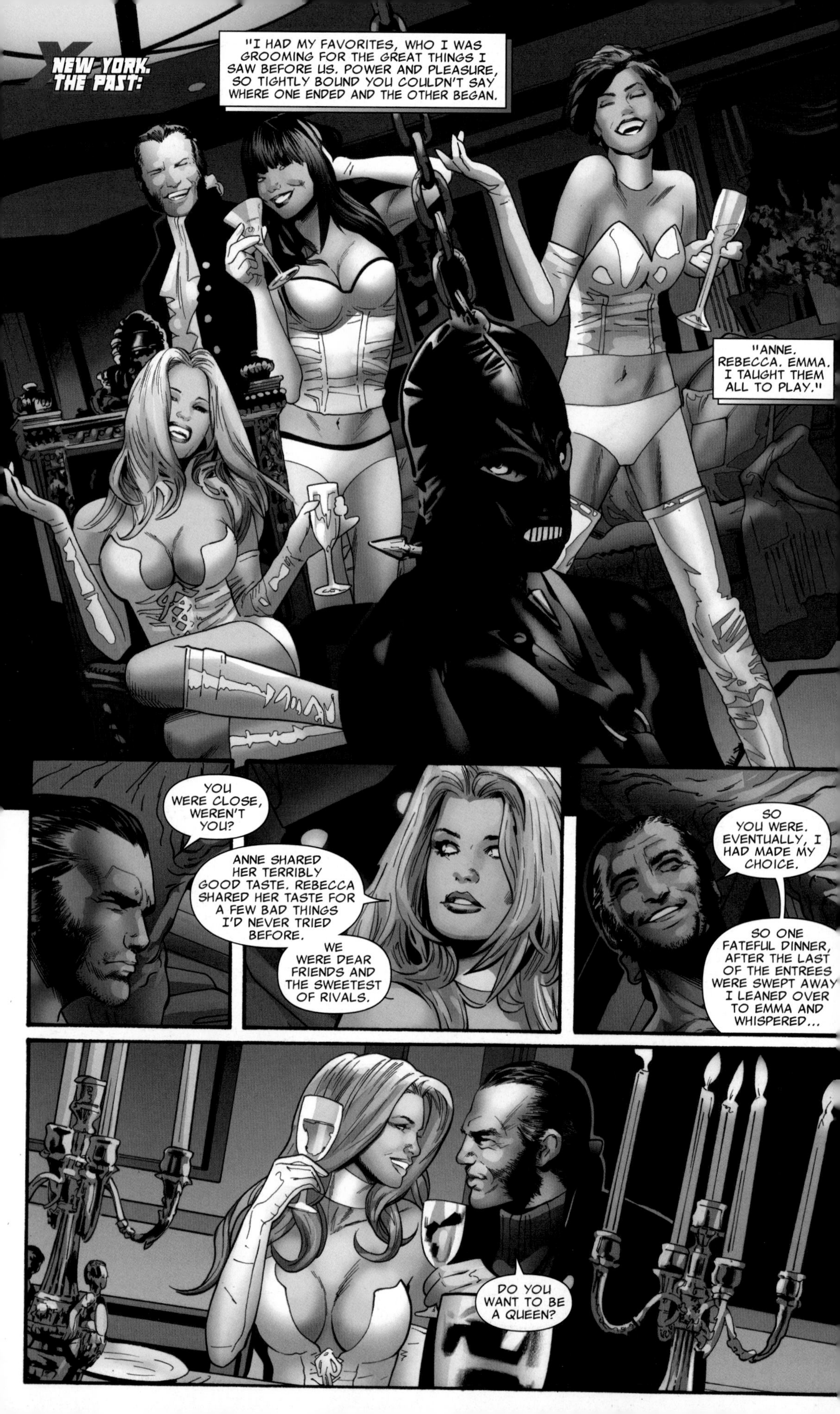

NEW YORK. THE PAST:
"I HAD MY FAVORITES, WHO I WAS GROOMING FOR THE GREAT THINGS I SAW BEFORE US. POWER AND PLEASURE, SO TIGHTLY BOUND YOU COULDN'T SAY WHERE ONE ENDED AND THE OTHER BEGAN.
"ANNE. REBECCA. EMMA. I TAUGHT THEM ALL TO PLAY."
YOU WERE CLOSE, WEREN'T YOU?
ANNE SHARED HER TERRIBLY GOOD TASTE. REBECCA SHARED HER TASTE FOR A FEW BAD THINGS I'D NEVER TRIED BEFORE.
WE WERE DEAR FRIENDS AND THE SWEETEST OF RIVALS.
SO YOU WERE. EVENTUALLY, I HAD MADE MY CHOICE.
SO ONE FATEFUL DINNER, AFTER THE LAST OF THE ENTREES WERE SWEPT AWAY I LEANED OVER TO EMMA AND WHISPERED...
DO YOU WANT TO BE A QUEEN?

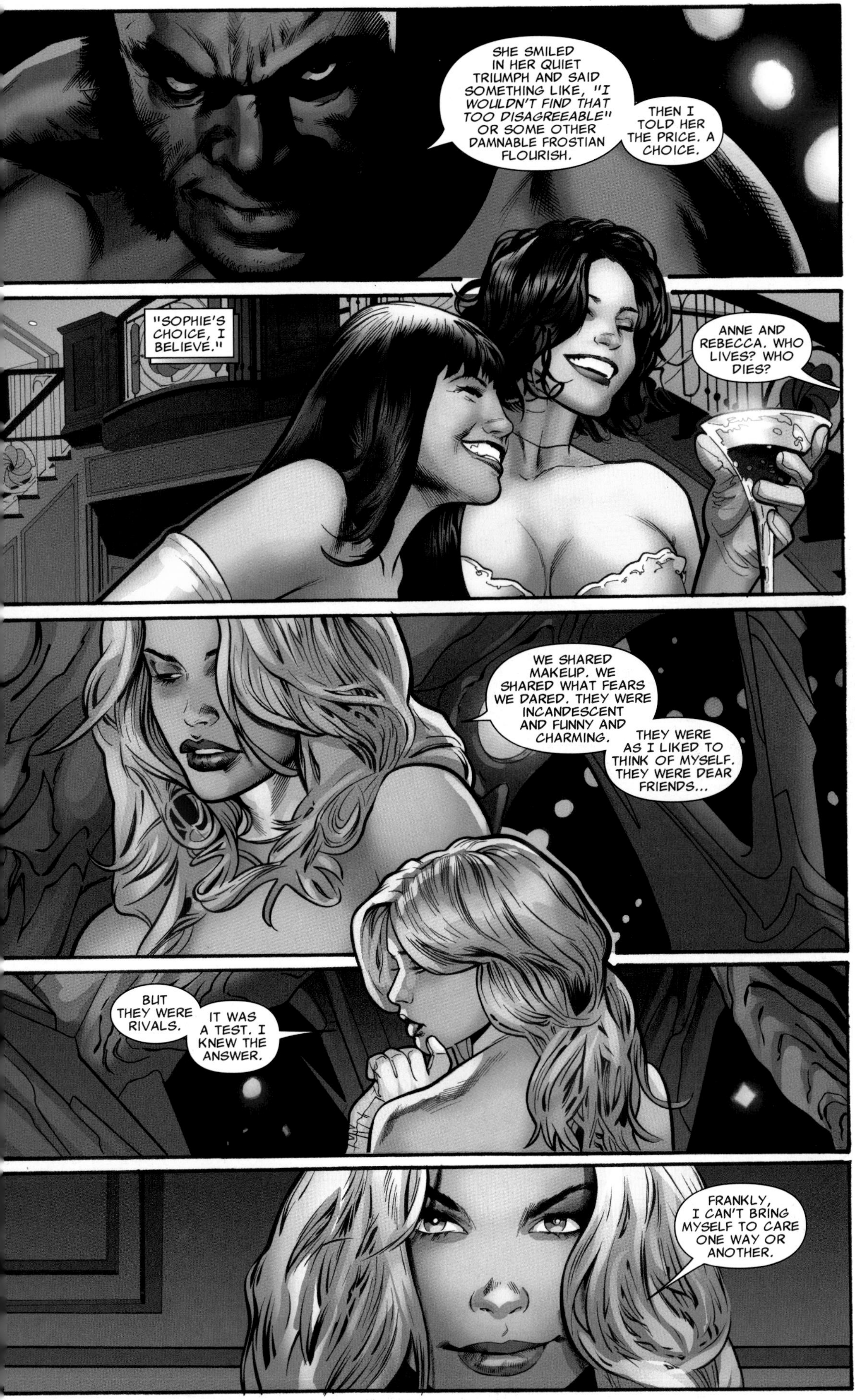

SHE SMILED IN HER QUIET TRIUMPH AND SAID SOMETHING LIKE, "I WOULDN'T FIND THAT TOO DISAGREEABLE" OR SOME OTHER DAMNABLE FROSTIAN FLOURISH.
THEN I TOLD HER THE PRICE. A CHOICE.
"SOPHIE'S CHOICE, I BELIEVE."
ANNE AND REBECCA. WHO LIVES? WHO DIES?
WE SHARED MAKEUP. WE SHARED WHAT FEARS WE DARED. THEY WERE INCANDESCENT AND FUNNY AND CHARMING.
THEY WERE AS I LIKED TO THINK OF MYSELF. THEY WERE DEAR FRIENDS...
BUT THEY WERE RIVALS.
IT WAS A TEST. I KNEW THE ANSWER.
FRANKLY, I CAN'T BRING MYSELF TO CARE ONE WAY OR ANOTHER.

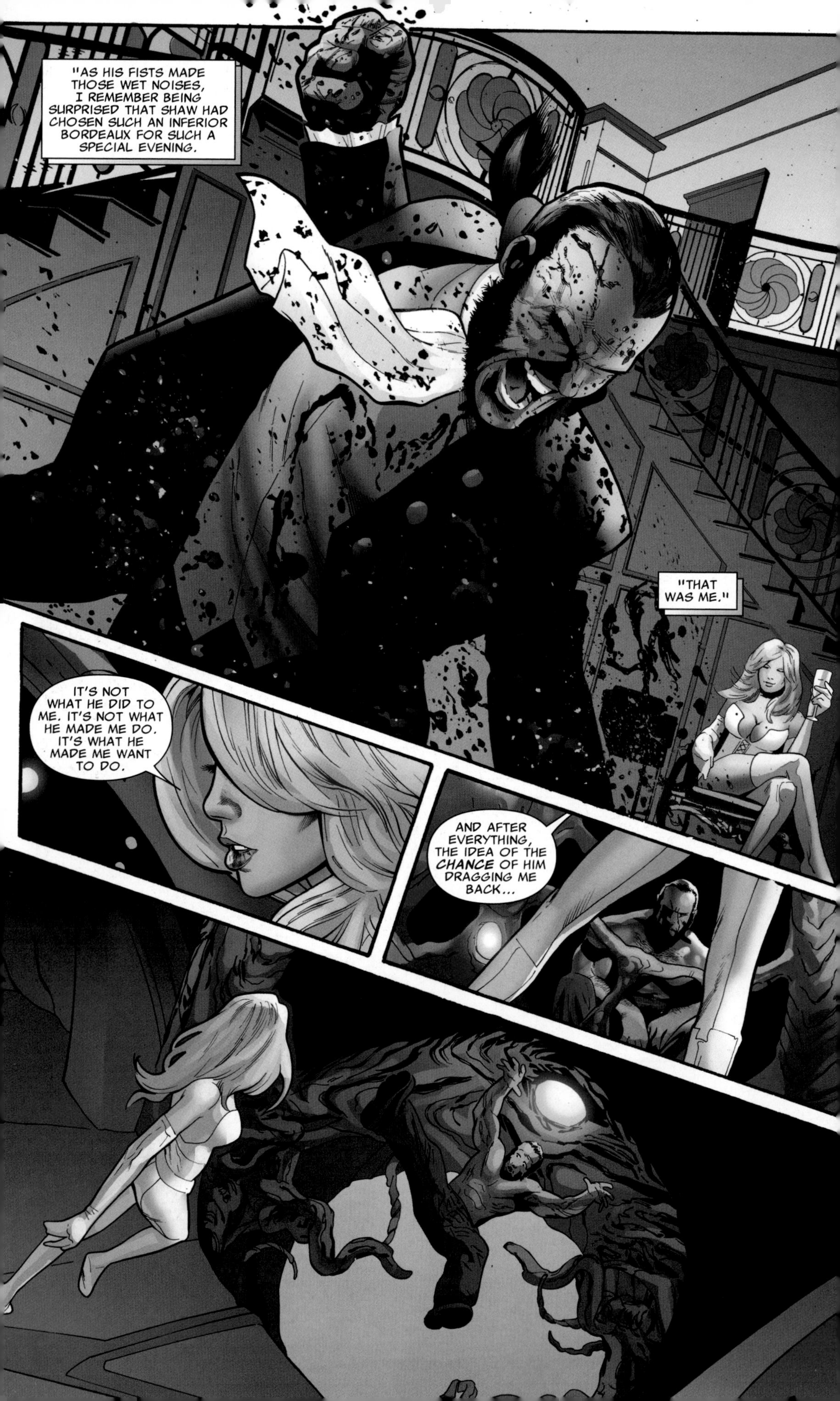
"AS HIS FISTS MADE THOSE WET NOISES, I REMEMBER BEING SURPRISED THAT SHAW HAD CHOSEN SUCH AN INFERIOR BORDEAUX FOR SUCH A SPECIAL EVENING.
"THAT WAS ME."
IT'S NOT WHAT HE DID TO ME. IT'S NOT WHAT HE MADE ME DO. IT'S WHAT HE MADE ME WANT TO DO.
AND AFTER EVERYTHING, THE IDEA OF THE *CHANCE* OF HIM DRAGGING ME BACK...

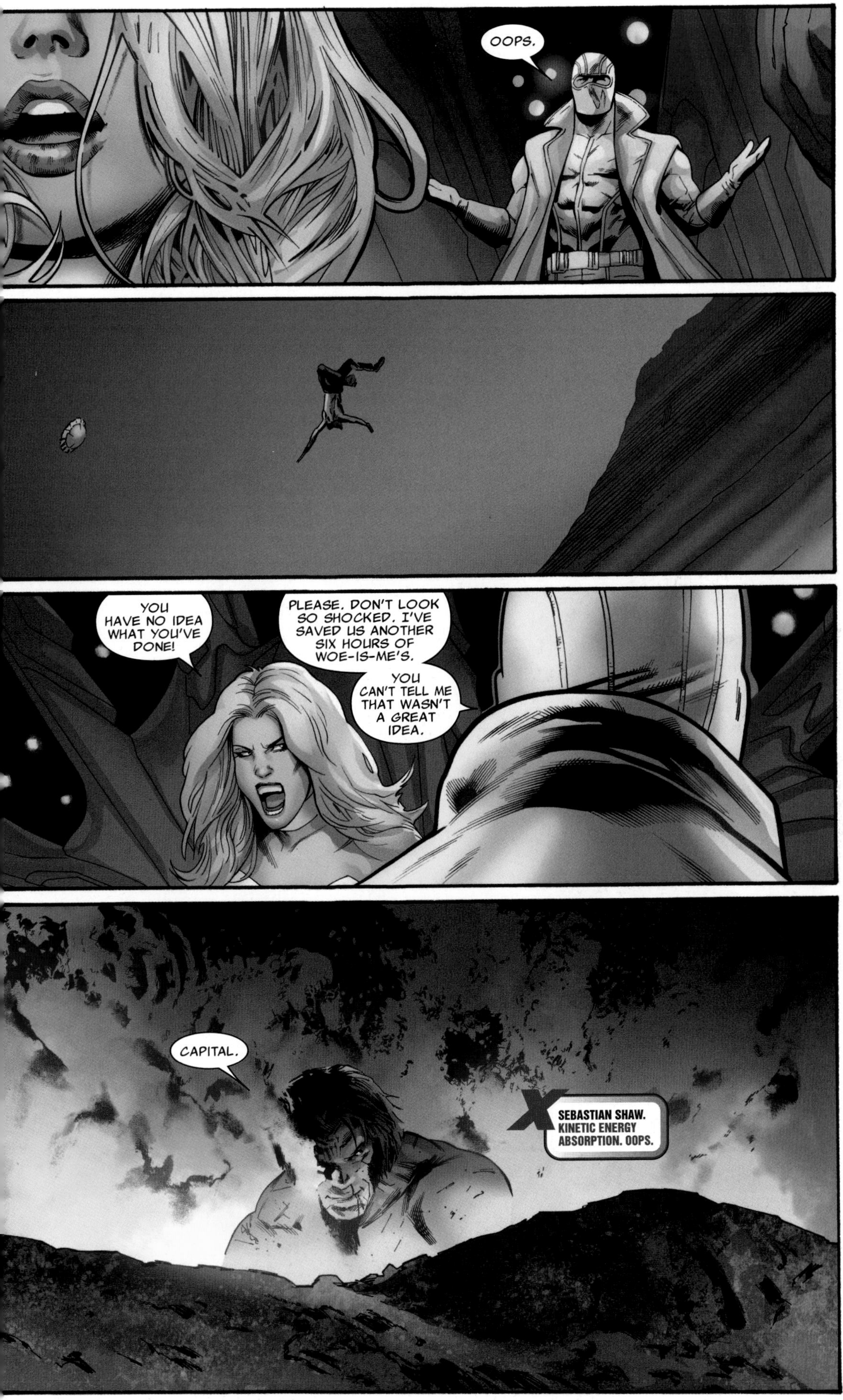
OOPS.
YOU HAVE NO IDEA WHAT YOU'VE DONE!
PLEASE. DON'T LOOK SO SHOCKED. I'VE SAVED US ANOTHER SIX HOURS OF WOE-IS-ME'S.
YOU CAN'T TELL ME THAT WASN'T A GREAT IDEA.
CAPITAL.
SEBASTIAN SHAW. KINETIC ENERGY ABSORPTION. OOPS.

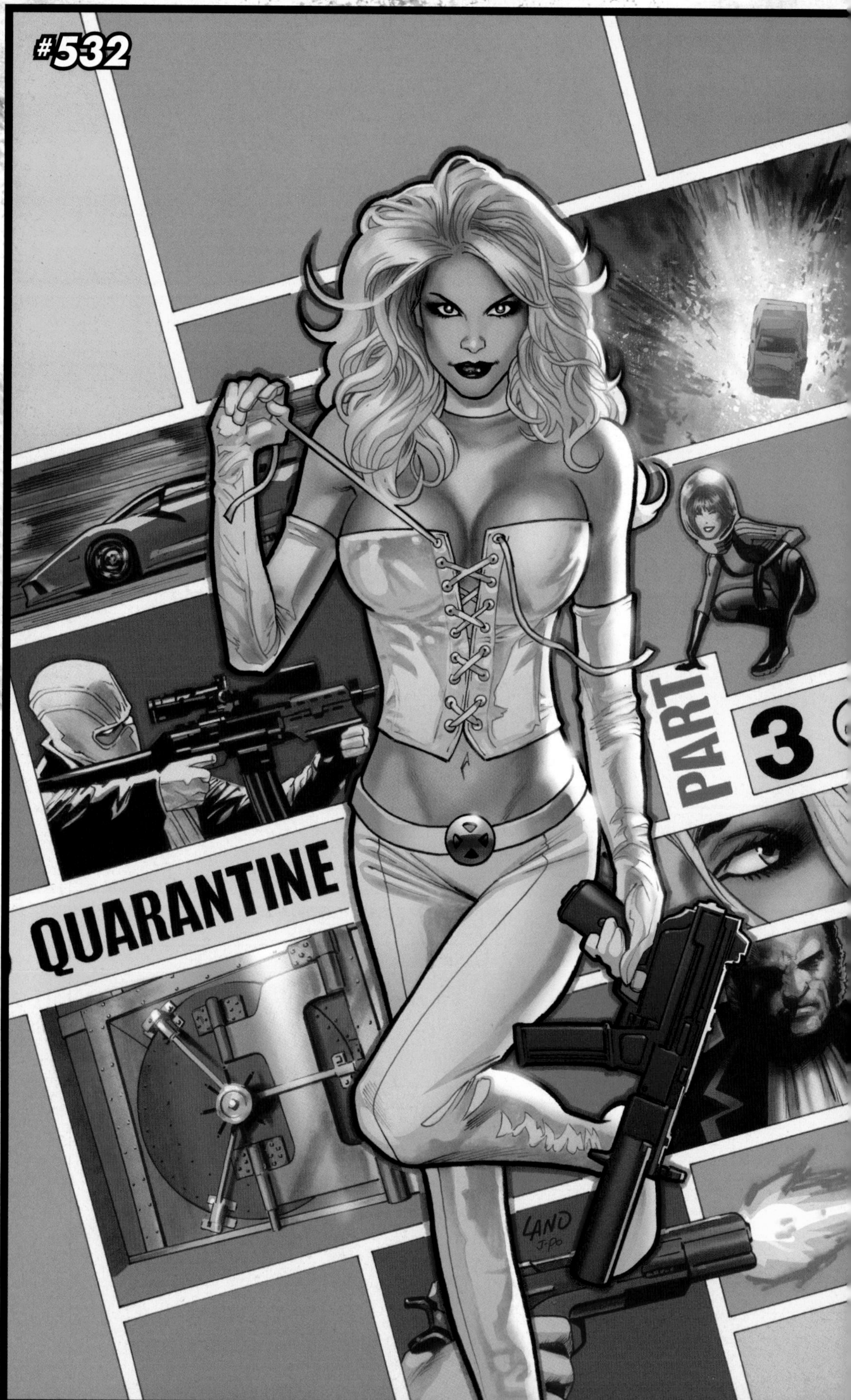

#532
QUARANTINE
PART 3
LAND J-Po

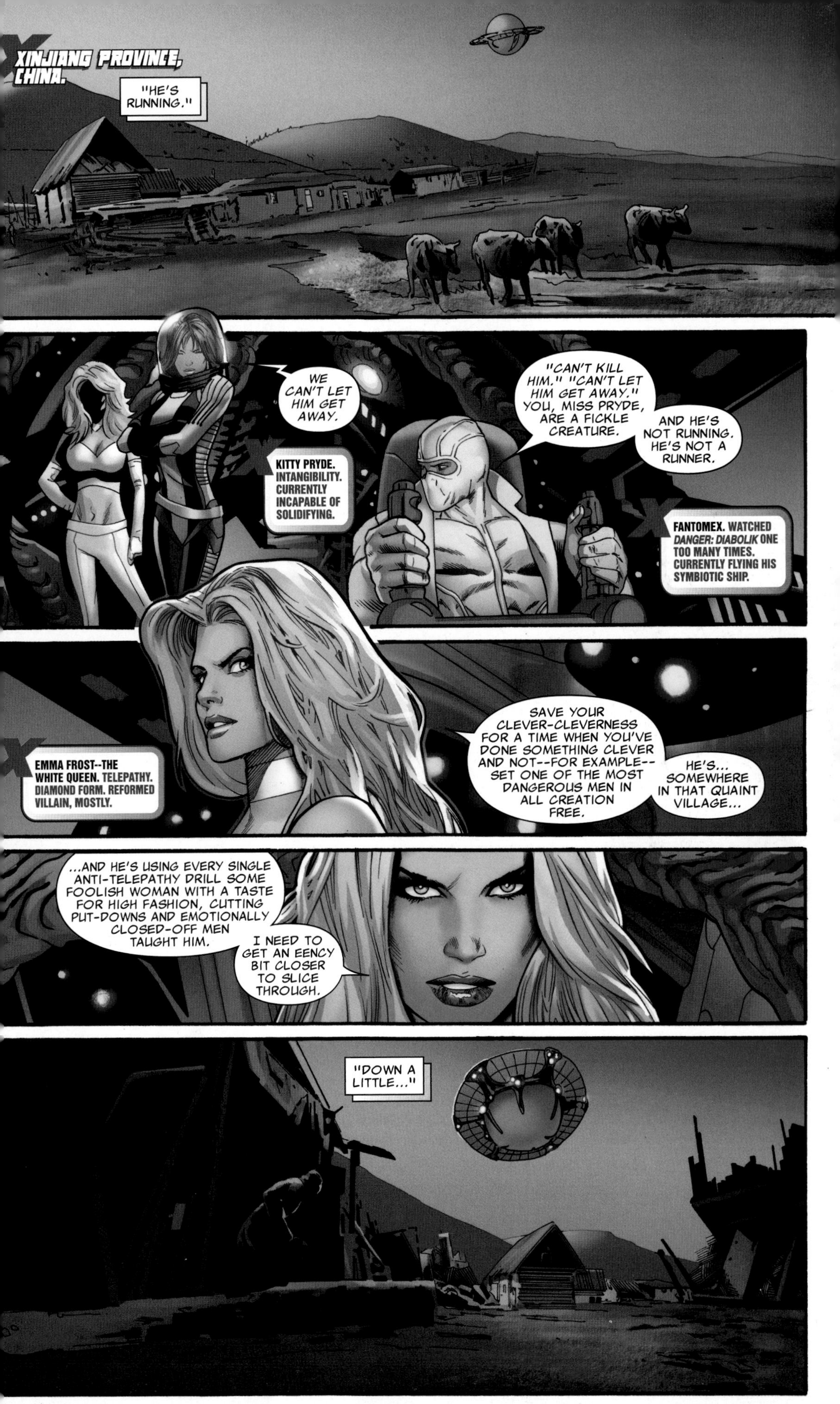

XINJIANG PROVINCE, CHINA.
"HE'S RUNNING."
WE CAN'T LET HIM GET AWAY.
KITTY PRYDE. INTANGIBILITY. CURRENTLY INCAPABLE OF SOLIDIFYING.
"CAN'T KILL HIM." "CAN'T LET HIM GET AWAY." YOU, MISS PRYDE, ARE A FICKLE CREATURE.
AND HE'S NOT RUNNING. HE'S NOT A RUNNER.
FANTOMEX. WATCHED DANGER: DIABOLIK ONE TOO MANY TIMES. CURRENTLY FLYING HIS SYMBIOTIC SHIP.
EMMA FROST--THE WHITE QUEEN. TELEPATHY. DIAMOND FORM. REFORMED VILLAIN, MOSTLY.
SAVE YOUR CLEVER-CLEVERNESS FOR A TIME WHEN YOU'VE DONE SOMETHING CLEVER AND NOT--FOR EXAMPLE--SET ONE OF THE MOST DANGEROUS MEN IN ALL CREATION FREE.
HE'S... SOMEWHERE IN THAT QUAINT VILLAGE...
...AND HE'S USING EVERY SINGLE ANTI-TELEPATHY DRILL SOME FOOLISH WOMAN WITH A TASTE FOR HIGH FASHION, CUTTING PUT-DOWNS AND EMOTIONALLY CLOSED-OFF MEN TAUGHT HIM.
I NEED TO GET AN EENCY BIT CLOSER TO SLICE THROUGH.
"DOWN A LITTLE..."

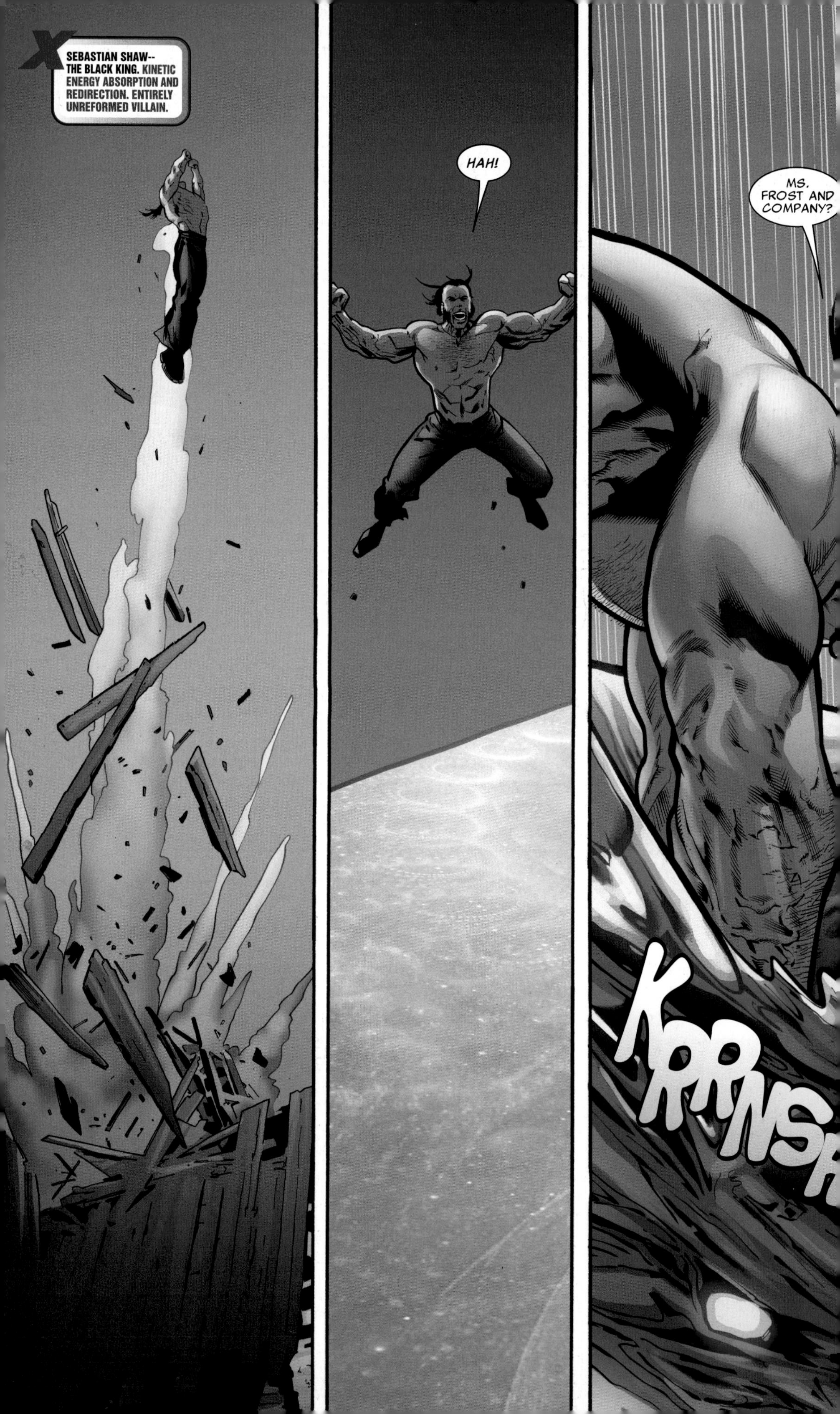
SEBASTIAN SHAW-- THE BLACK KING. KINETIC ENERGY ABSORPTION AND REDIRECTION. ENTIRELY UNREFORMED VILLAIN.
HAH!
MS. FROST AND COMPANY?
KRRNSH

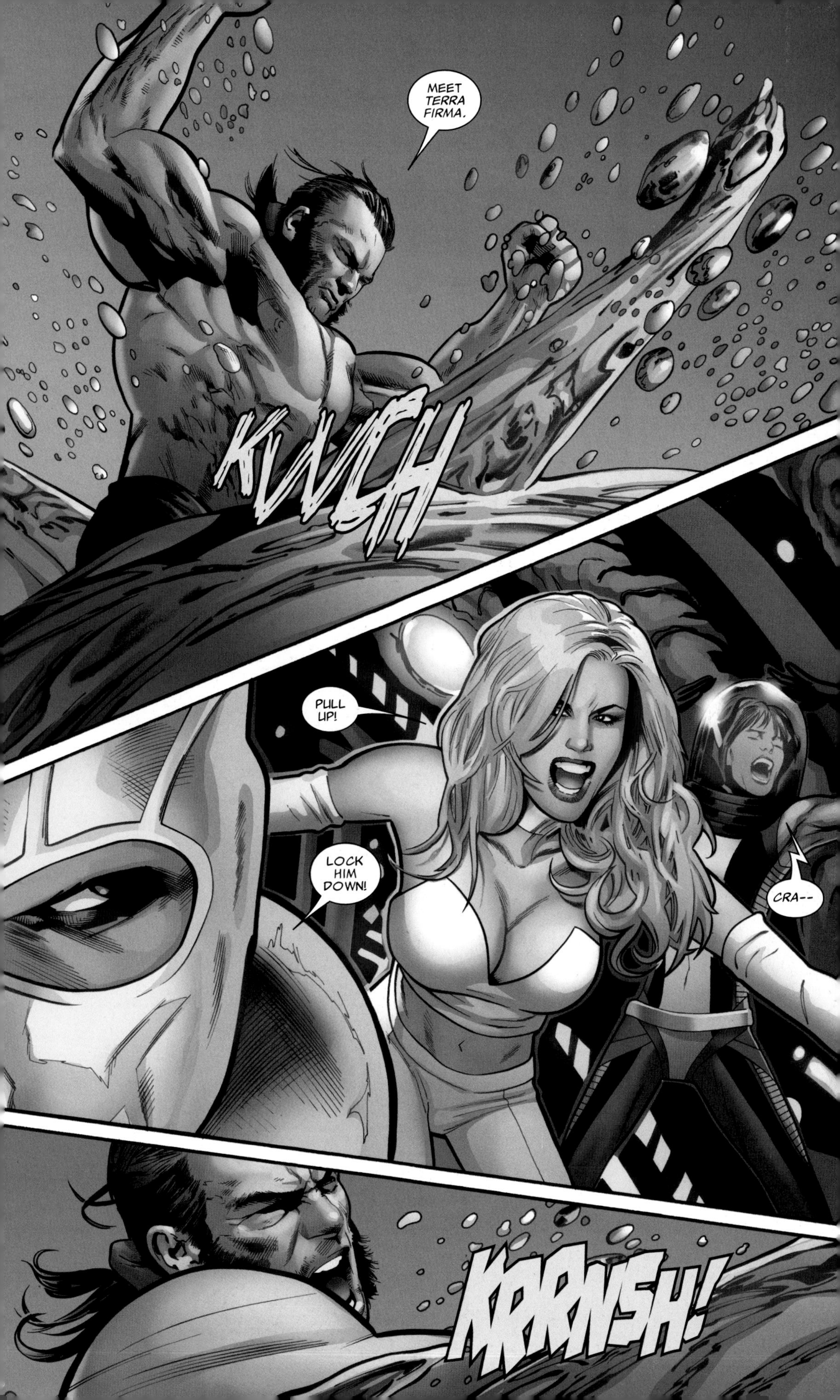
MEET TERRA FIRMA.
KWCH
PULL UP!
LOCK HIM DOWN!
CRA--
KRANSH!

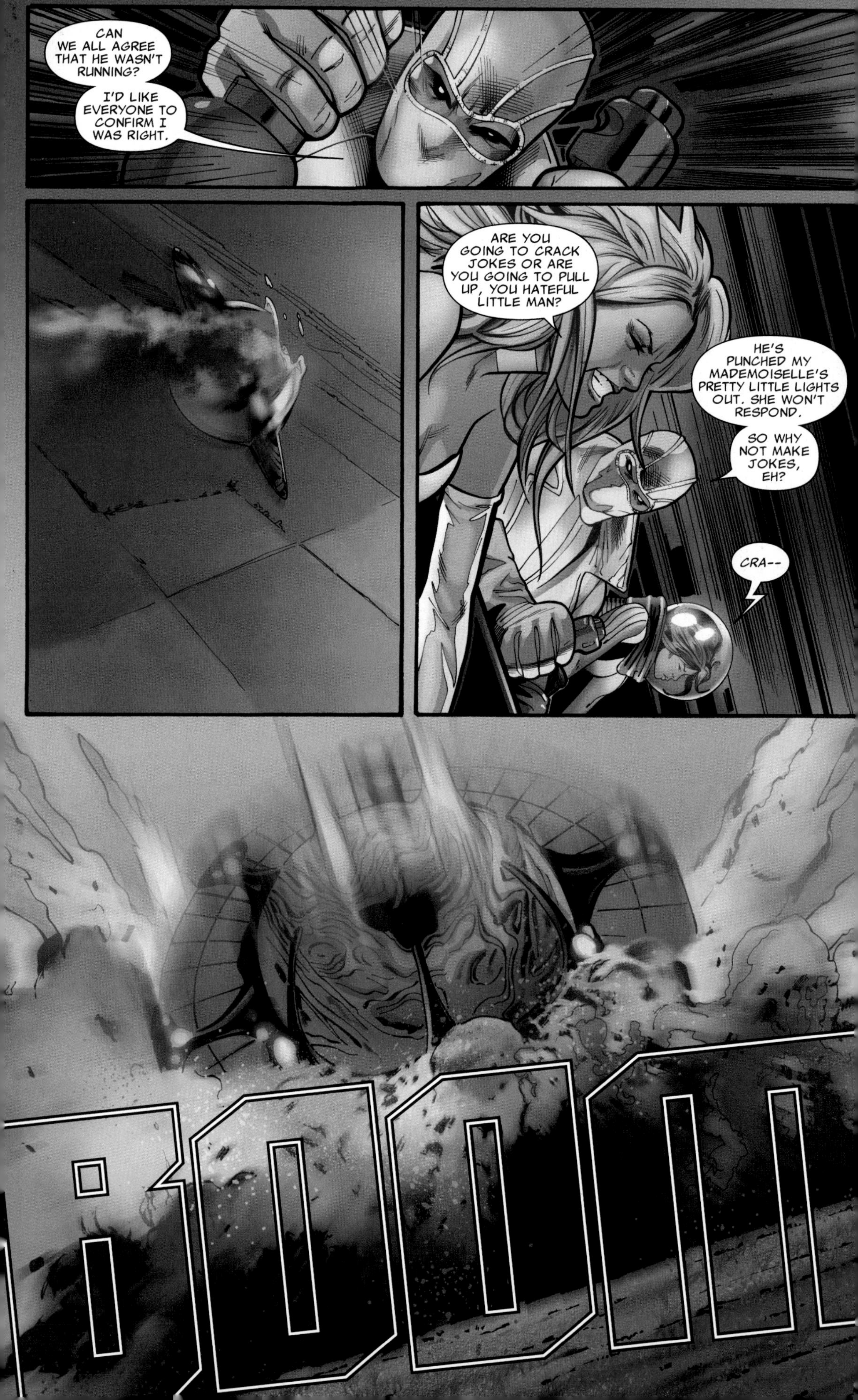
CAN WE ALL AGREE THAT HE WASN'T RUNNING?
I'D LIKE EVERYONE TO CONFIRM I WAS RIGHT.
ARE YOU GOING TO CRACK JOKES OR ARE YOU GOING TO PULL UP, YOU HATEFUL LITTLE MAN?
HE'S PUNCHED MY MADEMOISELLE'S PRETTY LITTLE LIGHTS OUT. SHE WON'T RESPOND.
SO WHY NOT MAKE JOKES, EH?
CRA--

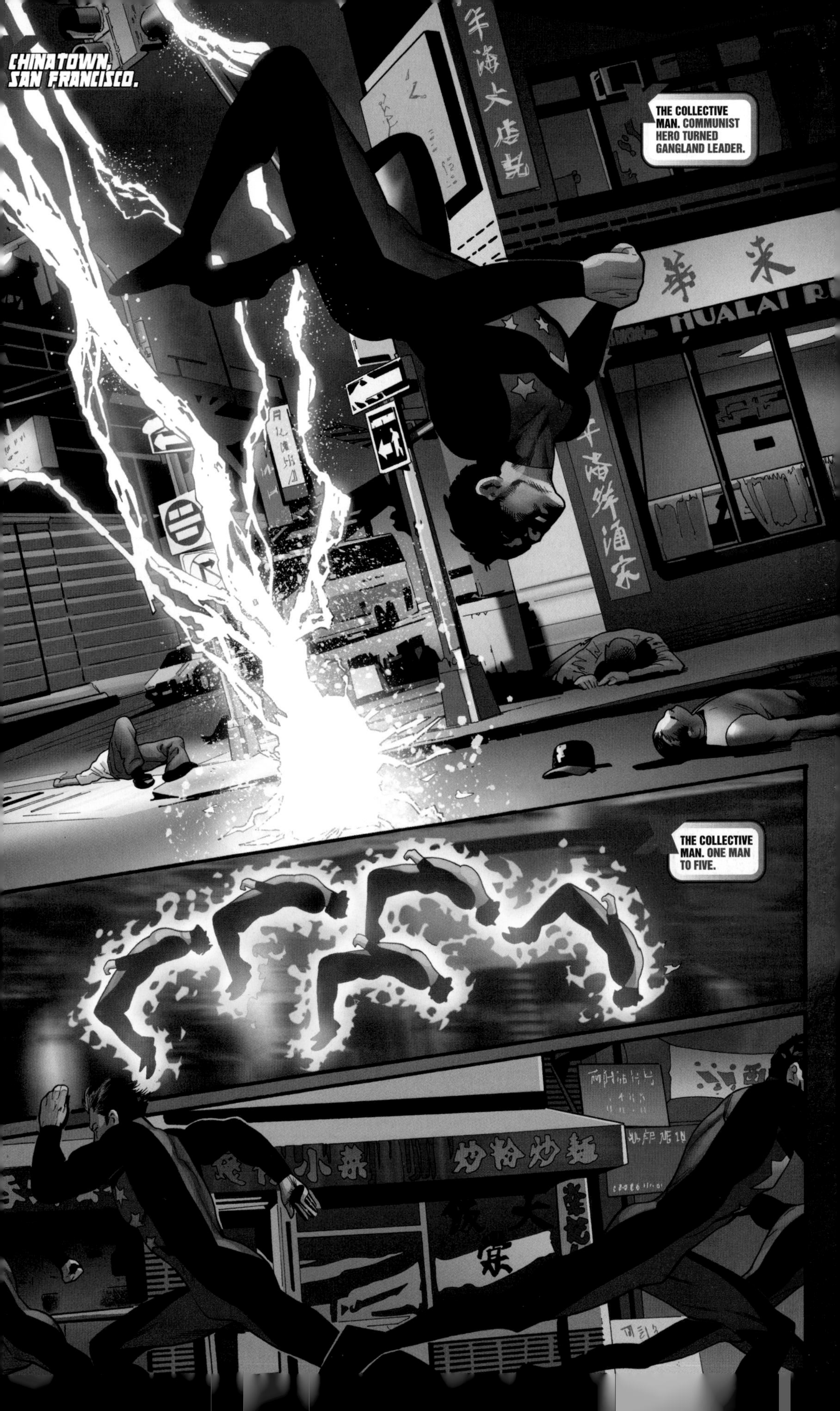
CHINATOWN, SAN FRANCISCO.
THE COLLECTIVE MAN. COMMUNIST HERO TURNED GANGLAND LEADER.
THE COLLECTIVE MAN. ONE MAN TO FIVE.

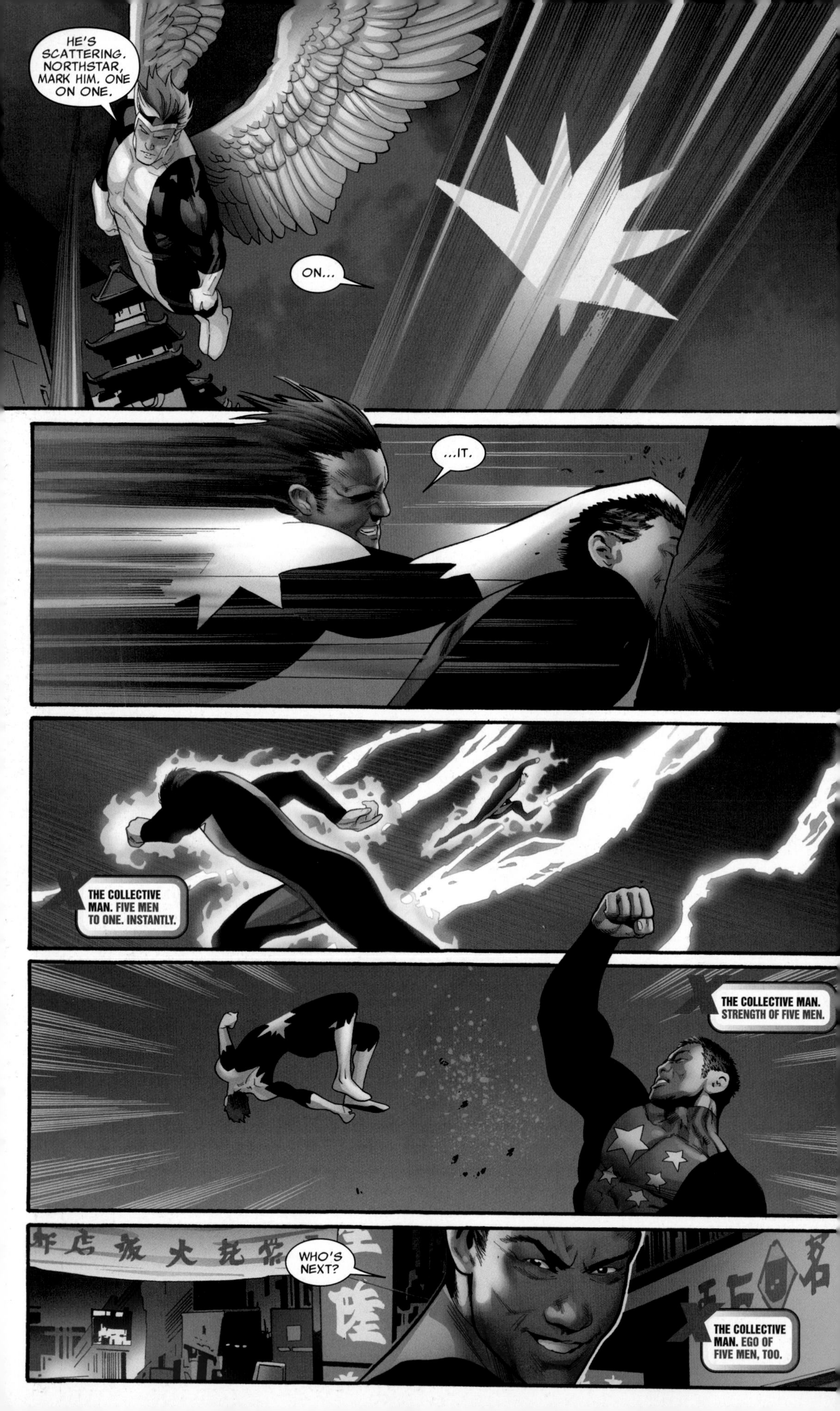
HE'S SCATTERING. NORTHSTAR, MARK HIM. ONE ON ONE.
ON...
...IT.
THE COLLECTIVE MAN. FIVE MEN TO ONE. INSTANTLY.
THE COLLECTIVE MAN. STRENGTH OF FIVE MEN.
WHO'S NEXT?
THE COLLECTIVE MAN. EGO OF FIVE MEN, TOO.

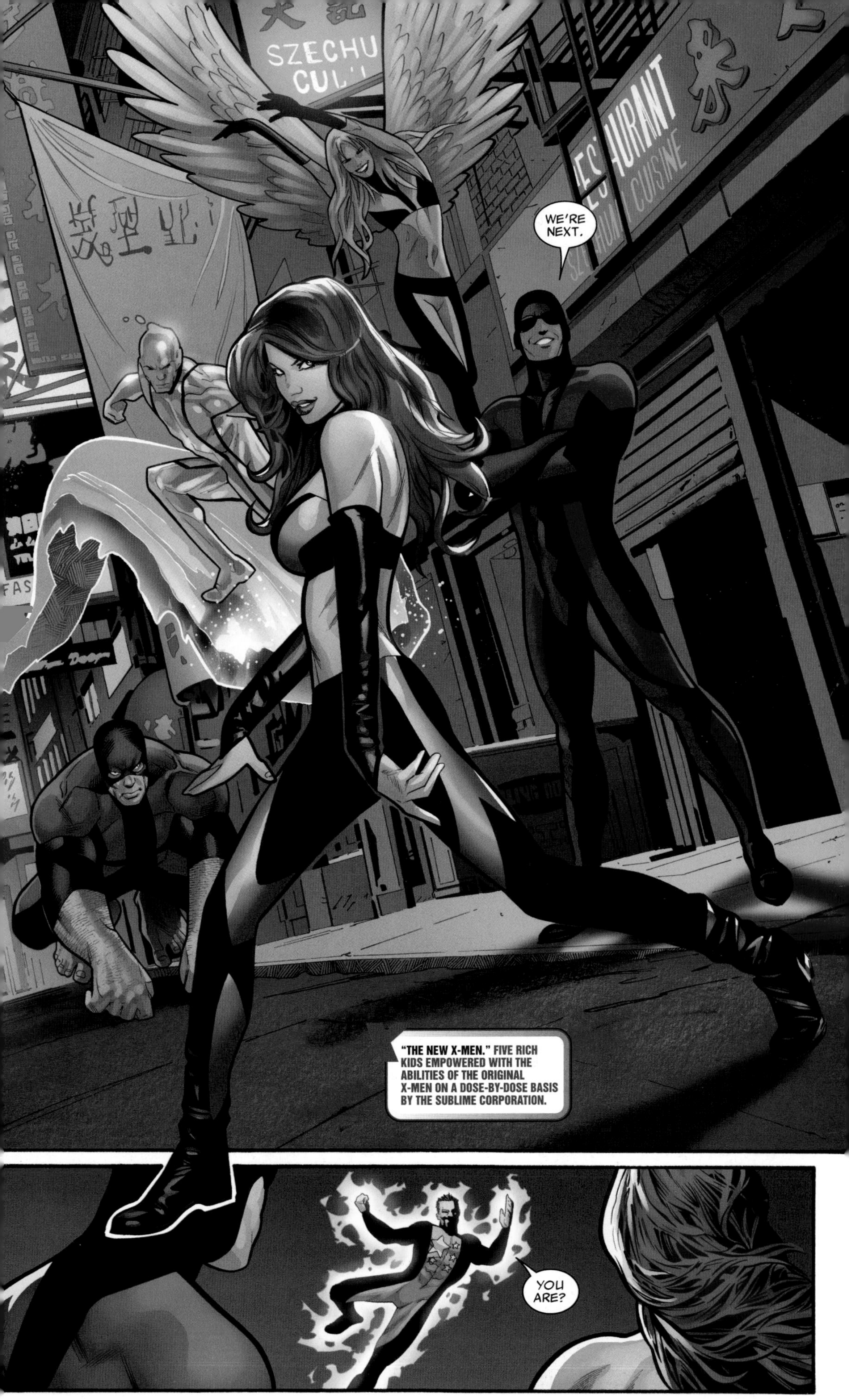
SZECHU
CUISINE
WE'RE NEXT.
"THE NEW X-MEN." FIVE RICH KIDS EMPOWERED WITH THE ABILITIES OF THE ORIGINAL X-MEN ON A DOSE-BY-DOSE BASIS BY THE SUBLIME CORPORATION.
YOU ARE?

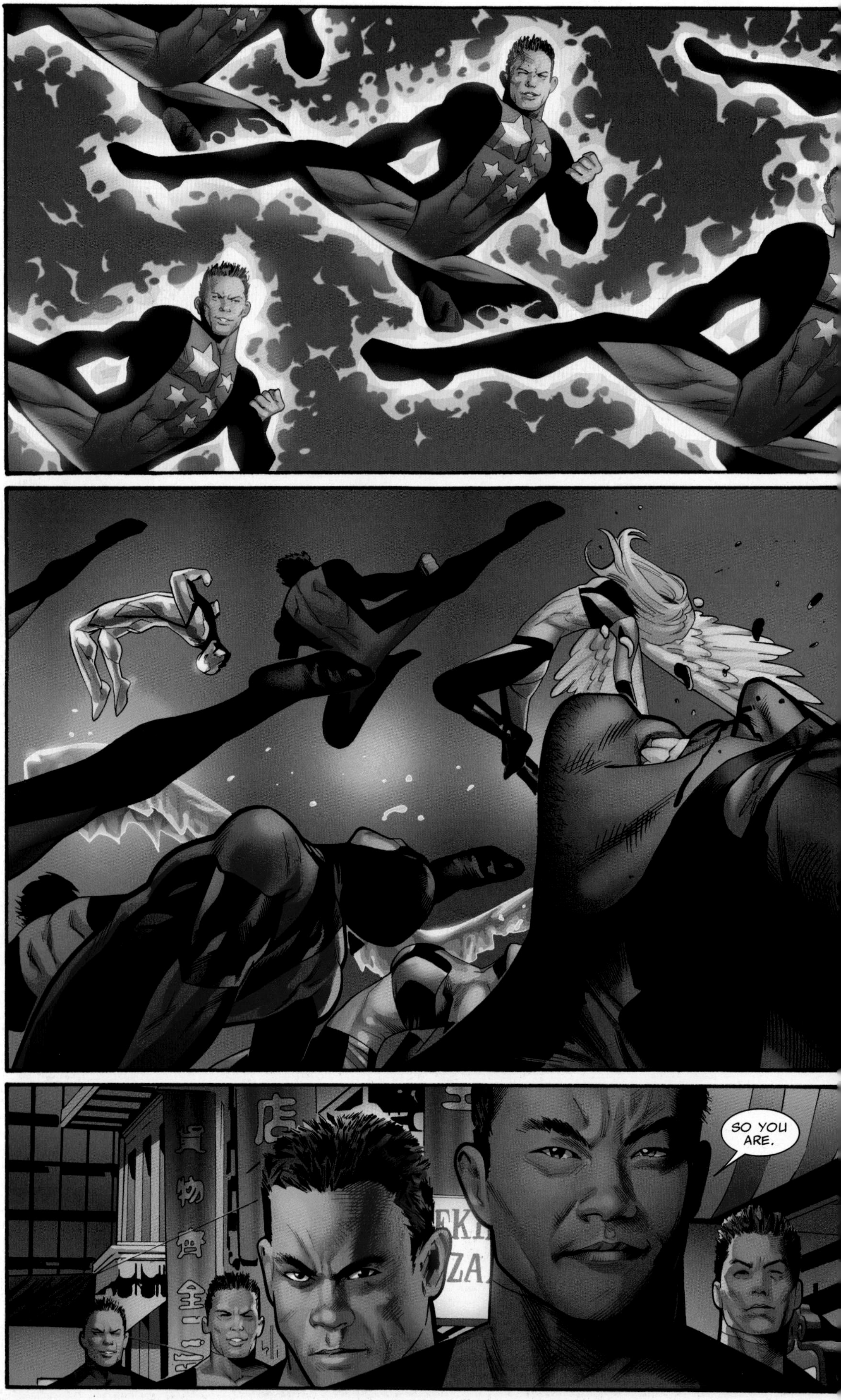
SO YOU
ARE.

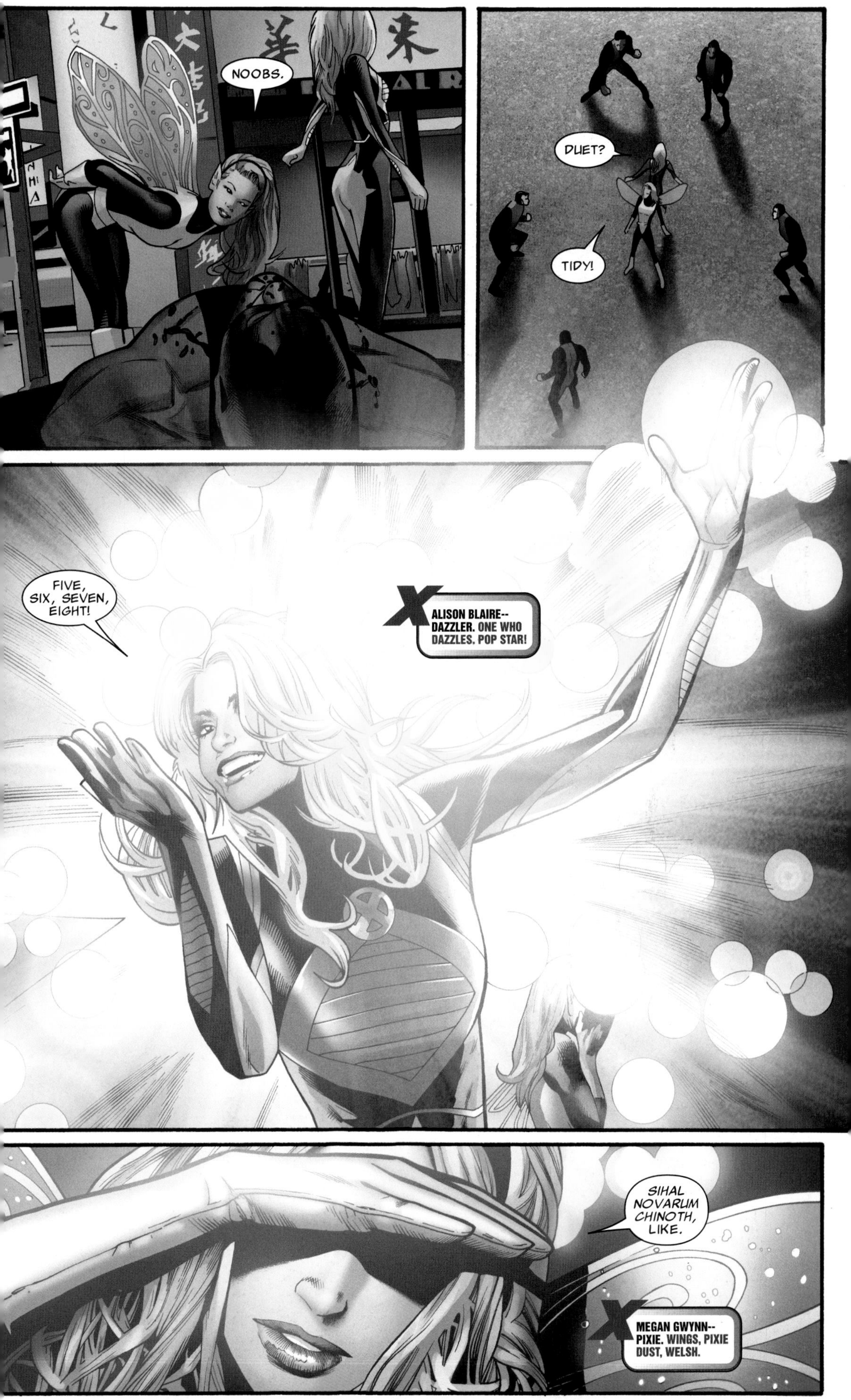
NOOBS.
DUET?
TIDY!
FIVE, SIX, SEVEN, EIGHT!
ALISON BLAIRE-- DAZZLER. ONE WHO DAZZLES. POP STAR!
SIHAL NOVARUM CHINOTH, LIKE.
MEGAN GWYNN-- PIXIE. WINGS, PIXIE DUST, WELSH.

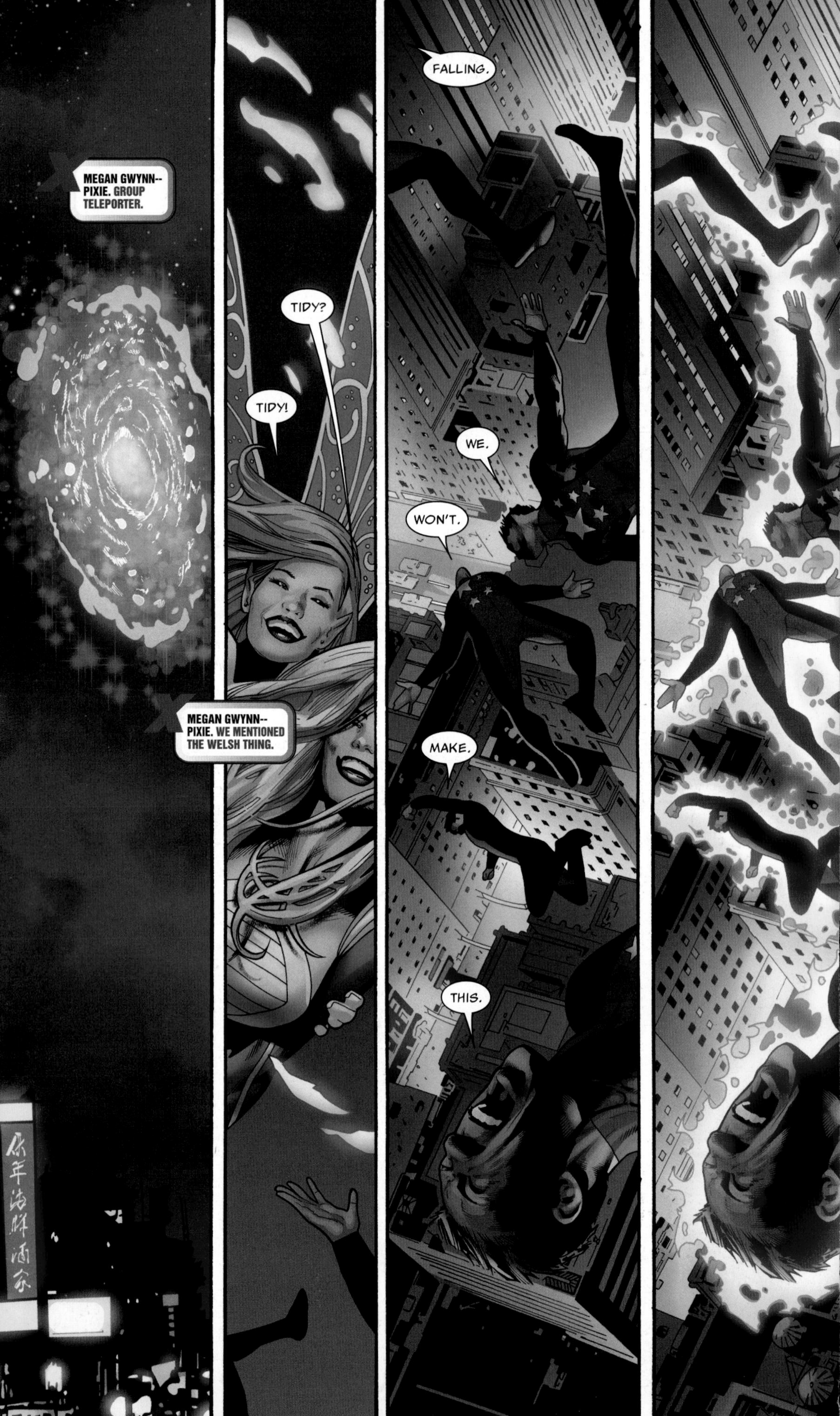
MEGAN GWYNN--
PIXIE. GROUP
TELEPORTER.
TIDY?
TIDY!
MEGAN GWYNN--
PIXIE. WE MENTIONED
THE WELSH THING.
FALLING.
WE.
WON'T.
MAKE.
THIS.

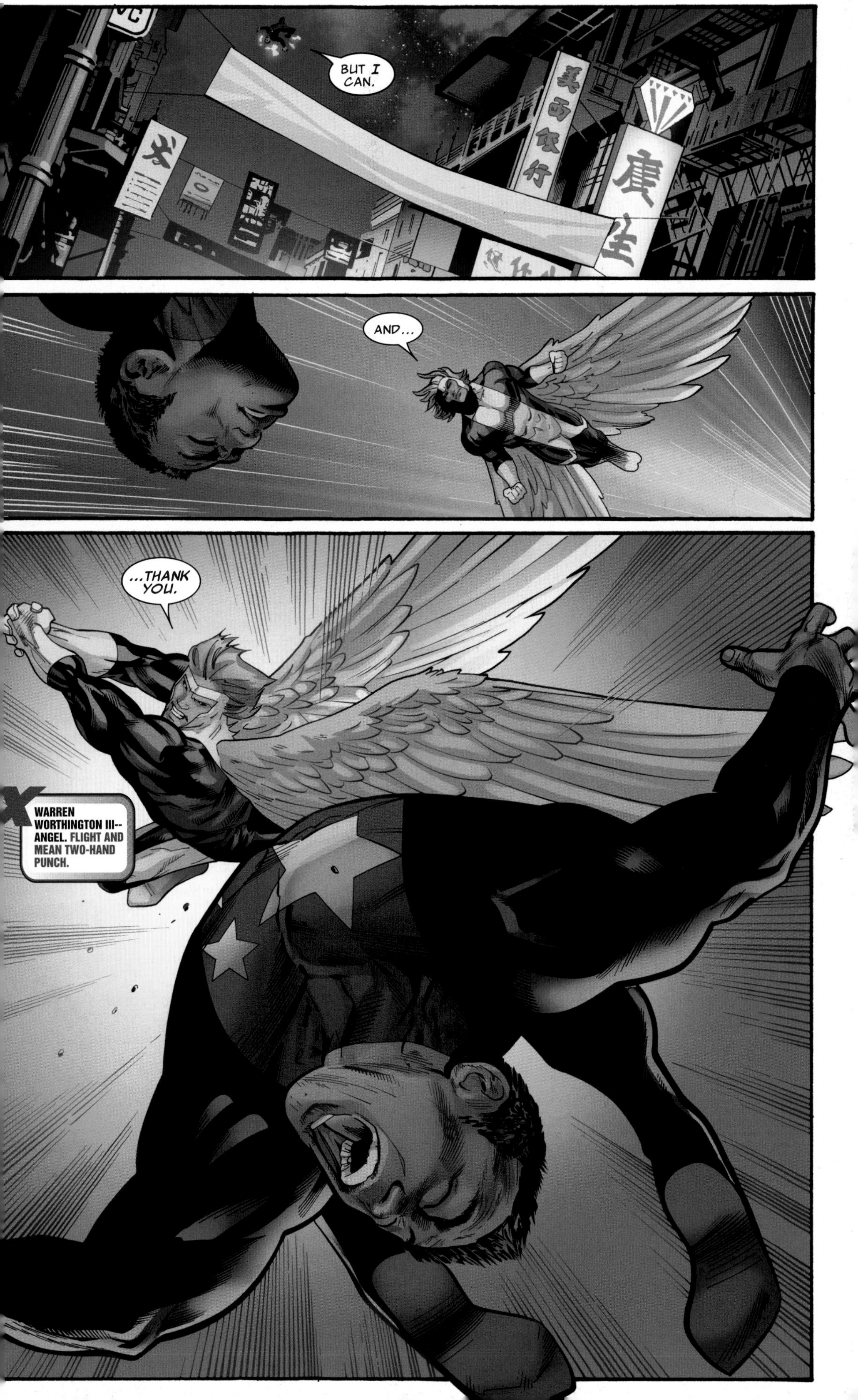
BUT I CAN.
AND...
...THANK YOU.
WARREN WORTHINGTON III--ANGEL. FLIGHT AND MEAN TWO-HAND PUNCH.

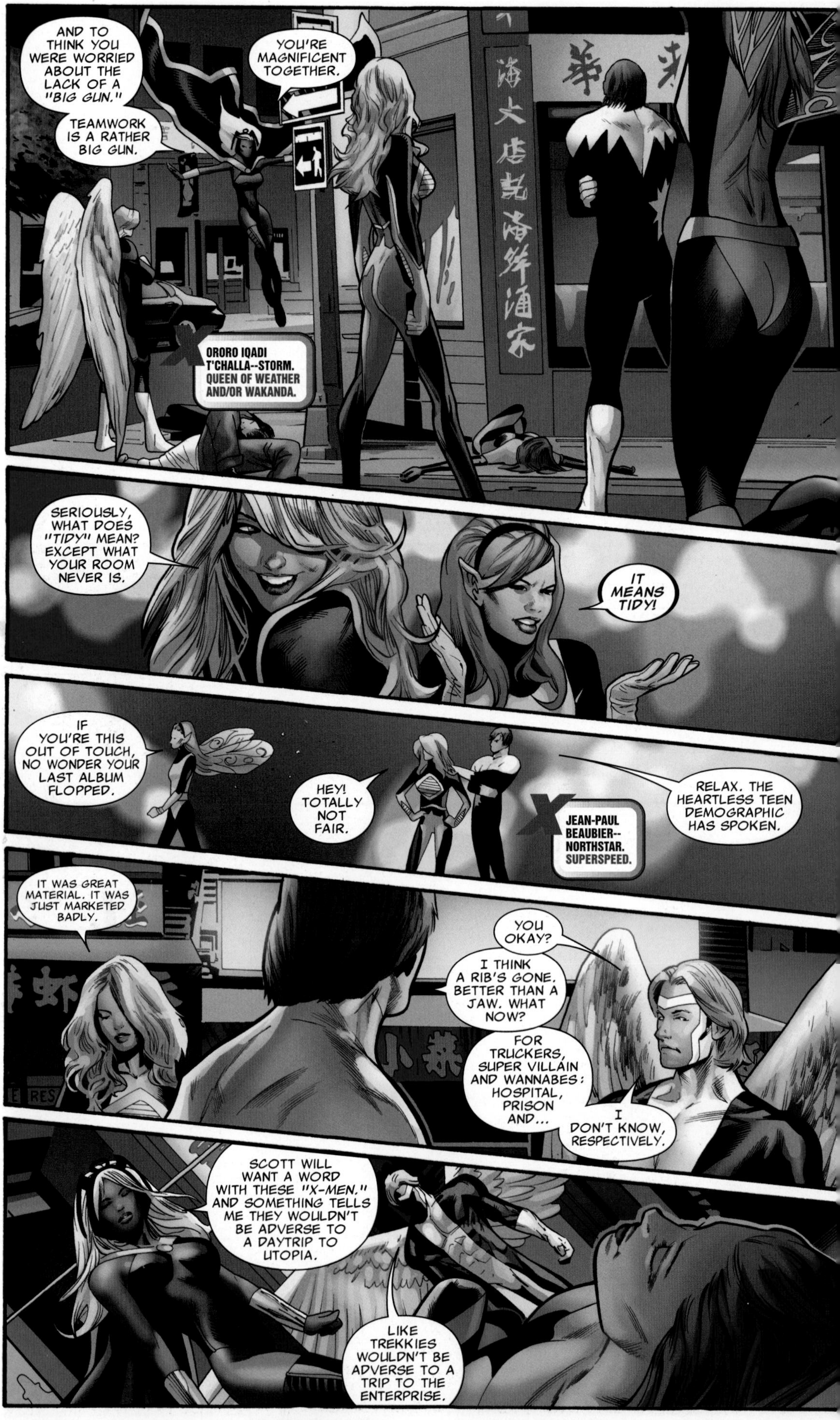
AND TO THINK YOU WERE WORRIED ABOUT THE LACK OF A "BIG GUN."
TEAMWORK IS A RATHER BIG GUN.
YOU'RE MAGNIFICENT TOGETHER.
ORORO IQADI T'CHALLA--STORM. QUEEN OF WEATHER AND/OR WAKANDA.
SERIOUSLY, WHAT DOES "TIDY" MEAN? EXCEPT WHAT YOUR ROOM NEVER IS.
IT MEANS TIDY!
IF YOU'RE THIS OUT OF TOUCH, NO WONDER YOUR LAST ALBUM FLOPPED.
HEY! TOTALLY NOT FAIR.
RELAX. THE HEARTLESS TEEN DEMOGRAPHIC HAS SPOKEN.
JEAN-PAUL BEAUBIER--NORTHSTAR. SUPERSPEED.
IT WAS GREAT MATERIAL. IT WAS JUST MARKETED BADLY.
YOU OKAY?
I THINK A RIB'S GONE. BETTER THAN A JAW. WHAT NOW?
FOR TRUCKERS, SUPER VILLAIN AND WANNABES: HOSPITAL, PRISON AND...
I DON'T KNOW, RESPECTIVELY.
SCOTT WILL WANT A WORD WITH THESE "X-MEN." AND SOMETHING TELLS ME THEY WOULDN'T BE ADVERSE TO A DAYTRIP TO UTOPIA.
LIKE TREKKIES WOULDN'T BE ADVERSE TO A TRIP TO THE ENTERPRISE.

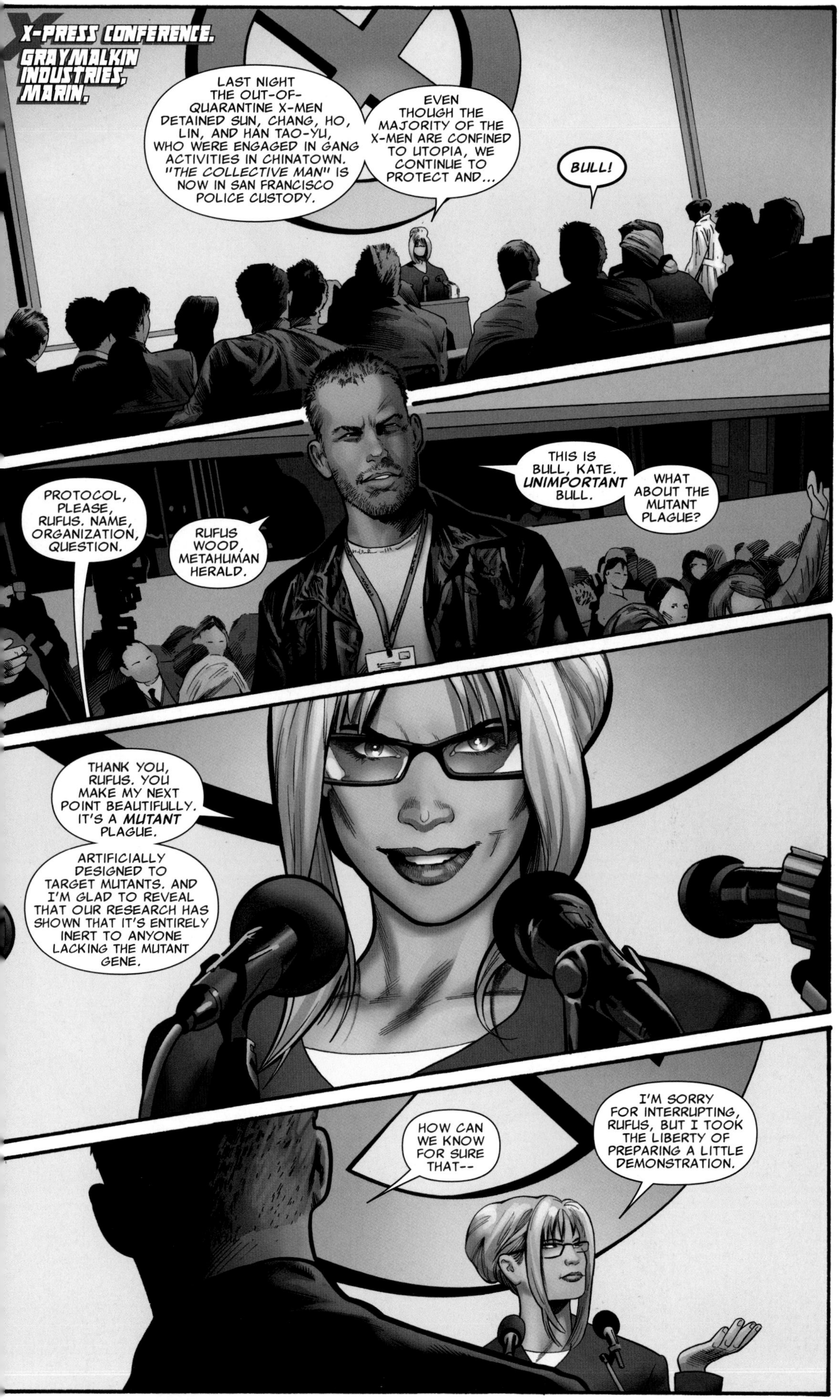
X-PRESS CONFERENCE.
GRAYMALKIN INDUSTRIES, MARIN.
LAST NIGHT THE OUT-OF-QUARANTINE X-MEN DETAINED SUN, CHANG, HO, LIN, AND HAN TAO-YU, WHO WERE ENGAGED IN GANG ACTIVITIES IN CHINATOWN. "THE COLLECTIVE MAN" IS NOW IN SAN FRANCISCO POLICE CUSTODY.
EVEN THOUGH THE MAJORITY OF THE X-MEN ARE CONFINED TO UTOPIA, WE CONTINUE TO PROTECT AND...
BULL!
PROTOCOL, PLEASE, RUFUS. NAME, ORGANIZATION, QUESTION.
RUFUS WOOD, METAHUMAN HERALD.
THIS IS BULL, KATE. UNIMPORTANT BULL.
WHAT ABOUT THE MUTANT PLAGUE?
THANK YOU, RUFUS. YOU MAKE MY NEXT POINT BEAUTIFULLY. IT'S A MUTANT PLAGUE.
ARTIFICIALLY DESIGNED TO TARGET MUTANTS. AND I'M GLAD TO REVEAL THAT OUR RESEARCH HAS SHOWN THAT IT'S ENTIRELY INERT TO ANYONE LACKING THE MUTANT GENE.
HOW CAN WE KNOW FOR SURE THAT--
I'M SORRY FOR INTERRUPTING, RUFUS, BUT I TOOK THE LIBERTY OF PREPARING A LITTLE DEMONSTRATION.

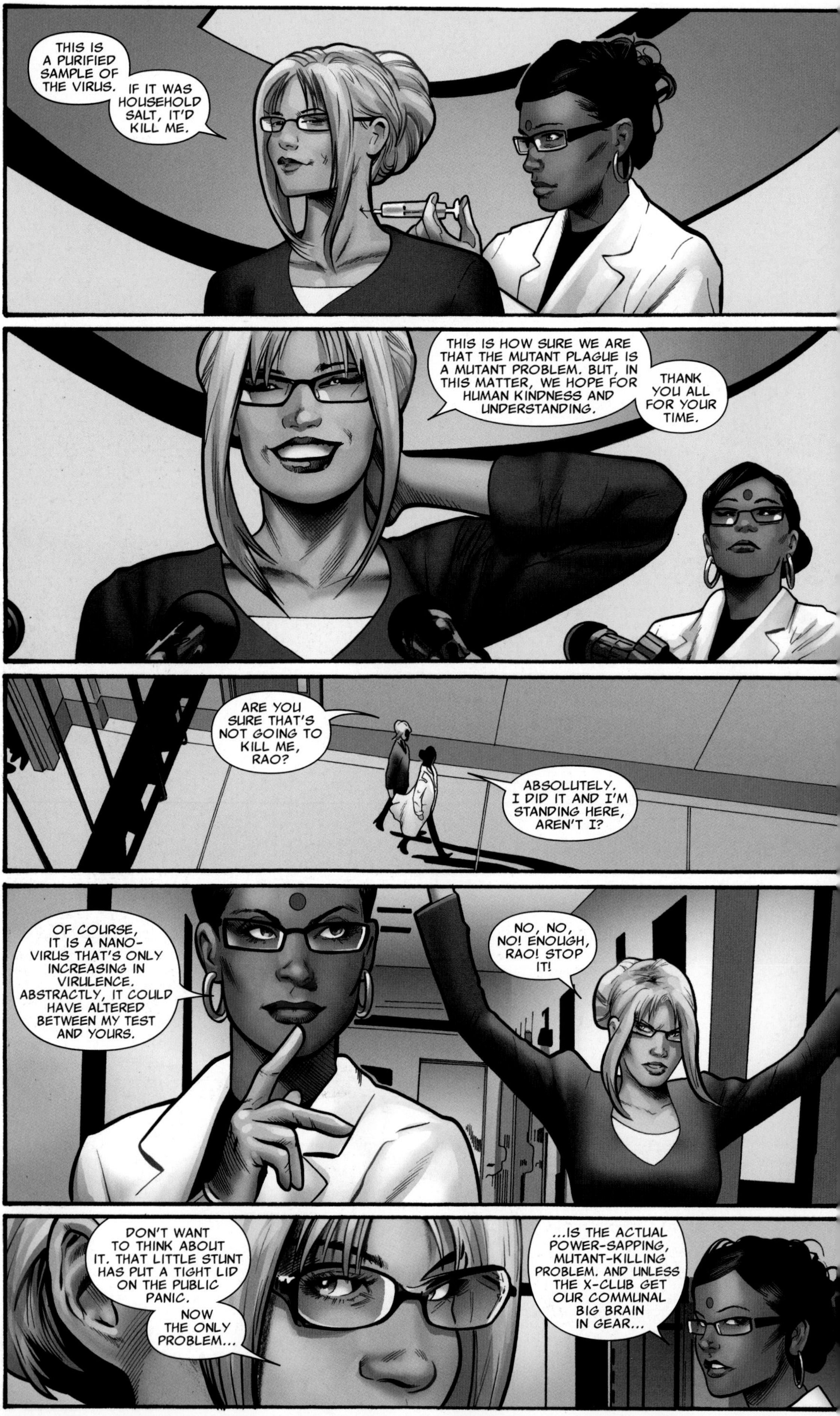
THIS IS A PURIFIED SAMPLE OF THE VIRUS.
IF IT WAS HOUSEHOLD SALT, IT'D KILL ME.
THIS IS HOW SURE WE ARE THAT THE MUTANT PLAGUE IS A MUTANT PROBLEM. BUT, IN THIS MATTER, WE HOPE FOR HUMAN KINDNESS AND UNDERSTANDING.
THANK YOU ALL FOR YOUR TIME.
ARE YOU SURE THAT'S NOT GOING TO KILL ME, RAO?
ABSOLUTELY. I DID IT AND I'M STANDING HERE, AREN'T I?
OF COURSE, IT IS A NANO-VIRUS THAT'S ONLY INCREASING IN VIRULENCE. ABSTRACTLY, IT COULD HAVE ALTERED BETWEEN MY TEST AND YOURS.
NO, NO, NO! ENOUGH, RAO! STOP IT!
DON'T WANT TO THINK ABOUT IT. THAT LITTLE STUNT HAS PUT A TIGHT LID ON THE PUBLIC PANIC.
NOW THE ONLY PROBLEM...
...IS THE ACTUAL POWER-SAPPING, MUTANT-KILLING PROBLEM. AND UNLESS THE X-CLUB GET OUR COMMUNAL BIG BRAIN IN GEAR...

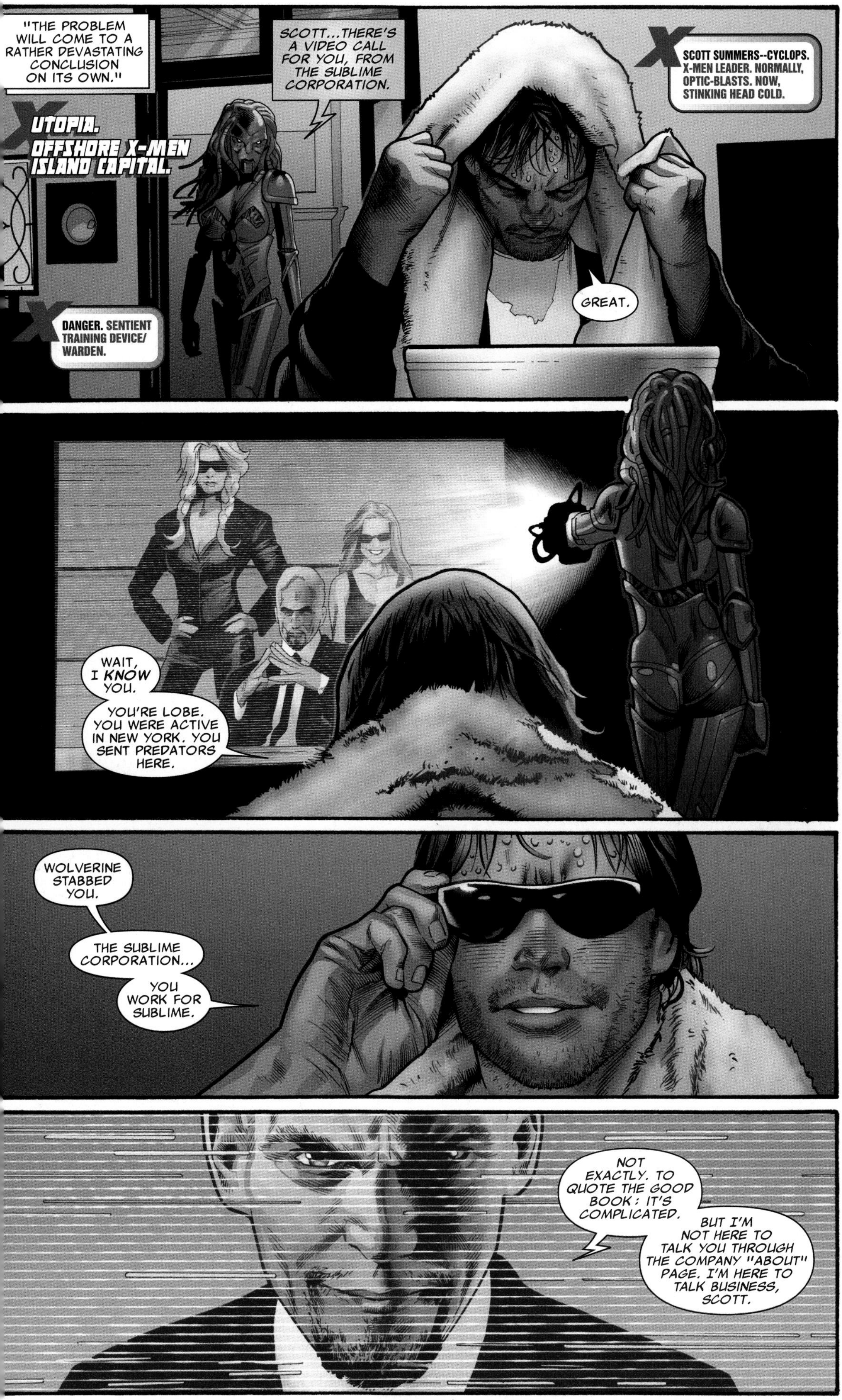
"THE PROBLEM WILL COME TO A RATHER DEVASTATING CONCLUSION ON ITS OWN."
UTOPIA. OFFSHORE X-MEN ISLAND CAPITAL.
SCOTT...THERE'S A VIDEO CALL FOR YOU, FROM THE SUBLIME CORPORATION.
SCOTT SUMMERS--CYCLOPS. X-MEN LEADER. NORMALLY, OPTIC-BLASTS. NOW, STINKING HEAD COLD.
DANGER. SENTIENT TRAINING DEVICE/ WARDEN.
GREAT.
WAIT, I KNOW YOU.
YOU'RE LOBE. YOU WERE ACTIVE IN NEW YORK. YOU SENT PREDATORS HERE.
WOLVERINE STABBED YOU.
THE SUBLIME CORPORATION...
YOU WORK FOR SUBLIME.
NOT EXACTLY. TO QUOTE THE GOOD BOOK: IT'S COMPLICATED.
BUT I'M NOT HERE TO TALK YOU THROUGH THE COMPANY "ABOUT" PAGE. I'M HERE TO TALK BUSINESS, SCOTT.

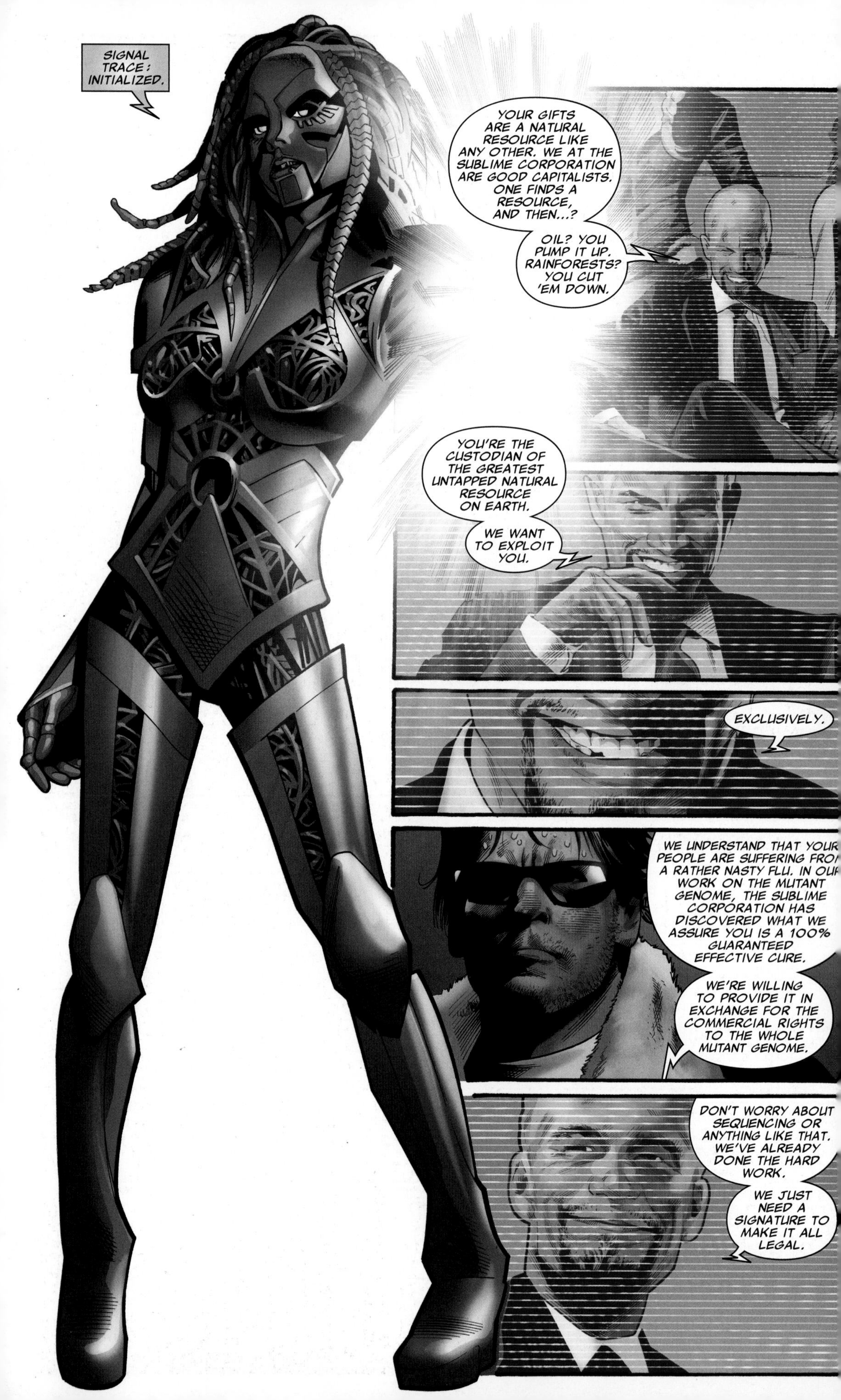

SIGNAL TRACE: INITIALIZED.
YOUR GIFTS ARE A NATURAL RESOURCE LIKE ANY OTHER. WE AT THE SUBLIME CORPORATION ARE GOOD CAPITALISTS. ONE FINDS A RESOURCE, AND THEN...?
OIL? YOU PUMP IT UP. RAINFORESTS? YOU CUT 'EM DOWN.
YOU'RE THE CUSTODIAN OF THE GREATEST UNTAPPED NATURAL RESOURCE ON EARTH.
WE WANT TO EXPLOIT YOU.
EXCLUSIVELY.
WE UNDERSTAND THAT YOUR PEOPLE ARE SUFFERING FROM A RATHER NASTY FLU. IN OUR WORK ON THE MUTANT GENOME, THE SUBLIME CORPORATION HAS DISCOVERED WHAT WE ASSURE YOU IS A 100% GUARANTEED EFFECTIVE CURE.
WE'RE WILLING TO PROVIDE IT IN EXCHANGE FOR THE COMMERCIAL RIGHTS TO THE WHOLE MUTANT GENOME.
DON'T WORRY ABOUT SEQUENCING OR ANYTHING LIKE THAT. WE'VE ALREADY DONE THE HARD WORK.
WE JUST NEED A SIGNATURE TO MAKE IT ALL LEGAL.

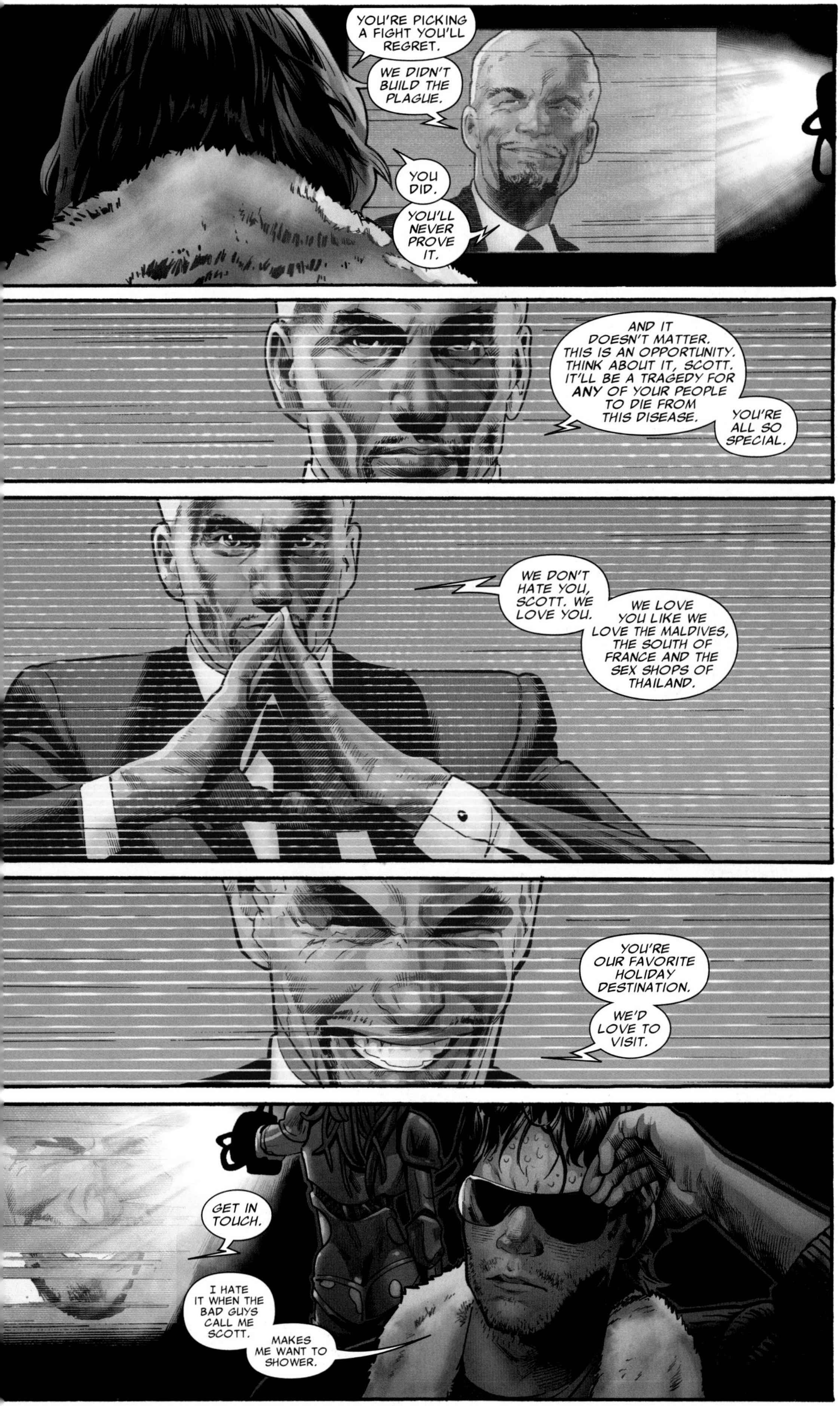

YOU'RE PICKING A FIGHT YOU'LL REGRET.
WE DIDN'T BUILD THE PLAGUE.
YOU DID.
YOU'LL NEVER PROVE IT.
AND IT DOESN'T MATTER. THIS IS AN OPPORTUNITY. THINK ABOUT IT, SCOTT. IT'LL BE A TRAGEDY FOR ANY OF YOUR PEOPLE TO DIE FROM THIS DISEASE.
YOU'RE ALL SO SPECIAL.
WE DON'T HATE YOU, SCOTT. WE LOVE YOU.
WE LOVE YOU LIKE WE LOVE THE MALDIVES, THE SOUTH OF FRANCE AND THE SEX SHOPS OF THAILAND.
YOU'RE OUR FAVORITE HOLIDAY DESTINATION.
WE'D LOVE TO VISIT.
GET IN TOUCH.
I HATE IT WHEN THE BAD GUYS CALL ME SCOTT.
MAKES ME WANT TO SHOWER.

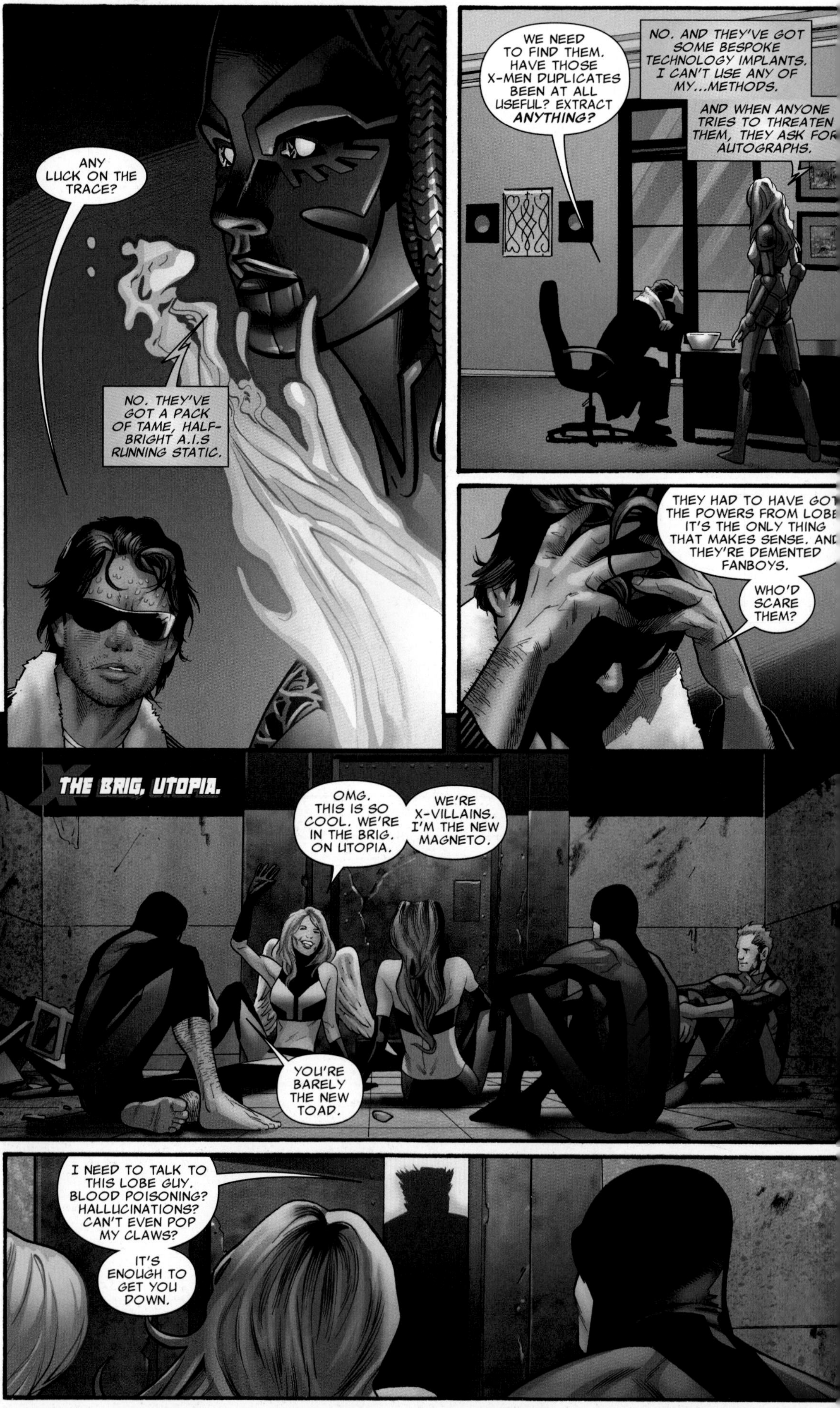
ANY LUCK ON THE TRACE?
NO. THEY'VE GOT A PACK OF TAME, HALF-BRIGHT A.I.S RUNNING STATIC.
WE NEED TO FIND THEM. HAVE THOSE X-MEN DUPLICATES BEEN AT ALL USEFUL? EXTRACT ANYTHING?
NO. AND THEY'VE GOT SOME BESPOKE TECHNOLOGY IMPLANTS. I CAN'T USE ANY OF MY...METHODS.
AND WHEN ANYONE TRIES TO THREATEN THEM, THEY ASK FOR AUTOGRAPHS.
THEY HAD TO HAVE GOT THE POWERS FROM LOBE. IT'S THE ONLY THING THAT MAKES SENSE. AND THEY'RE DEMENTED FANBOYS.
WHO'D SCARE THEM?
THE BRIG, UTOPIA.
OMG. THIS IS SO COOL. WE'RE IN THE BRIG. ON UTOPIA.
WE'RE X-VILLAINS. I'M THE NEW MAGNETO.
YOU'RE BARELY THE NEW TOAD.
I NEED TO TALK TO THIS LOBE GUY. BLOOD POISONING? HALLUCINATIONS? CAN'T EVEN POP MY CLAWS?
IT'S ENOUGH TO GET YOU DOWN.

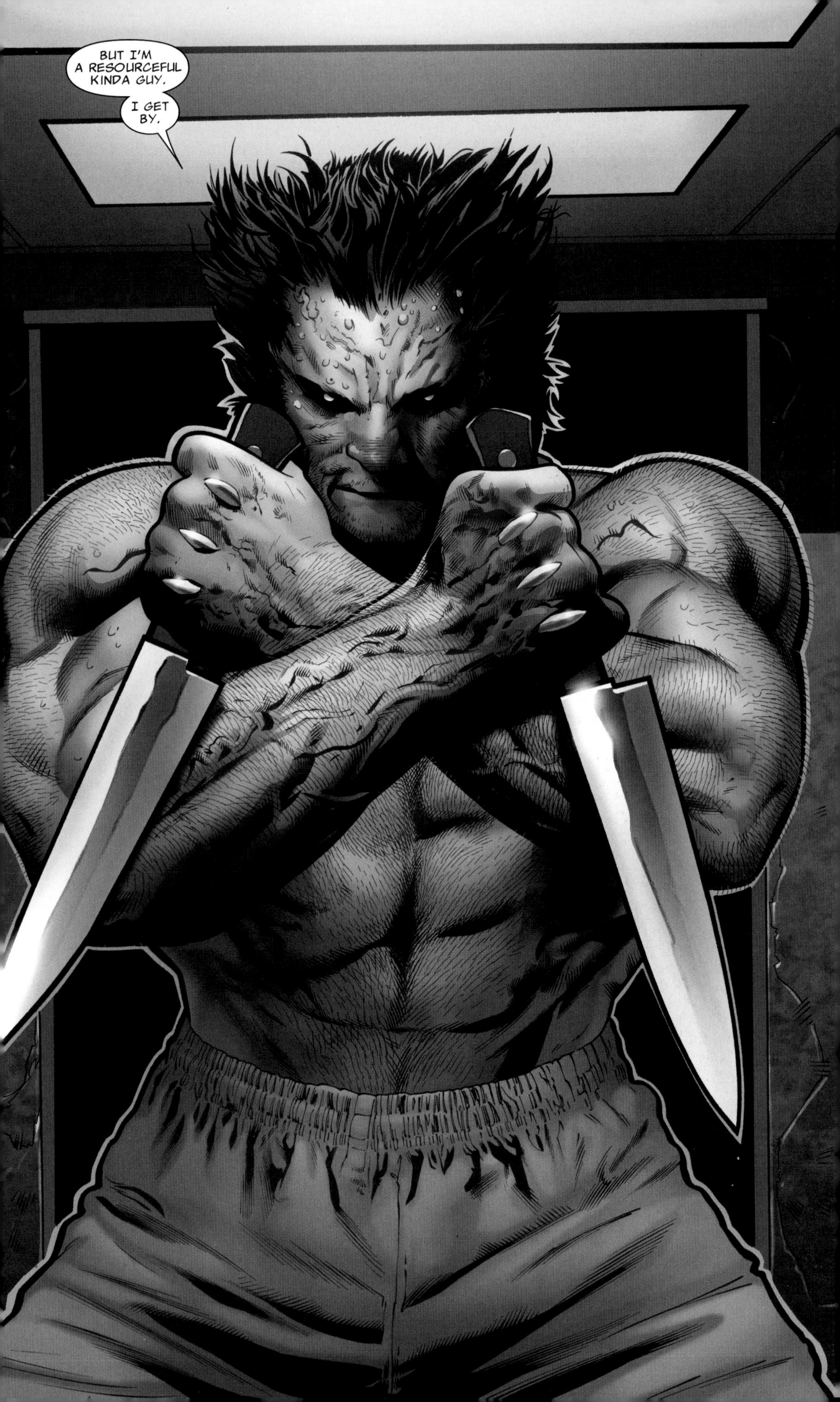
BUT I'M A RESOURCEFUL KINDA GUY.
I GET BY.

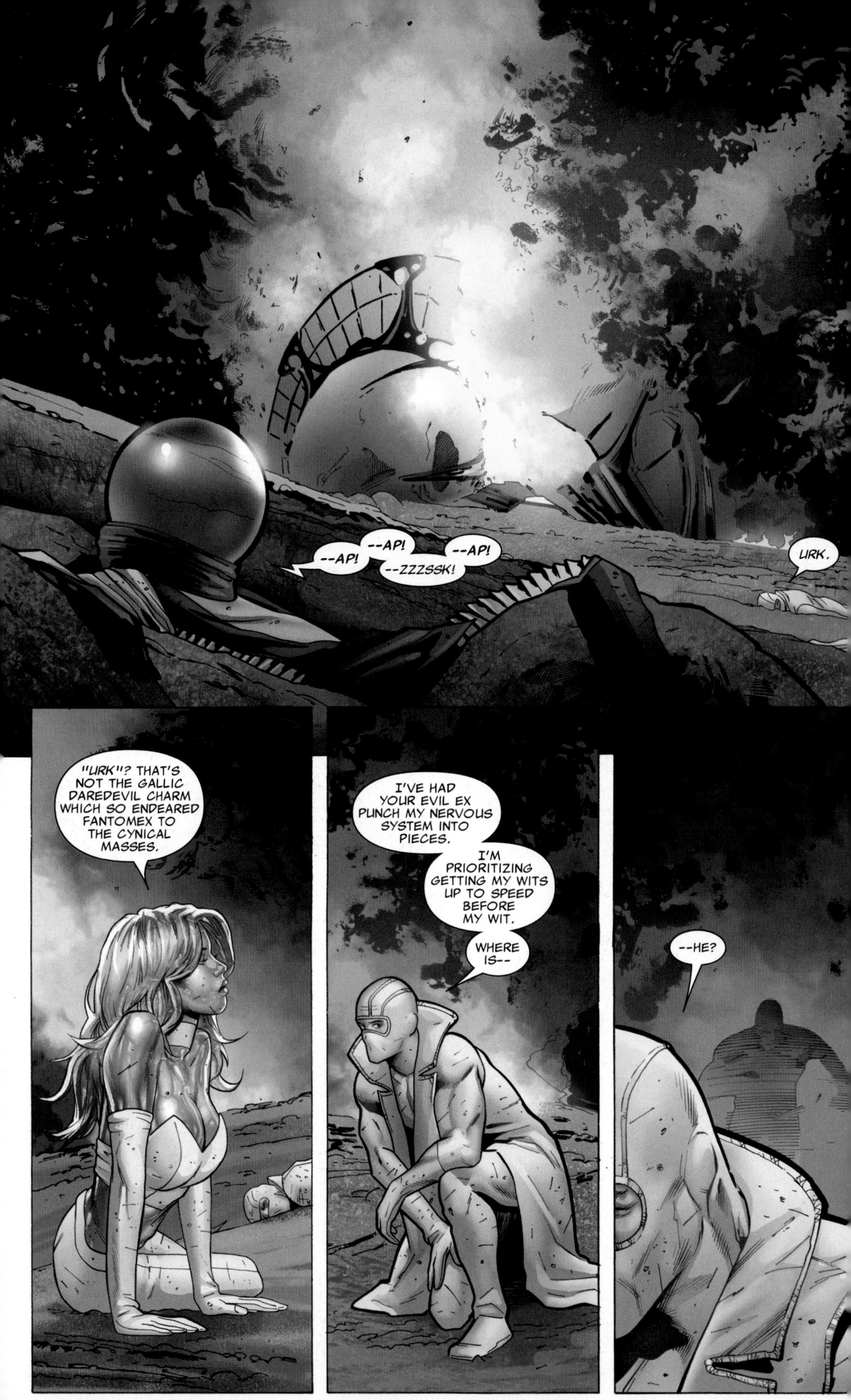
--AP!
--AP!
--ZZZSSK!
--AP!
URK.
"URK"? THAT'S NOT THE GALLIC DAREDEVIL CHARM WHICH SO ENDEARED FANTOMEX TO THE CYNICAL MASSES.
I'VE HAD YOUR EVIL EX PUNCH MY NERVOUS SYSTEM INTO PIECES.
I'M PRIORITIZING GETTING MY WITS UP TO SPEED BEFORE MY WIT.
WHERE IS--
--HE?

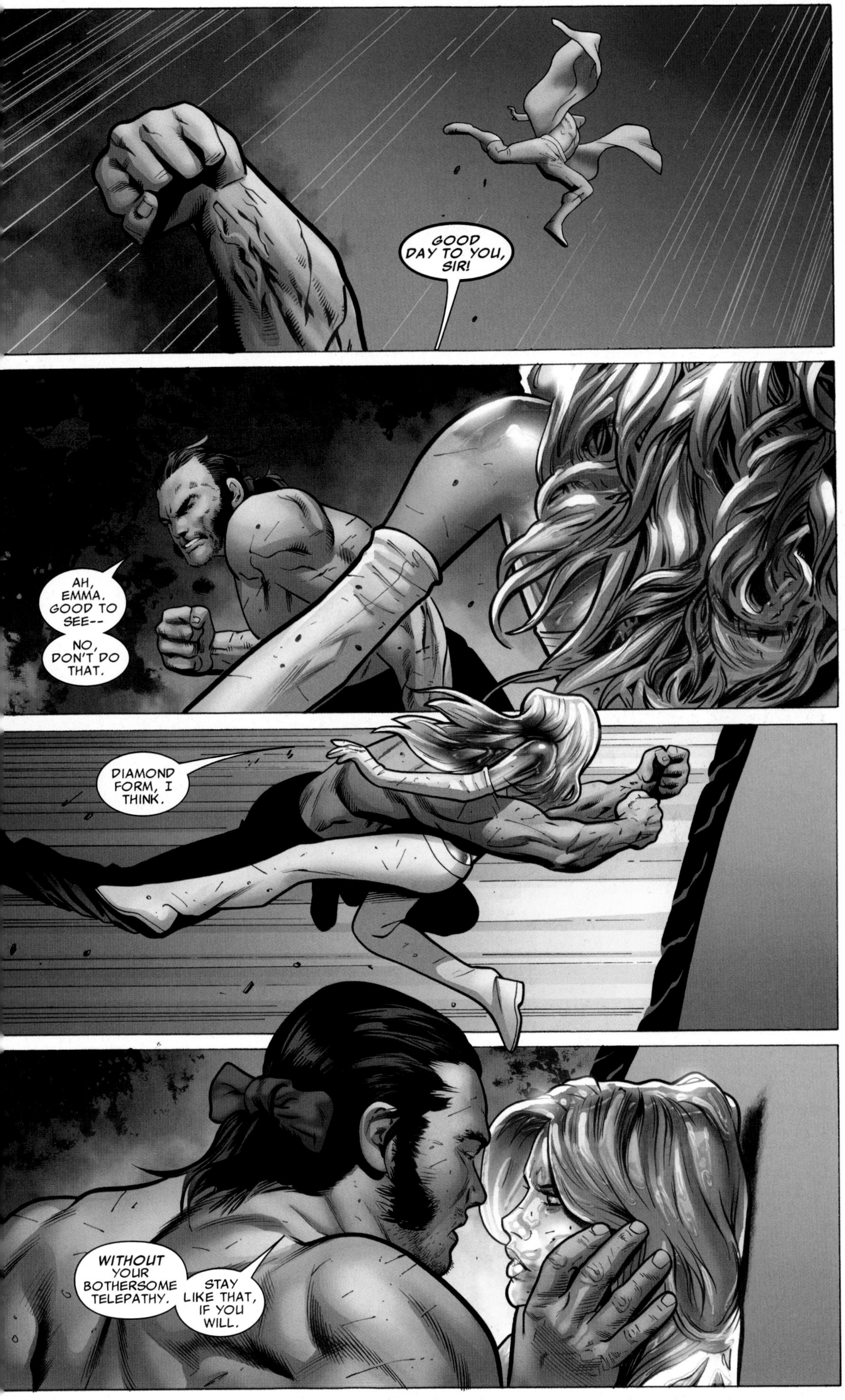
GOOD DAY TO YOU, SIR!
AH, EMMA. GOOD TO SEE--
NO, DON'T DO THAT.
DIAMOND FORM, I THINK.
WITHOUT YOUR BOTHERSOME TELEPATHY.
STAY LIKE THAT, IF YOU WILL.

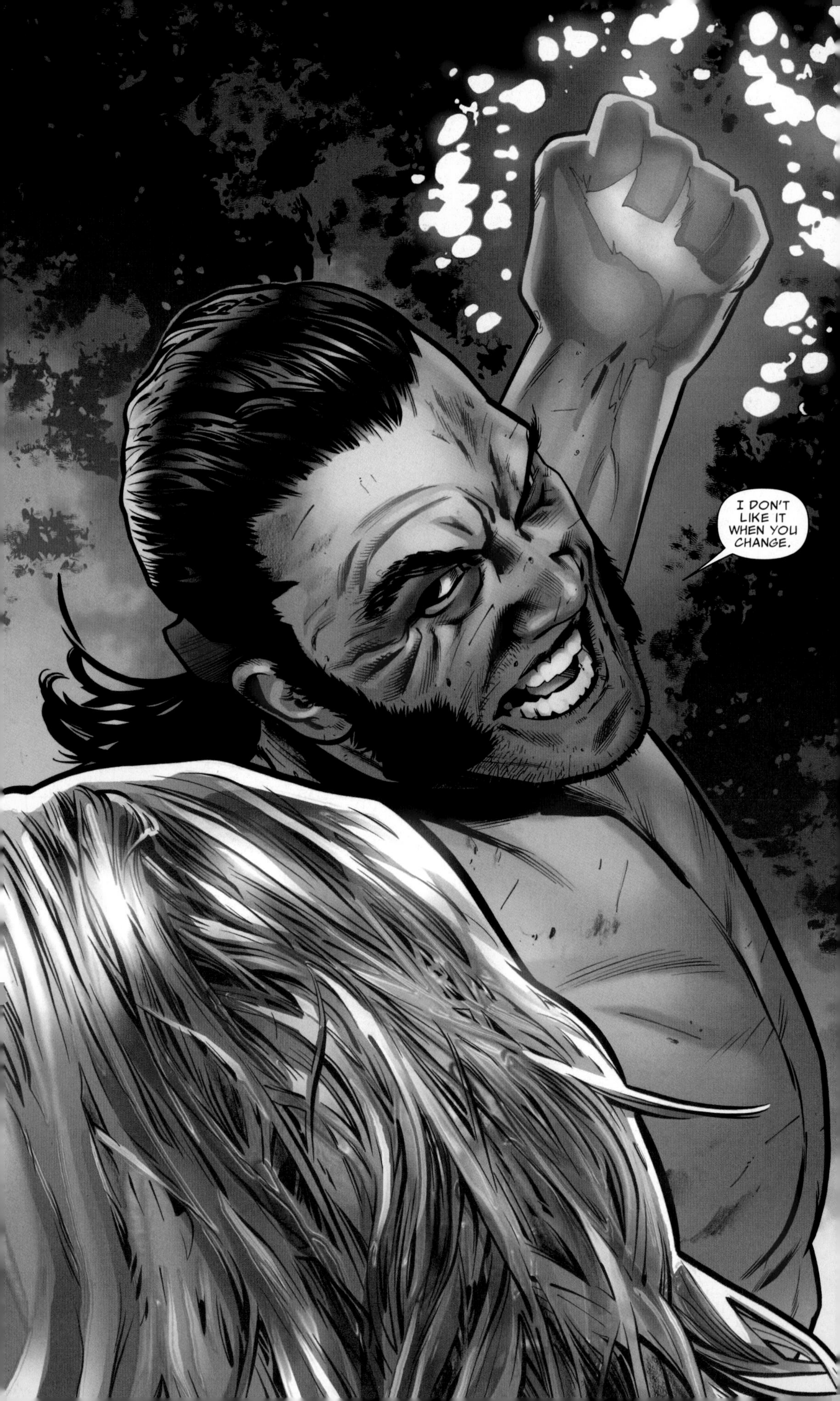
I DON'T LIKE IT WHEN YOU CHANGE.

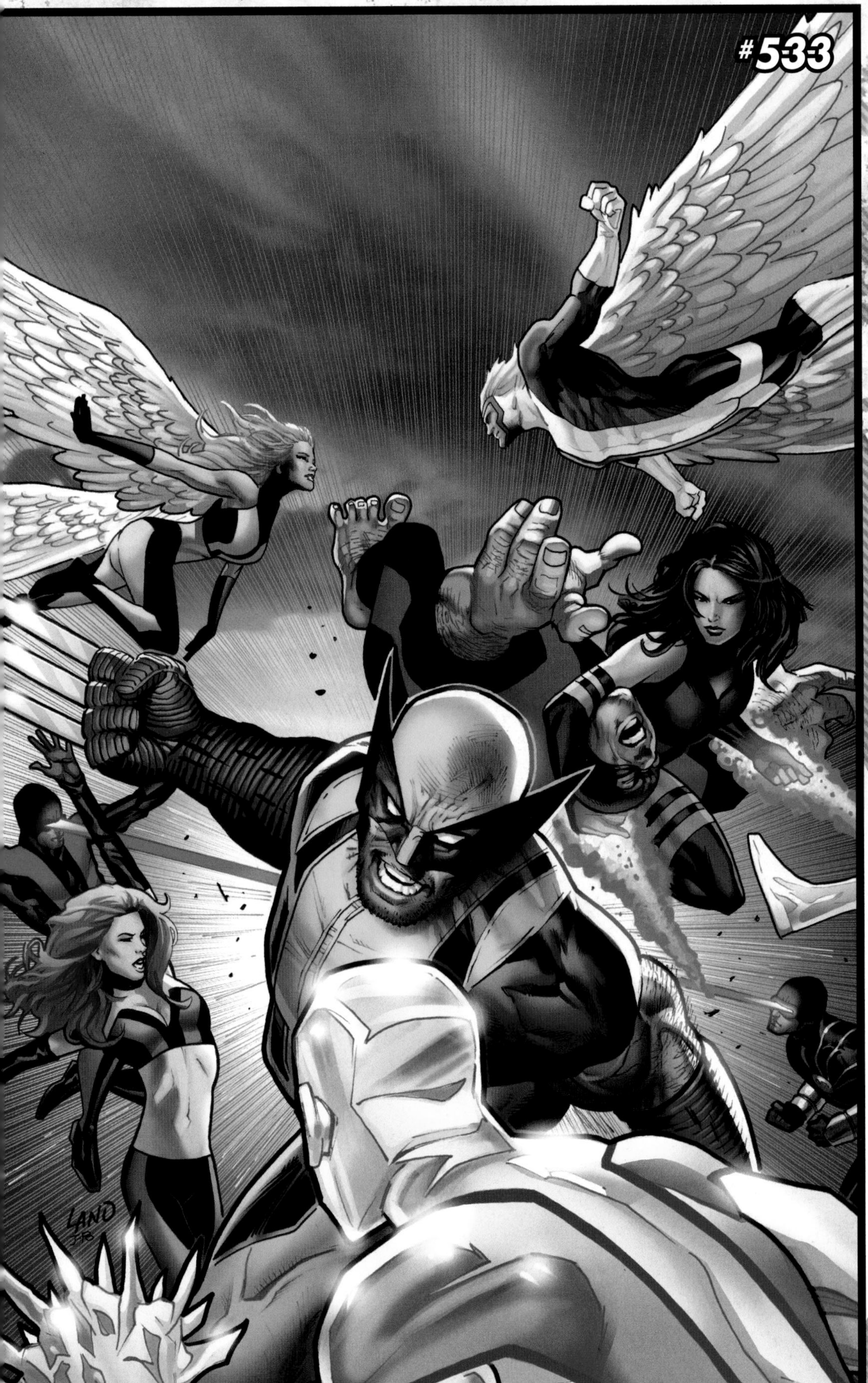
#533
LAND

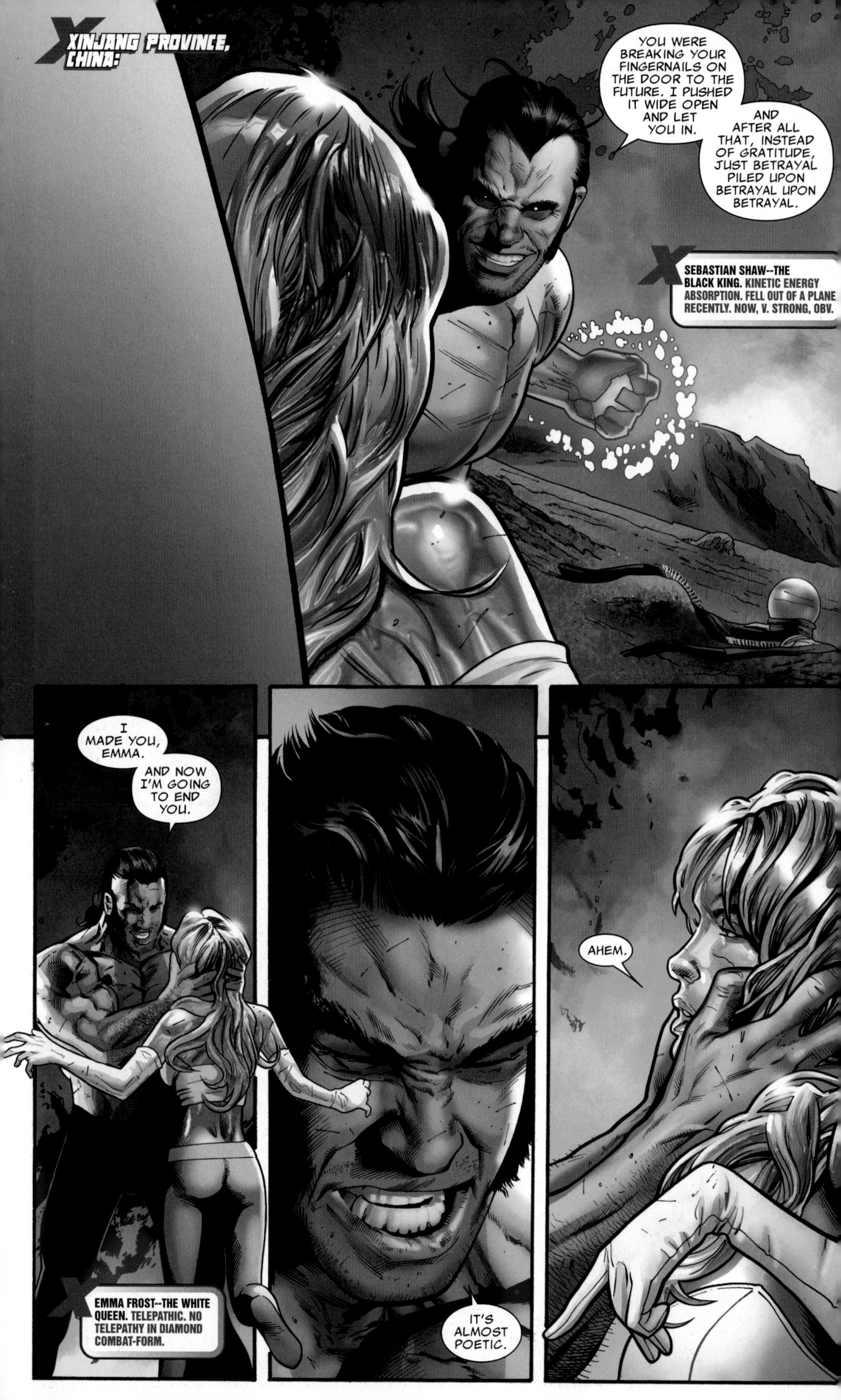
XINJANG PROVINCE, CHINA:
YOU WERE BREAKING YOUR FINGERNAILS ON THE DOOR TO THE FUTURE. I PUSHED IT WIDE OPEN AND LET YOU IN.
AND AFTER ALL THAT, INSTEAD OF GRATITUDE, JUST BETRAYAL PILED UPON BETRAYAL UPON BETRAYAL.
SEBASTIAN SHAW--THE BLACK KING. KINETIC ENERGY ABSORPTION. FELL OUT OF A PLANE RECENTLY. NOW, V. STRONG, OBV.
I MADE YOU, EMMA.
AND NOW I'M GOING TO END YOU.
EMMA FROST--THE WHITE QUEEN. TELEPATHIC. NO TELEPATHY IN DIAMOND COMBAT-FORM.
IT'S ALMOST POETIC.
AHEM.

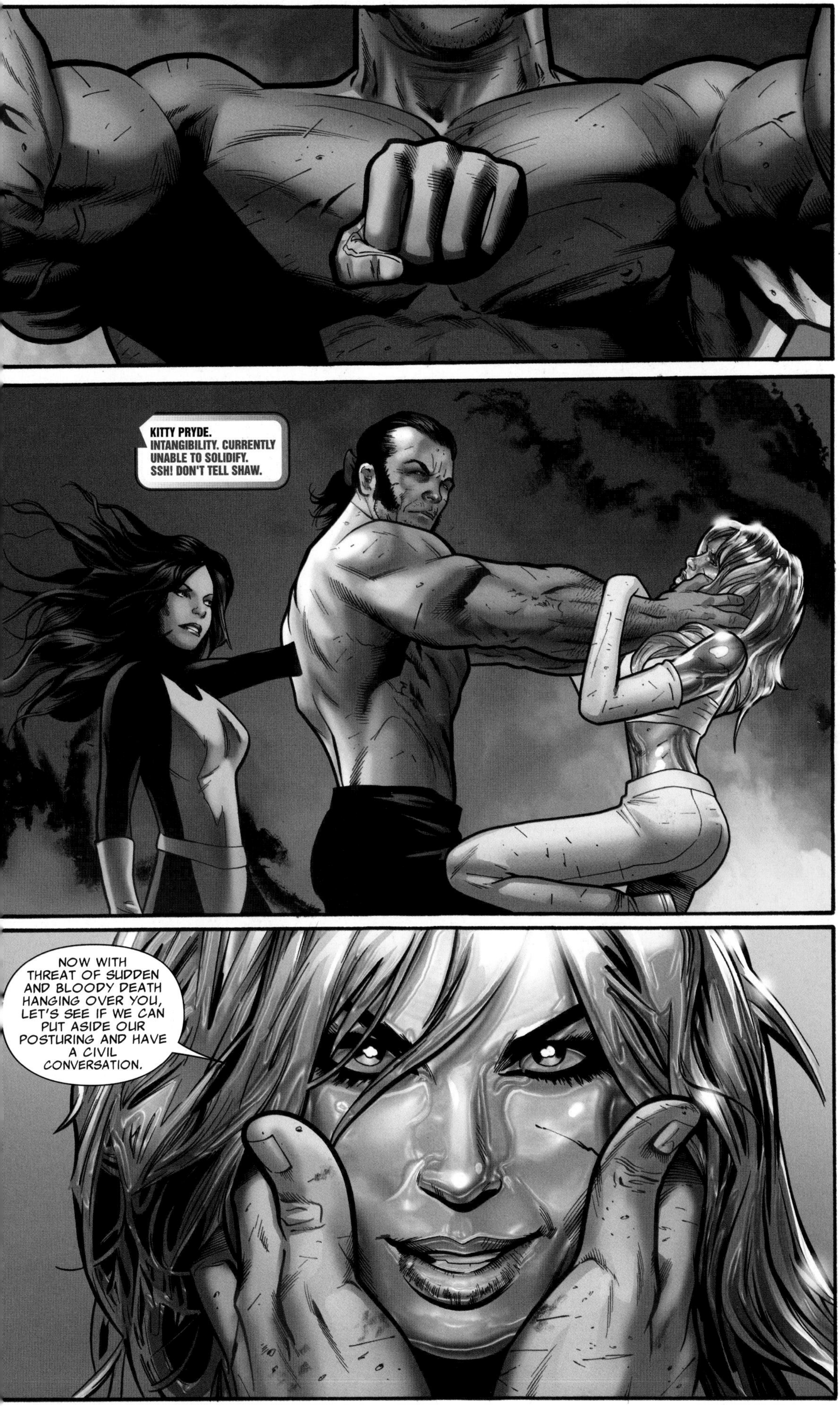
KITTY PRYDE. INTANGIBILITY. CURRENTLY UNABLE TO SOLIDIFY. SSH! DON'T TELL SHAW.
NOW WITH THREAT OF SUDDEN AND BLOODY DEATH HANGING OVER YOU, LET'S SEE IF WE CAN PUT ASIDE OUR POSTURING AND HAVE A CIVIL CONVERSATION.

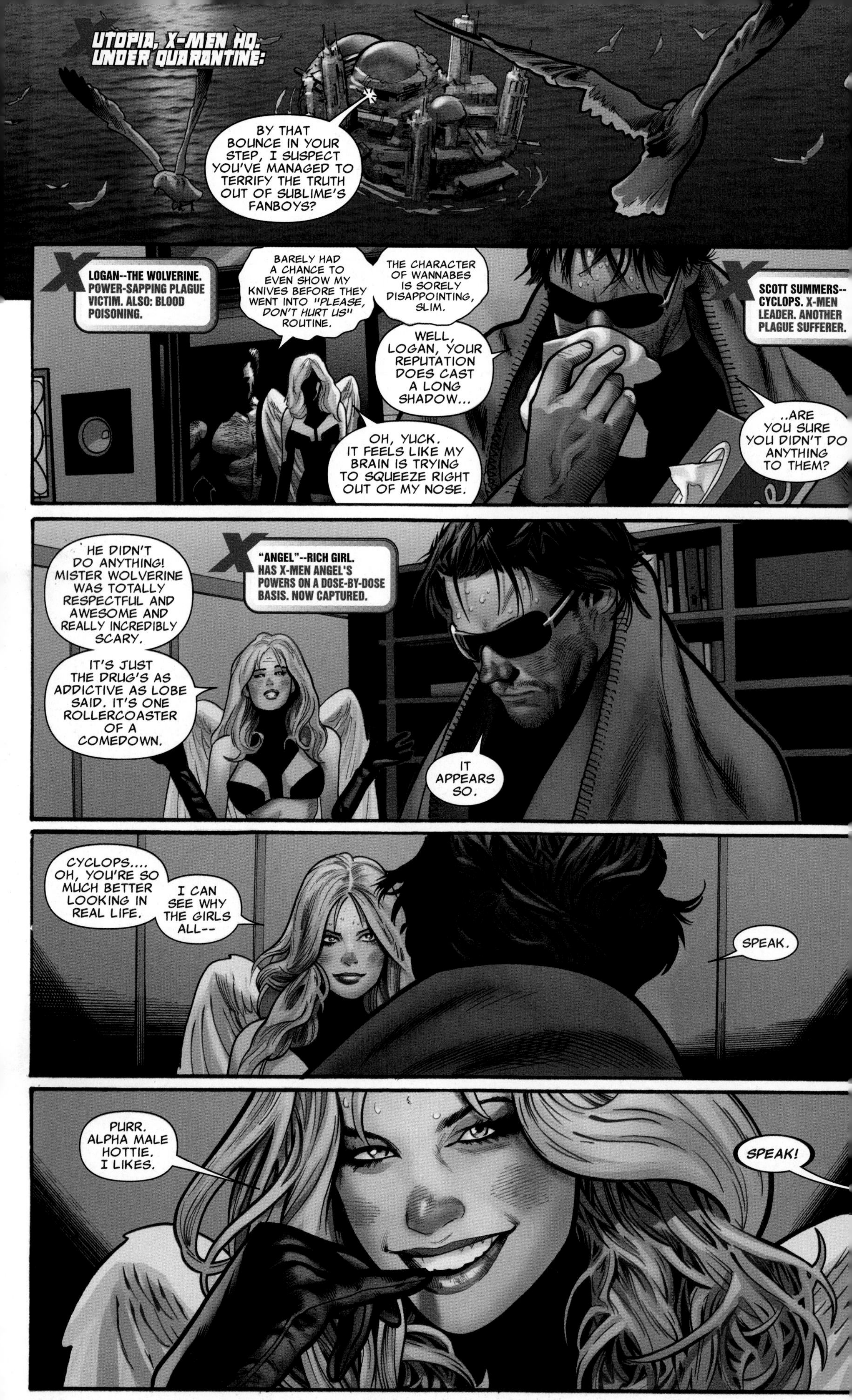
UTOPIA, X-MEN HQ: UNDER QUARANTINE:
BY THAT BOUNCE IN YOUR STEP, I SUSPECT YOU'VE MANAGED TO TERRIFY THE TRUTH OUT OF SUBLIME'S FANBOYS?
LOGAN--THE WOLVERINE. POWER-SAPPING PLAGUE VICTIM. ALSO: BLOOD POISONING.
BARELY HAD A CHANCE TO EVEN SHOW MY KNIVES BEFORE THEY WENT INTO "PLEASE, DON'T HURT US" ROUTINE.
THE CHARACTER OF WANNABES IS SORELY DISAPPOINTING, SLIM.
SCOTT SUMMERS--CYCLOPS. X-MEN LEADER. ANOTHER PLAGUE SUFFERER.
WELL, LOGAN, YOUR REPUTATION DOES CAST A LONG SHADOW...
..ARE YOU SURE YOU DIDN'T DO ANYTHING TO THEM?
OH, YUCK. IT FEELS LIKE MY BRAIN IS TRYING TO SQUEEZE RIGHT OUT OF MY NOSE.
HE DIDN'T DO ANYTHING! MISTER WOLVERINE WAS TOTALLY RESPECTFUL AND AWESOME AND REALLY INCREDIBLY SCARY.
"ANGEL"--RICH GIRL. HAS X-MEN ANGEL'S POWERS ON A DOSE-BY-DOSE BASIS. NOW CAPTURED.
IT'S JUST THE DRUG'S AS ADDICTIVE AS LOBE SAID. IT'S ONE ROLLERCOASTER OF A COMEDOWN.
IT APPEARS SO.
CYCLOPS.... OH, YOU'RE SO MUCH BETTER LOOKING IN REAL LIFE.
I CAN SEE WHY THE GIRLS ALL--
SPEAK.
PURR. ALPHA MALE HOTTIE. I LIKES.
SPEAK!

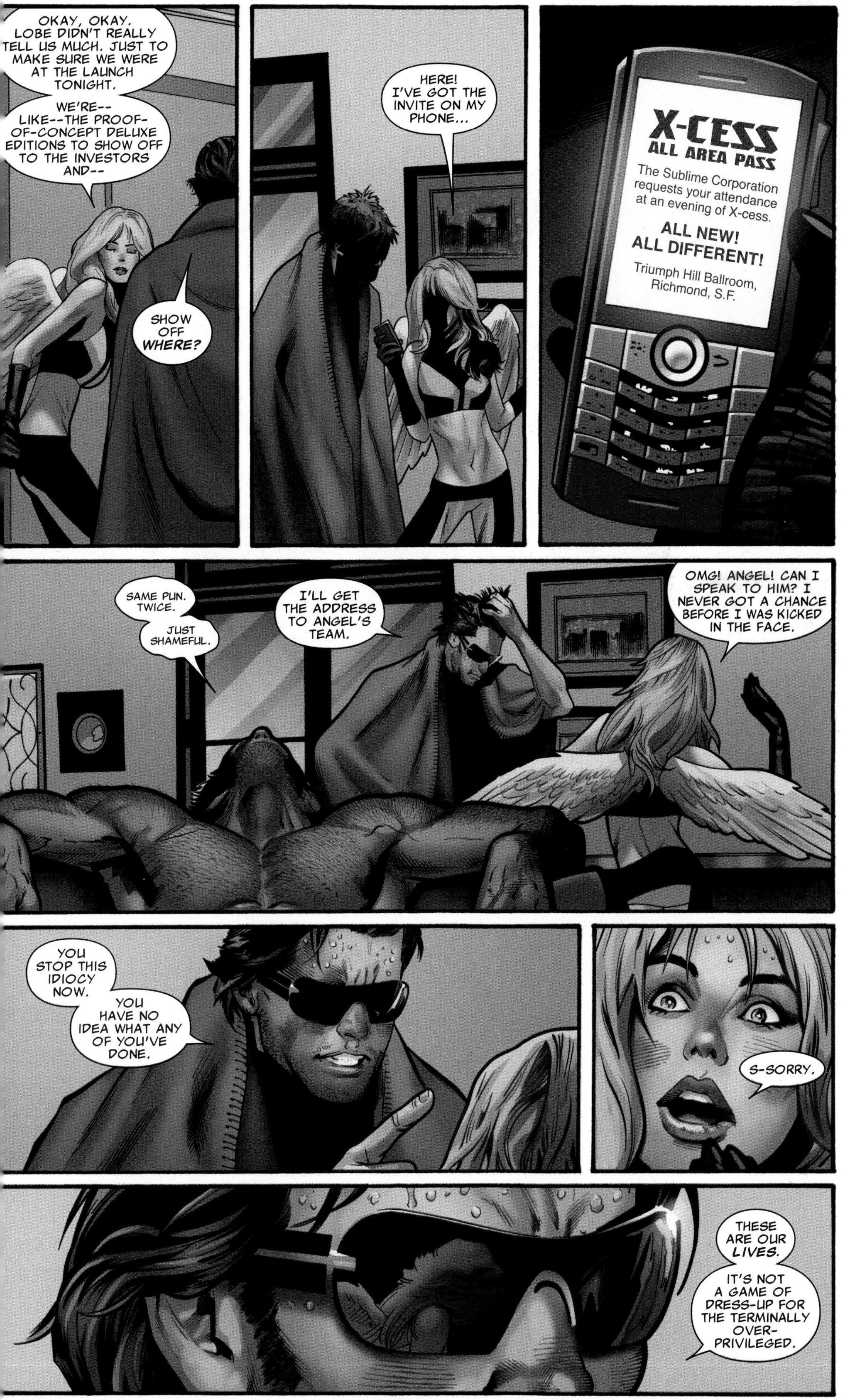

OKAY, OKAY. LOBE DIDN'T REALLY TELL US MUCH. JUST TO MAKE SURE WE WERE AT THE LAUNCH TONIGHT.
WE'RE-- LIKE--THE PROOF-OF-CONCEPT DELUXE EDITIONS TO SHOW OFF TO THE INVESTORS AND--
SHOW OFF WHERE?
HERE! I'VE GOT THE INVITE ON MY PHONE...
X-CESS
ALL AREA PASS
The Sublime Corporation requests your attendance at an evening of X-cess.
ALL NEW! ALL DIFFERENT!
Triumph Hill Ballroom, Richmond, S.F.
SAME PUN. TWICE.
JUST SHAMEFUL.
I'LL GET THE ADDRESS TO ANGEL'S TEAM.
OMG! ANGEL! CAN I SPEAK TO HIM? I NEVER GOT A CHANCE BEFORE I WAS KICKED IN THE FACE.
YOU STOP THIS IDIOCY NOW.
YOU HAVE NO IDEA WHAT ANY OF YOU'VE DONE.
S-SORRY.
THESE ARE OUR LIVES.
IT'S NOT A GAME OF DRESS-UP FOR THE TERMINALLY OVER-PRIVILEGED.

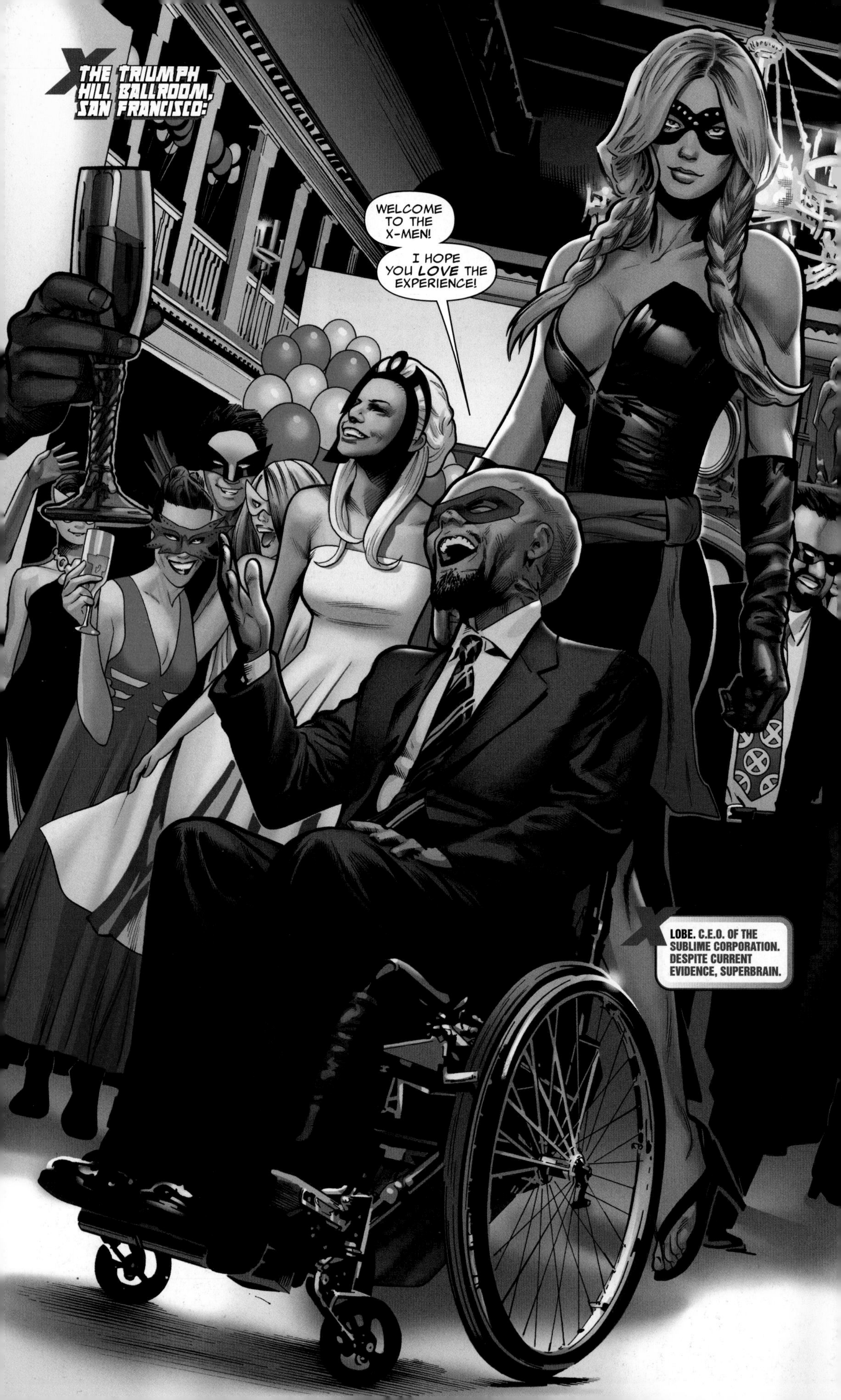
THE TRIUMPH HILL BALLROOM, SAN FRANCISCO:
WELCOME TO THE X-MEN!
I HOPE YOU LOVE THE EXPERIENCE!
LOBE. C.E.O. OF THE SUBLIME CORPORATION. DESPITE CURRENT EVIDENCE, SUPERBRAIN.

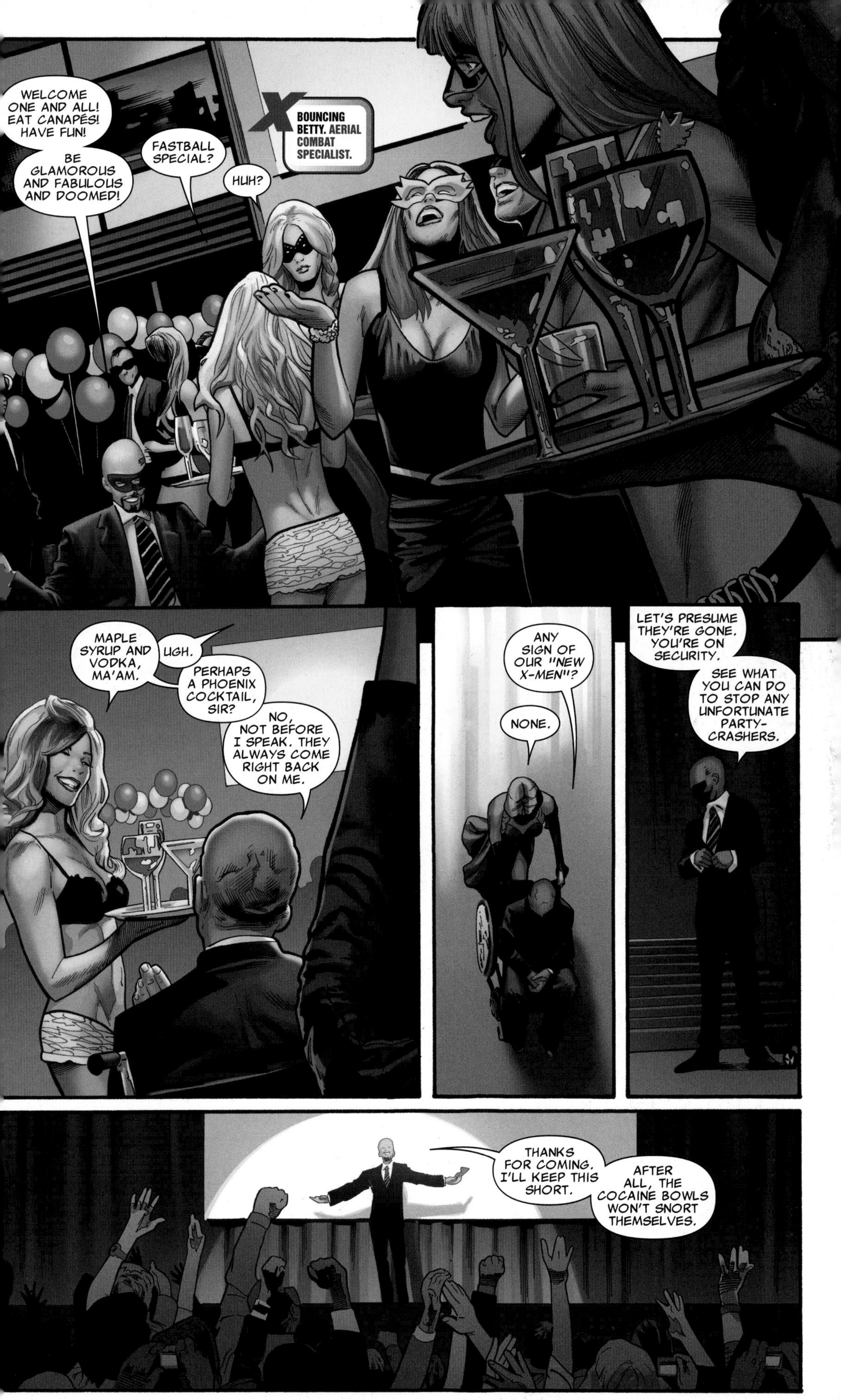

WELCOME ONE AND ALL! EAT CANAPÉS! HAVE FUN!
BE GLAMOROUS AND FABULOUS AND DOOMED!
FASTBALL SPECIAL?
HUH?
BOUNCING BETTY. AERIAL COMBAT SPECIALIST.
MAPLE SYRUP AND VODKA, MA'AM.
UGH.
PERHAPS A PHOENIX COCKTAIL, SIR?
NO, NOT BEFORE I SPEAK. THEY ALWAYS COME RIGHT BACK ON ME.
ANY SIGN OF OUR "NEW X-MEN"?
NONE.
LET'S PRESUME THEY'RE GONE. YOU'RE ON SECURITY.
SEE WHAT YOU CAN DO TO STOP ANY UNFORTUNATE PARTY-CRASHERS.
THANKS FOR COMING. I'LL KEEP THIS SHORT.
AFTER ALL, THE COCAINE BOWLS WON'T SNORT THEMSELVES.

I WAS A TOP-FLIGHT M.B.A. SPECIALIST WHEN I HEARD JOHN SUBLIME TALK ABOUT THE THIRD SPECIES. IT CHANGED MY LIFE. HUMANS *BECOMING* MUTANTS.

AND THE U-MEN WHO PUT THAT INTO PRACTICE. BRILLIANCE.

BUT... SURGERY? ALL THAT NASTY CUTTING? AND THE RELIGIOUS STUFF?

UGGGG-LY. THERE HAD TO BE A BETTER WAY.

STILL...HE WAS MY INSPIRATION. ALAS, HE ISN'T AROUND ANY MORE.

THANKFULLY, THE SUBLIME CORPORATION IS CARRYING ON HIS GOOD WORK.

FOR PROFIT.

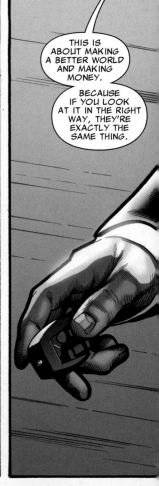

THIS IS ABOUT MAKING A BETTER WORLD AND MAKING MONEY.

BECAUSE IF YOU LOOK AT IT IN THE RIGHT WAY, THEY'RE EXACTLY THE SAME THING.

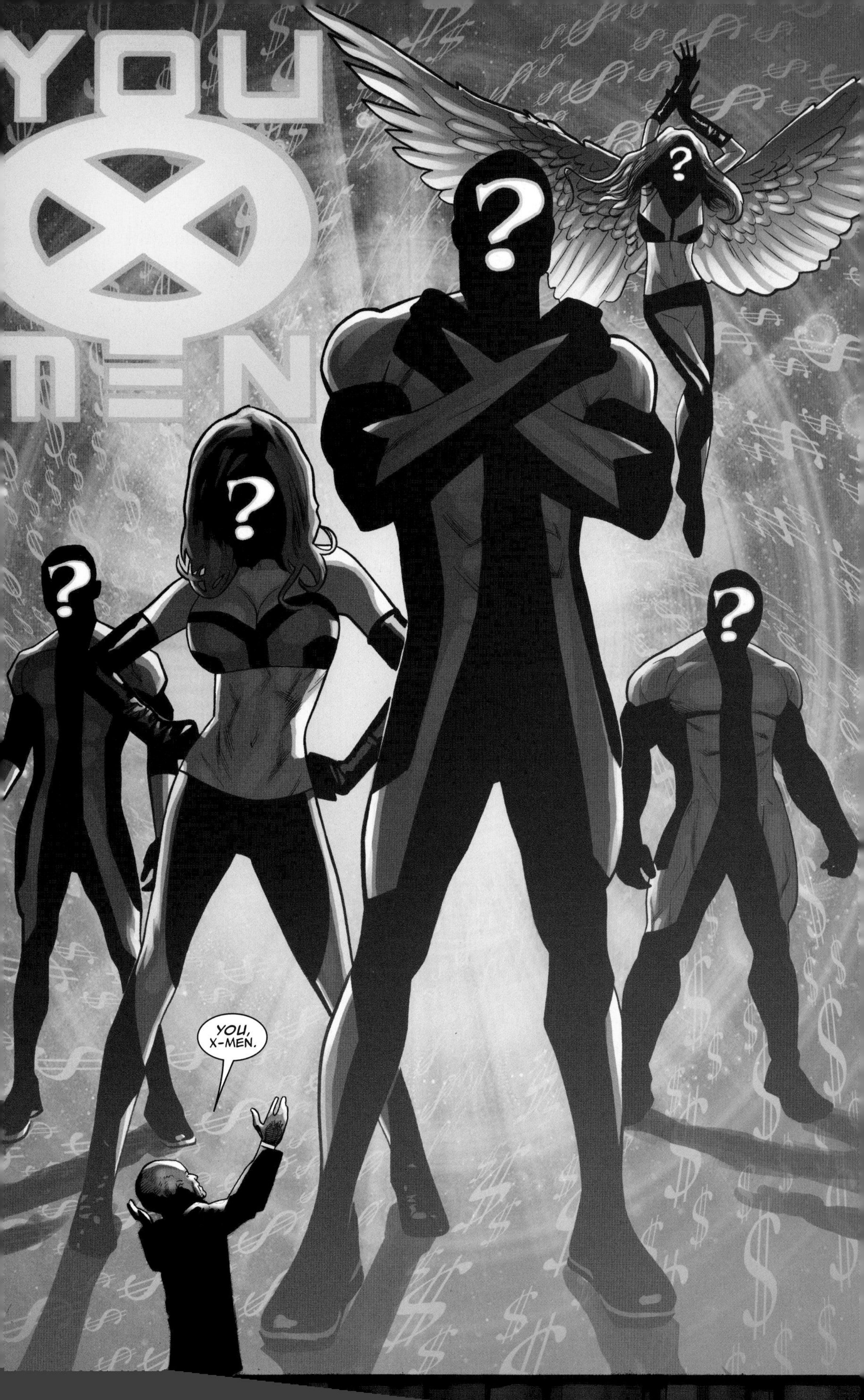
YOU
MEN
?
?
?
?
?
?
YOU, X-MEN.

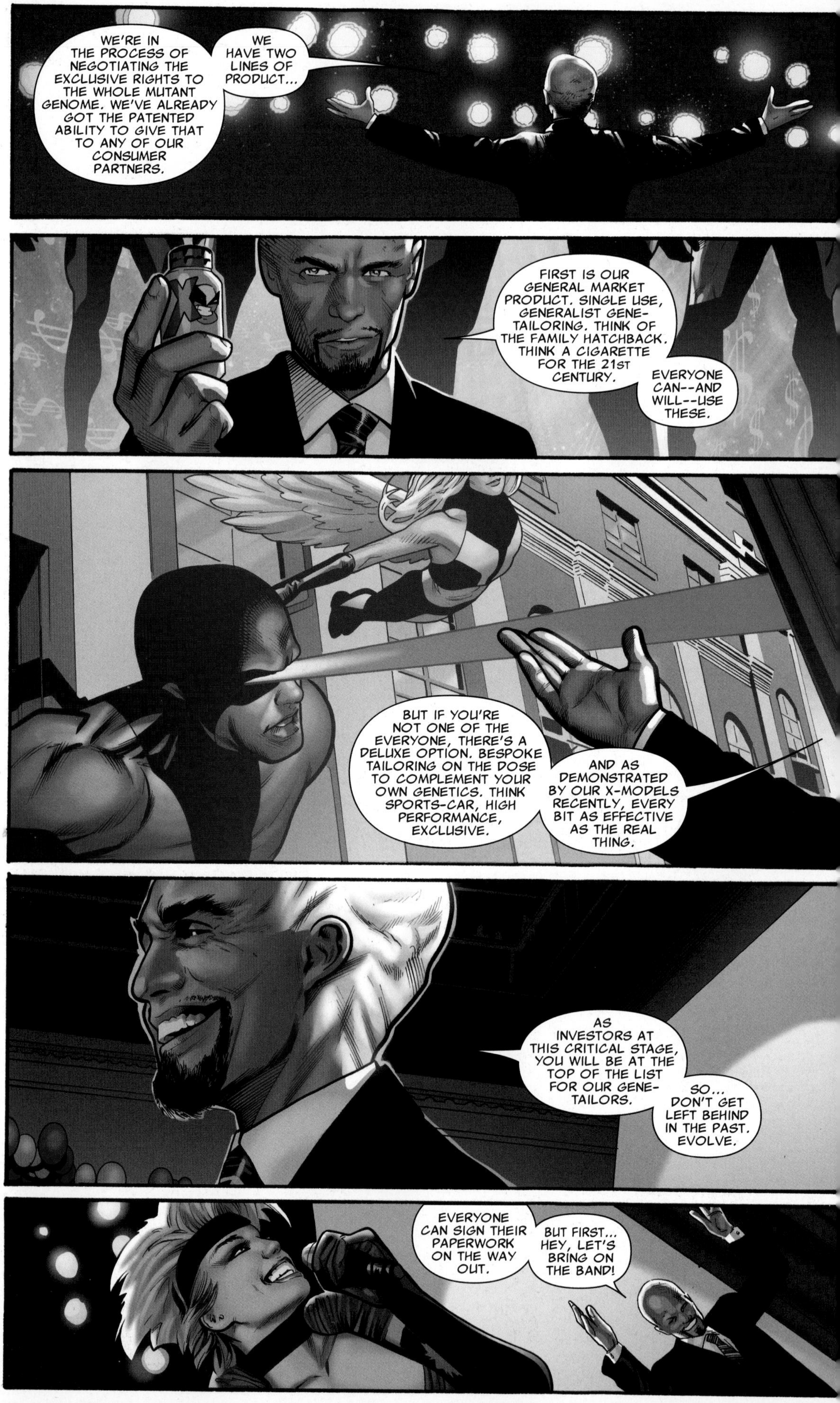
WE'RE IN THE PROCESS OF NEGOTIATING THE EXCLUSIVE RIGHTS TO THE WHOLE MUTANT GENOME. WE'VE ALREADY GOT THE PATENTED ABILITY TO GIVE THAT TO ANY OF OUR CONSUMER PARTNERS.
WE HAVE TWO LINES OF PRODUCT...
FIRST IS OUR GENERAL MARKET PRODUCT. SINGLE USE, GENERALIST GENE-TAILORING. THINK OF THE FAMILY HATCHBACK. THINK A CIGARETTE FOR THE 21ST CENTURY.
EVERYONE CAN--AND WILL--USE THESE.
BUT IF YOU'RE NOT ONE OF THE EVERYONE, THERE'S A DELUXE OPTION. BESPOKE TAILORING ON THE DOSE TO COMPLEMENT YOUR OWN GENETICS. THINK SPORTS-CAR, HIGH PERFORMANCE, EXCLUSIVE.
AND AS DEMONSTRATED BY OUR X-MODELS RECENTLY, EVERY BIT AS EFFECTIVE AS THE REAL THING.
AS INVESTORS AT THIS CRITICAL STAGE, YOU WILL BE AT THE TOP OF THE LIST FOR OUR GENE-TAILORS.
SO... DON'T GET LEFT BEHIND IN THE PAST. EVOLVE.
EVERYONE CAN SIGN THEIR PAPERWORK ON THE WAY OUT.
BUT FIRST... HEY, LET'S BRING ON THE BAND!

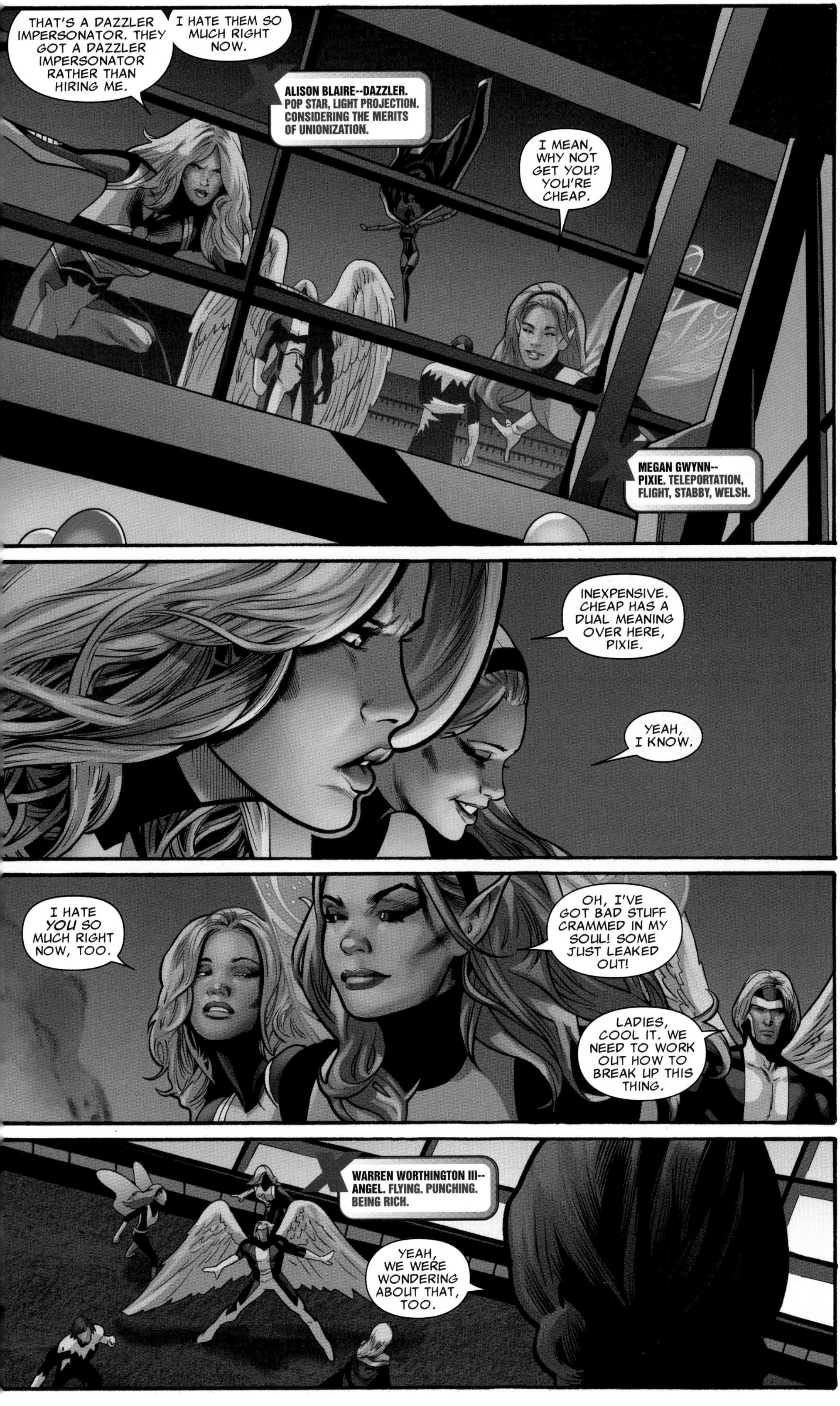
THAT'S A DAZZLER IMPERSONATOR. THEY GOT A DAZZLER IMPERSONATOR RATHER THAN HIRING ME.
I HATE THEM SO MUCH RIGHT NOW.
ALISON BLAIRE--DAZZLER. POP STAR, LIGHT PROJECTION. CONSIDERING THE MERITS OF UNIONIZATION.
I MEAN, WHY NOT GET YOU? YOU'RE CHEAP.
MEGAN GWYNN--PIXIE. TELEPORTATION, FLIGHT, STABBY, WELSH.
INEXPENSIVE. CHEAP HAS A DUAL MEANING OVER HERE, PIXIE.
YEAH, I KNOW.
I HATE YOU SO MUCH RIGHT NOW, TOO.
OH, I'VE GOT BAD STUFF CRAMMED IN MY SOUL! SOME JUST LEAKED OUT!
LADIES, COOL IT. WE NEED TO WORK OUT HOW TO BREAK UP THIS THING.
WARREN WORTHINGTON III--ANGEL. FLYING. PUNCHING. BEING RICH.
YEAH, WE WERE WONDERING ABOUT THAT, TOO.

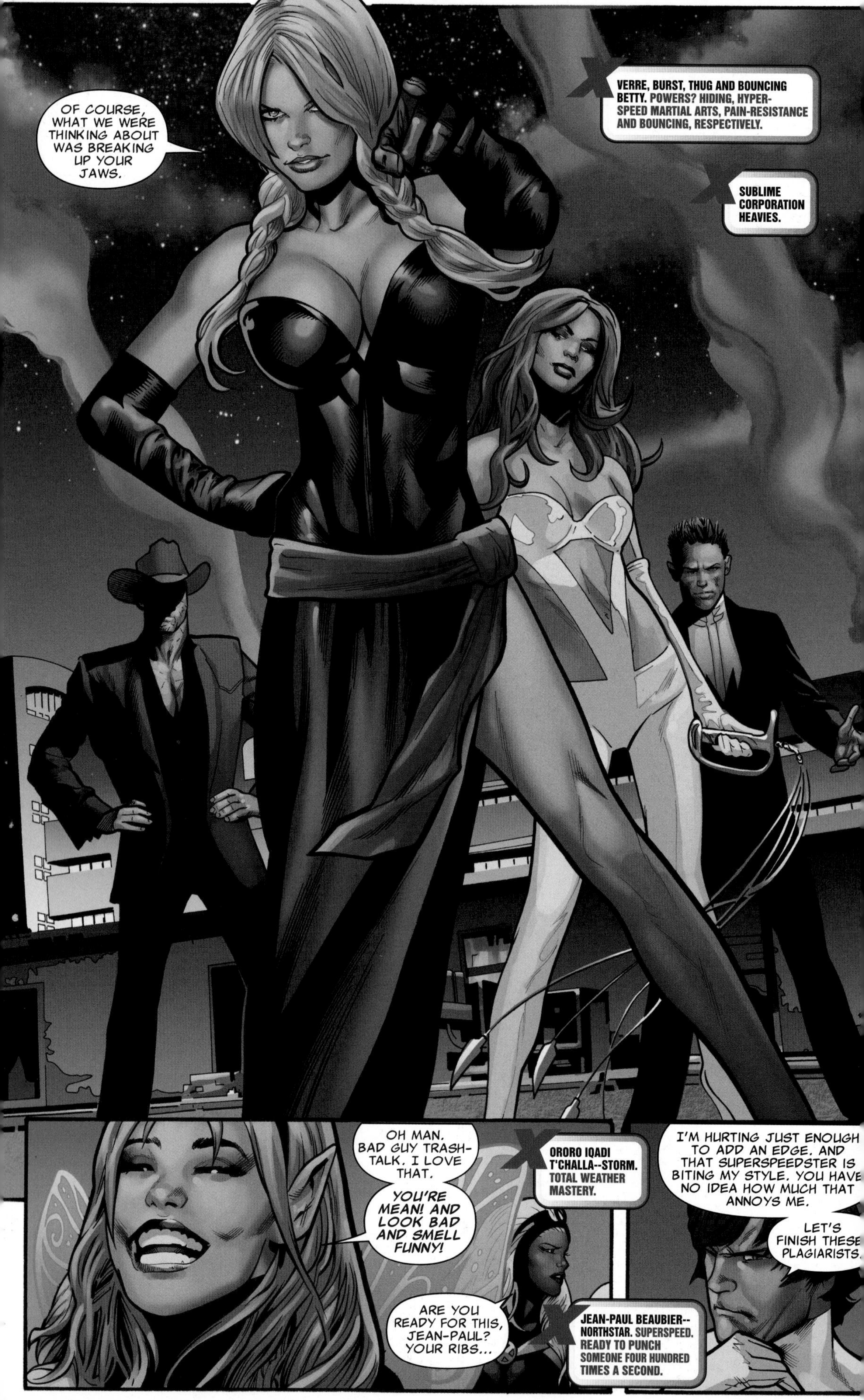
OF COURSE, WHAT WE WERE THINKING ABOUT WAS BREAKING UP YOUR JAWS.
VERRE, BURST, THUG AND BOUNCING BETTY. POWERS? HIDING, HYPER-SPEED MARTIAL ARTS, PAIN-RESISTANCE AND BOUNCING, RESPECTIVELY.
SUBLIME CORPORATION HEAVIES.
OH MAN. BAD GUY TRASH-TALK. I LOVE THAT.
YOU'RE MEAN! AND LOOK BAD AND SMELL FUNNY!
ORORO IQADI T'CHALLA--STORM. TOTAL WEATHER MASTERY.
I'M HURTING JUST ENOUGH TO ADD AN EDGE. AND THAT SUPERSPEEDSTER IS BITING MY STYLE. YOU HAVE NO IDEA HOW MUCH THAT ANNOYS ME.
LET'S FINISH THESE PLAGIARISTS.
ARE YOU READY FOR THIS, JEAN-PAUL? YOUR RIBS...
JEAN-PAUL BEAUBIER--NORTHSTAR. SUPERSPEED. READY TO PUNCH SOMEONE FOUR HUNDRED TIMES A SECOND.

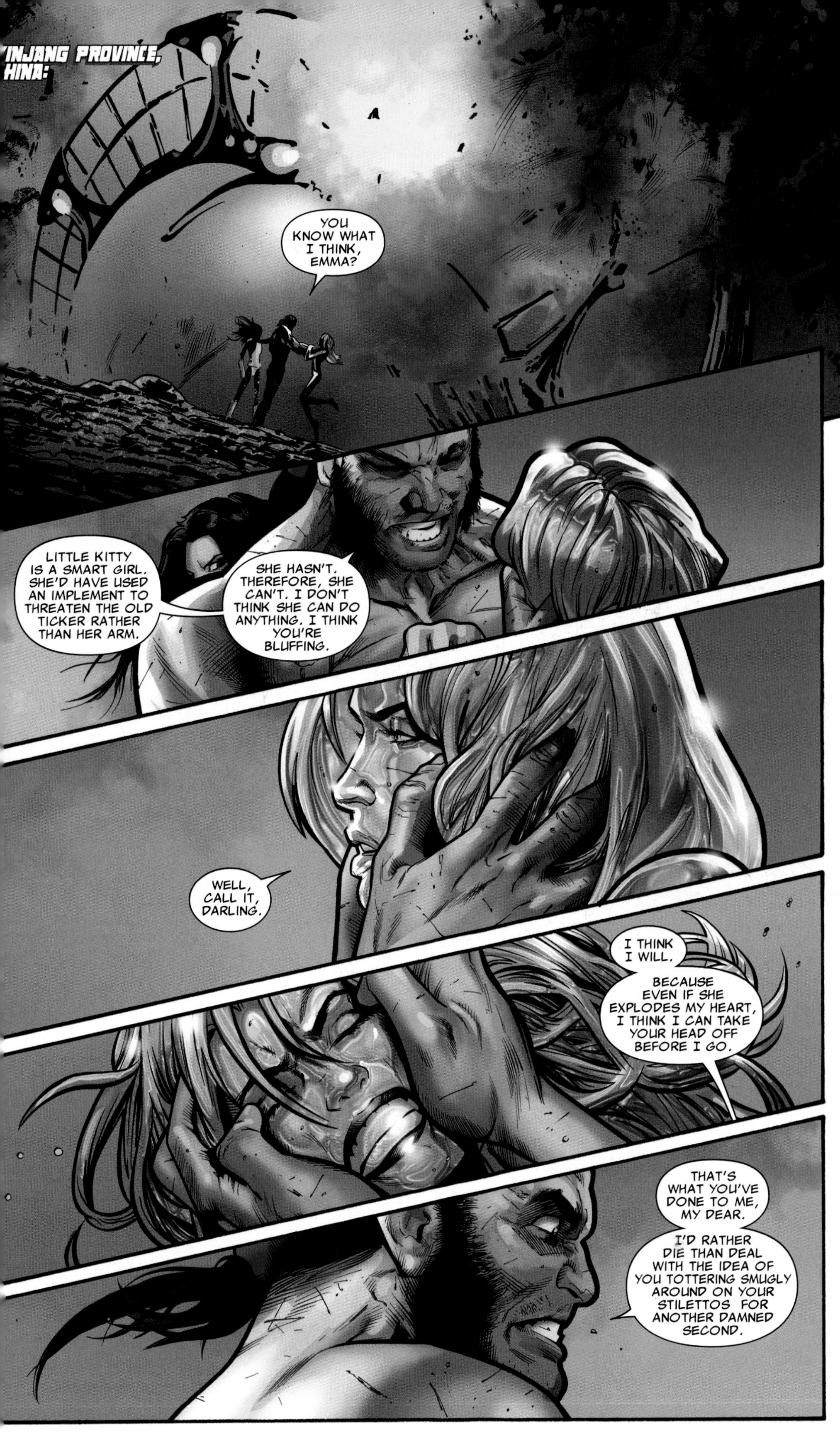
INJANG PROVINCE, HINA:
YOU KNOW WHAT I THINK, EMMA?
LITTLE KITTY IS A SMART GIRL. SHE'D HAVE USED AN IMPLEMENT TO THREATEN THE OLD TICKER RATHER THAN HER ARM.
SHE HASN'T. THEREFORE, SHE CAN'T. I DON'T THINK SHE CAN DO ANYTHING. I THINK YOU'RE BLUFFING.
WELL, CALL IT, DARLING.
I THINK I WILL.
BECAUSE EVEN IF SHE EXPLODES MY HEART, I THINK I CAN TAKE YOUR HEAD OFF BEFORE I GO.
THAT'S WHAT YOU'VE DONE TO ME, MY DEAR.
I'D RATHER DIE THAN DEAL WITH THE IDEA OF YOU TOTTERING SMUGLY AROUND ON YOUR STILETTOS FOR ANOTHER DAMNED SECOND.

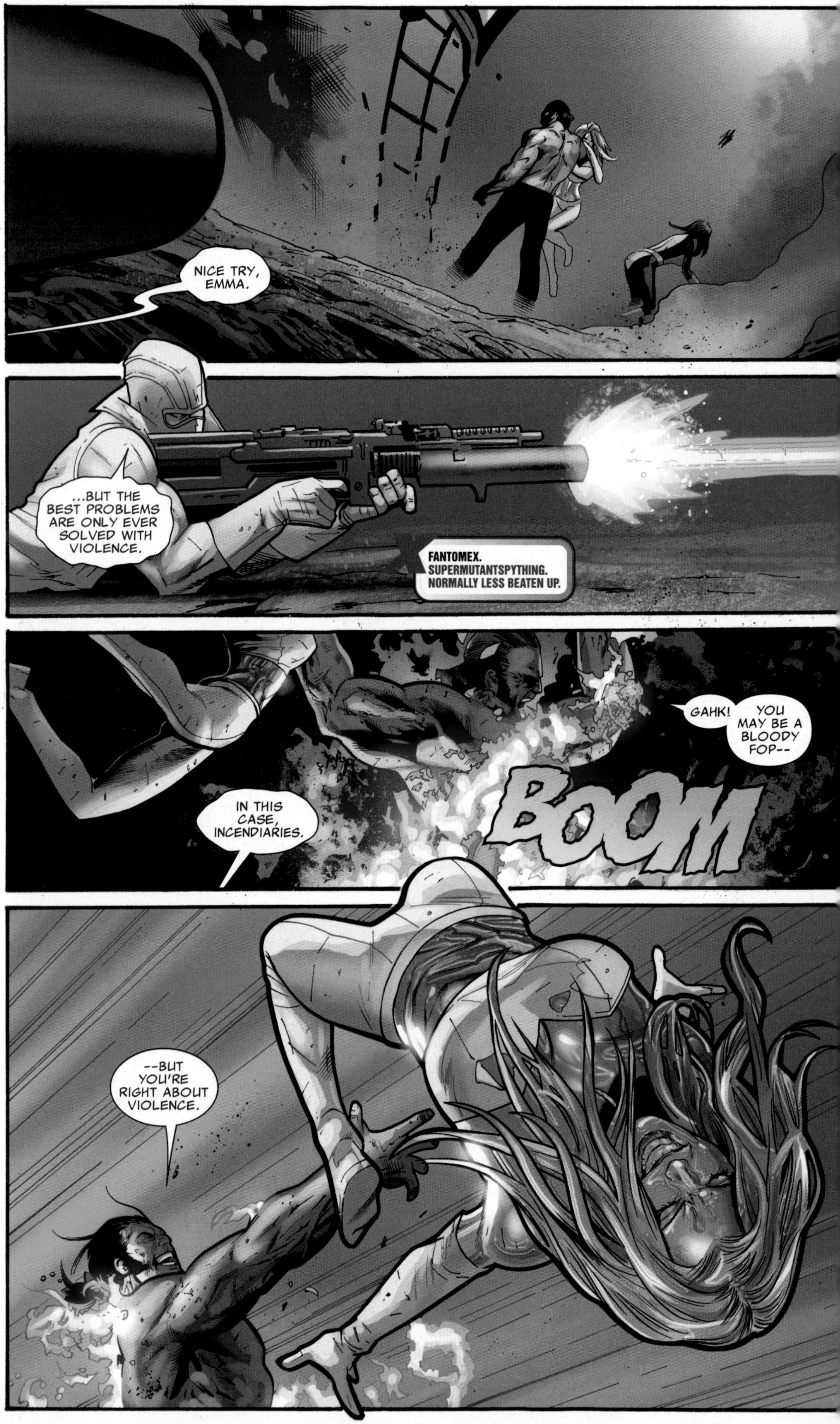
NICE TRY, EMMA.
...BUT THE BEST PROBLEMS ARE ONLY EVER SOLVED WITH VIOLENCE.
FANTOMEX. SUPERMUTANTSPYTHING. NORMALLY LESS BEATEN UP.
GAHK!
YOU MAY BE A BLOODY FOP--
BOOM
IN THIS CASE, INCENDIARIES.
--BUT YOU'RE RIGHT ABOUT VIOLENCE.

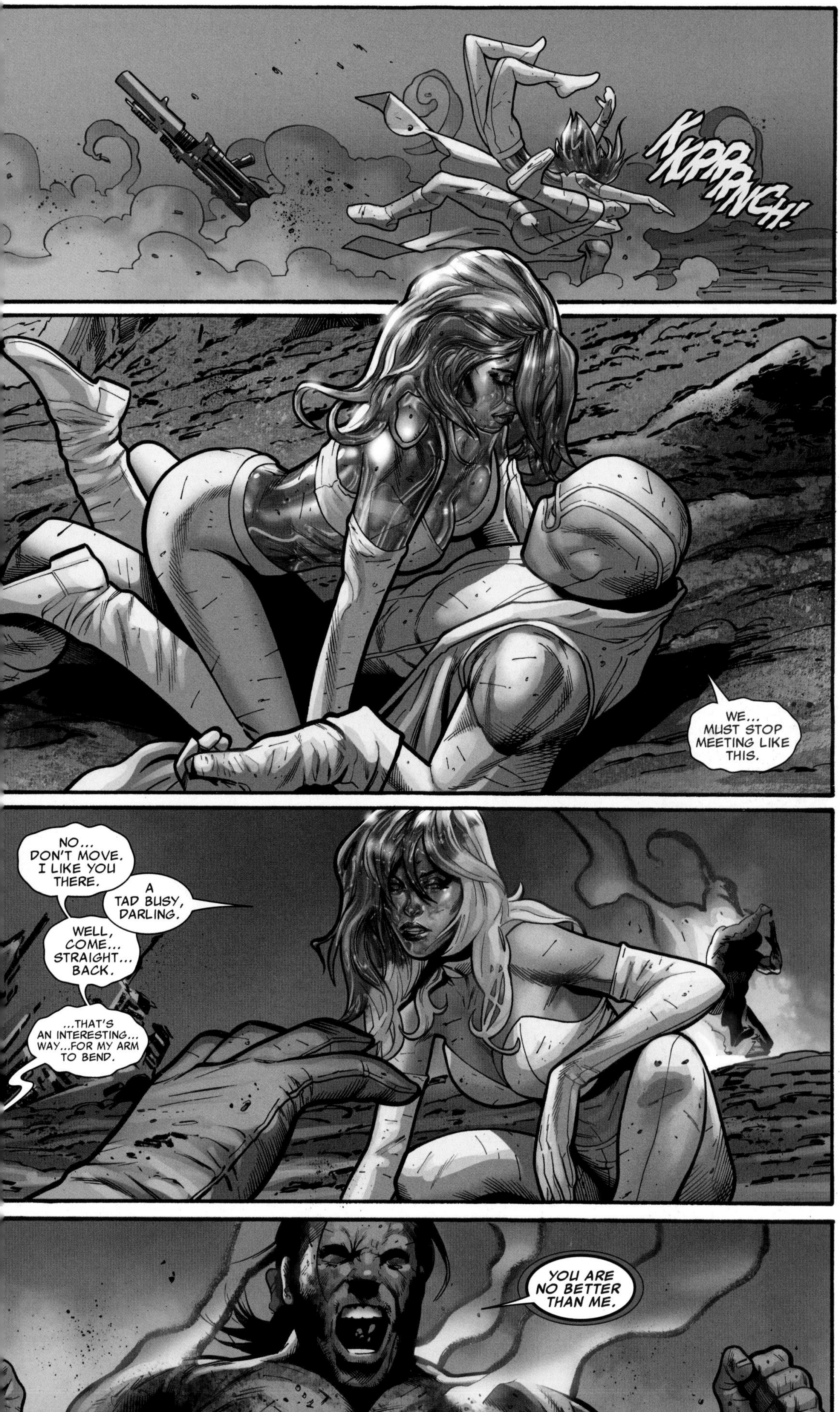
KKPRRNCH!
WE... MUST STOP MEETING LIKE THIS.
NO... DON'T MOVE. I LIKE YOU THERE.
A TAD BUSY, DARLING.
WELL, COME... STRAIGHT... BACK.
...THAT'S AN INTERESTING... WAY...FOR MY ARM TO BEND.
YOU ARE NO BETTER THAN ME.

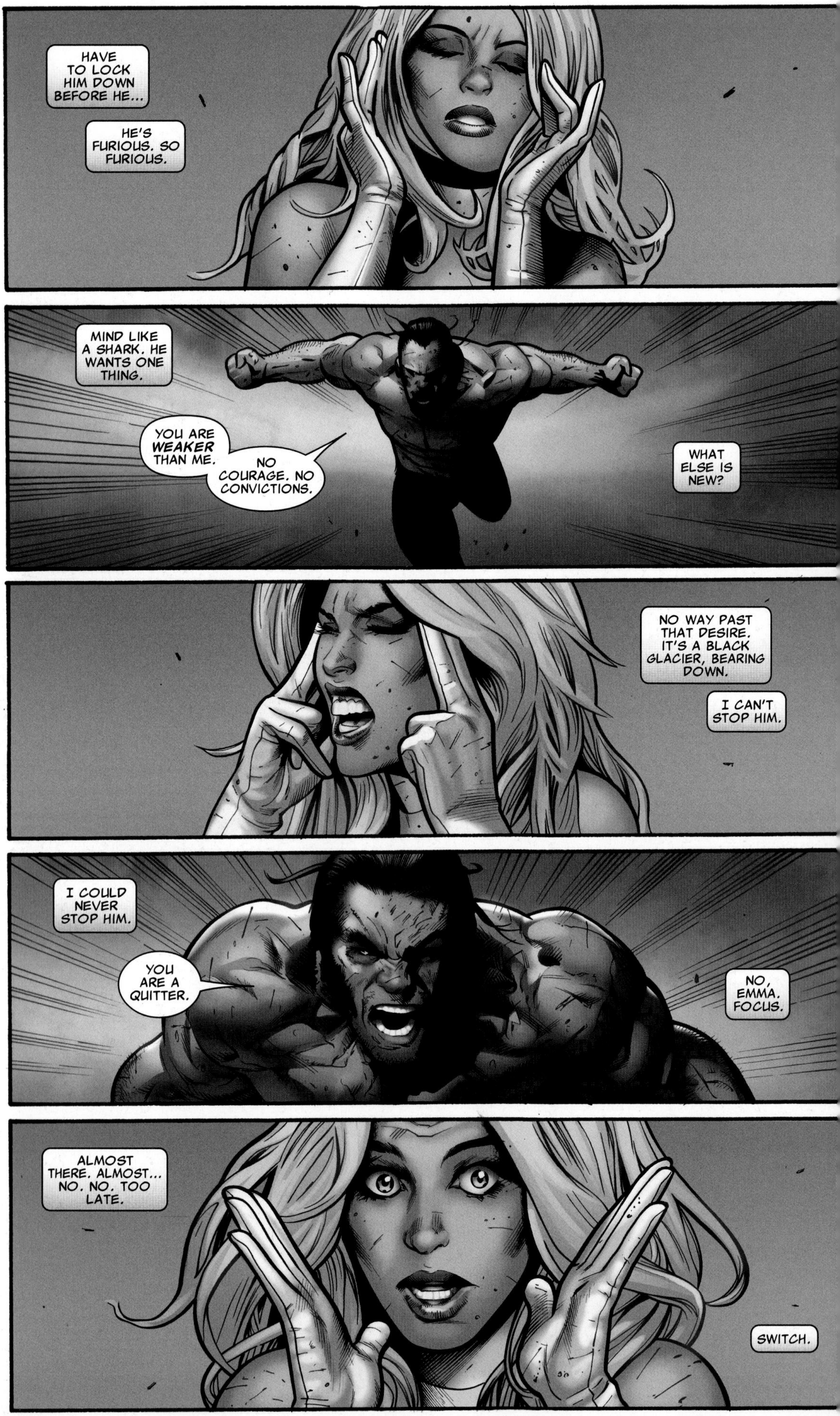

HAVE TO LOCK HIM DOWN BEFORE HE...
HE'S FURIOUS. SO FURIOUS.
MIND LIKE A SHARK. HE WANTS ONE THING.
YOU ARE WEAKER THAN ME.
NO COURAGE. NO CONVICTIONS.
WHAT ELSE IS NEW?
NO WAY PAST THAT DESIRE. IT'S A BLACK GLACIER, BEARING DOWN.
I CAN'T STOP HIM.
I COULD NEVER STOP HIM.
YOU ARE A QUITTER.
NO, EMMA. FOCUS.
ALMOST THERE. ALMOST... NO. NO. TOO LATE.
SWITCH.

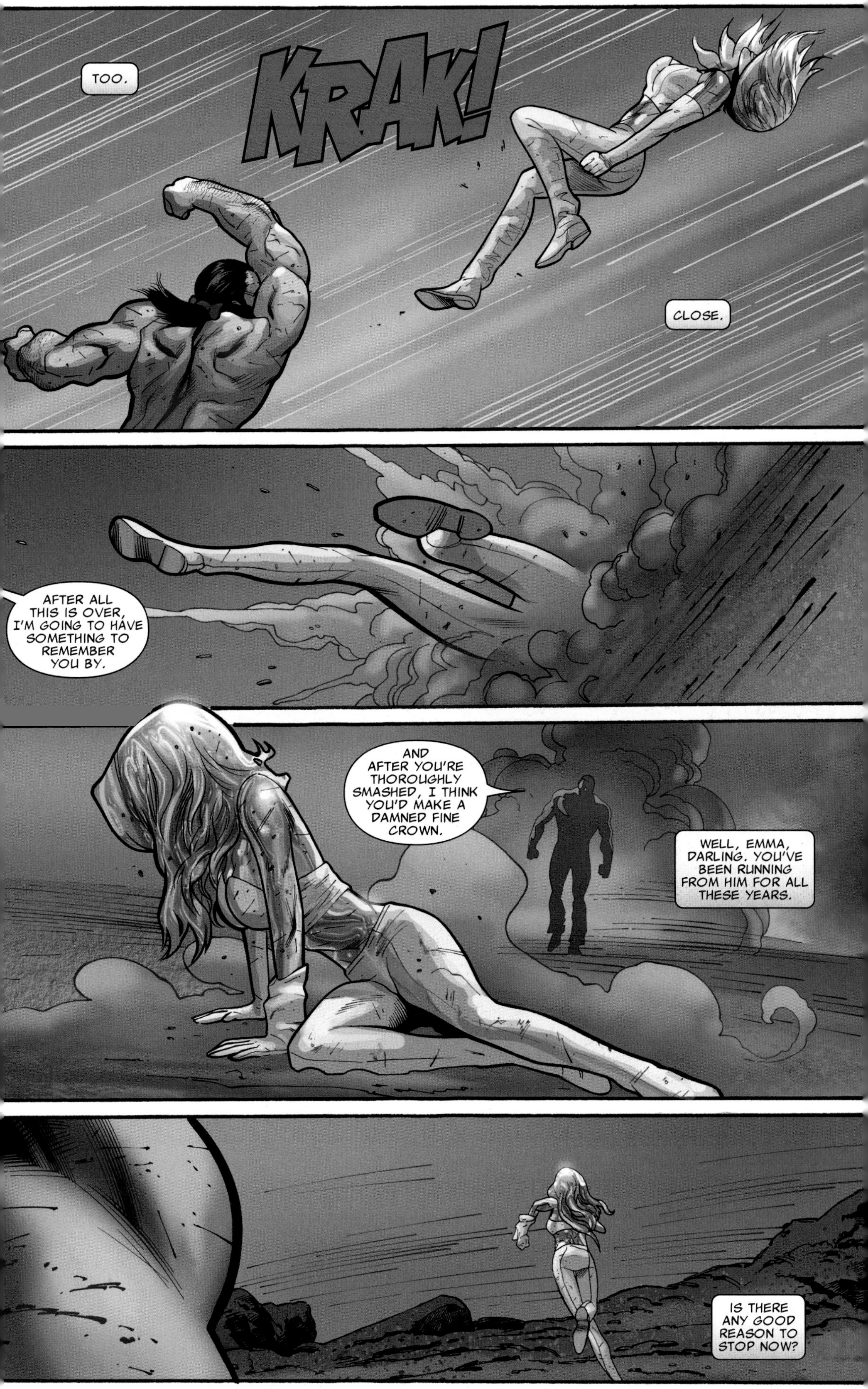
TOO.
KRAK!
CLOSE.
AFTER ALL THIS IS OVER, I'M GOING TO HAVE SOMETHING TO REMEMBER YOU BY.
AND AFTER YOU'RE THOROUGHLY SMASHED, I THINK YOU'D MAKE A DAMNED FINE CROWN.
WELL, EMMA, DARLING. YOU'VE BEEN RUNNING FROM HIM FOR ALL THESE YEARS.
IS THERE ANY GOOD REASON TO STOP NOW?

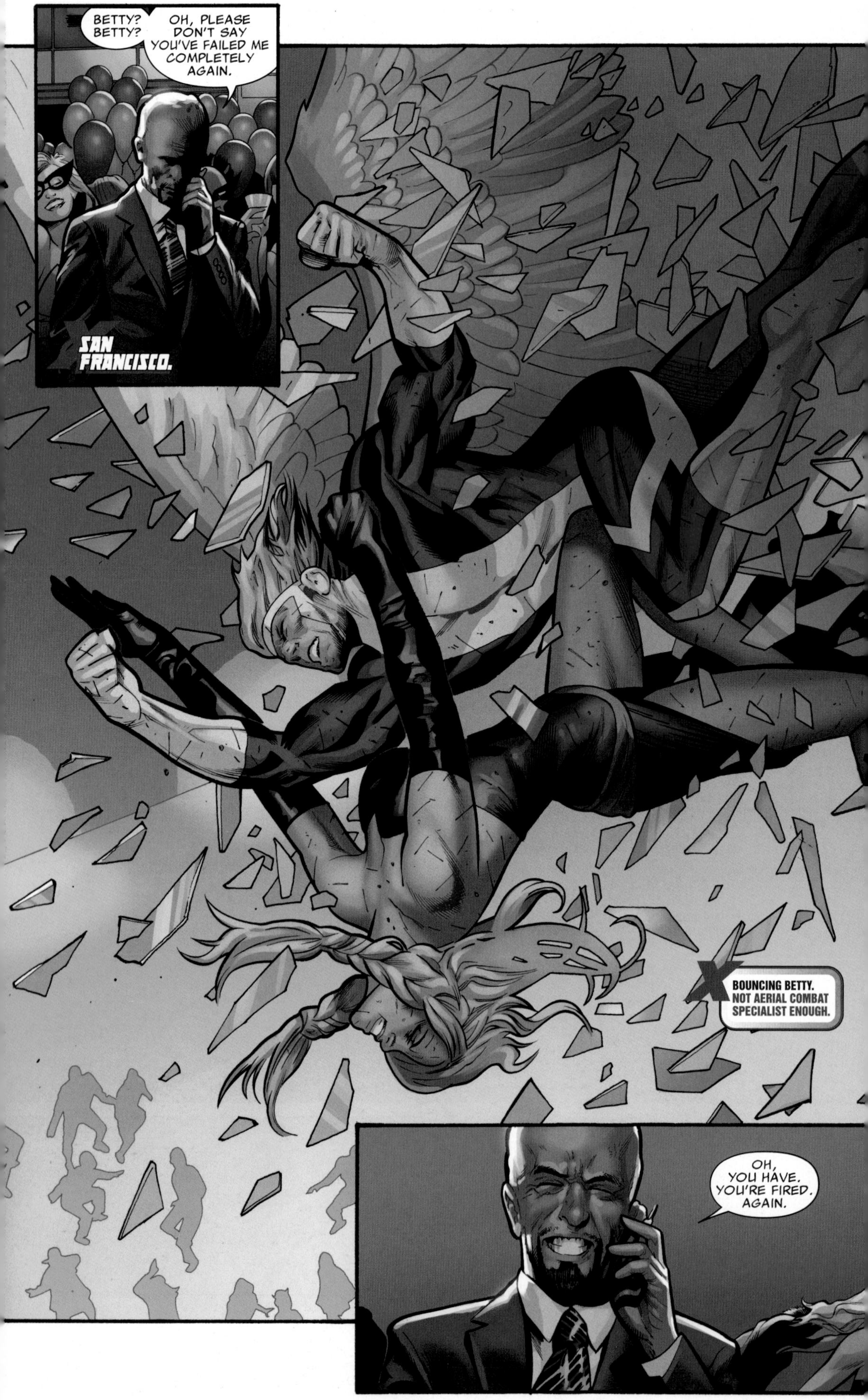
BETTY? BETTY?
OH, PLEASE DON'T SAY YOU'VE FAILED ME COMPLETELY AGAIN.
SAN FRANCISCO.
BOUNCING BETTY. NOT AERIAL COMBAT SPECIALIST ENOUGH.
OH, YOU HAVE. YOU'RE FIRED. AGAIN.

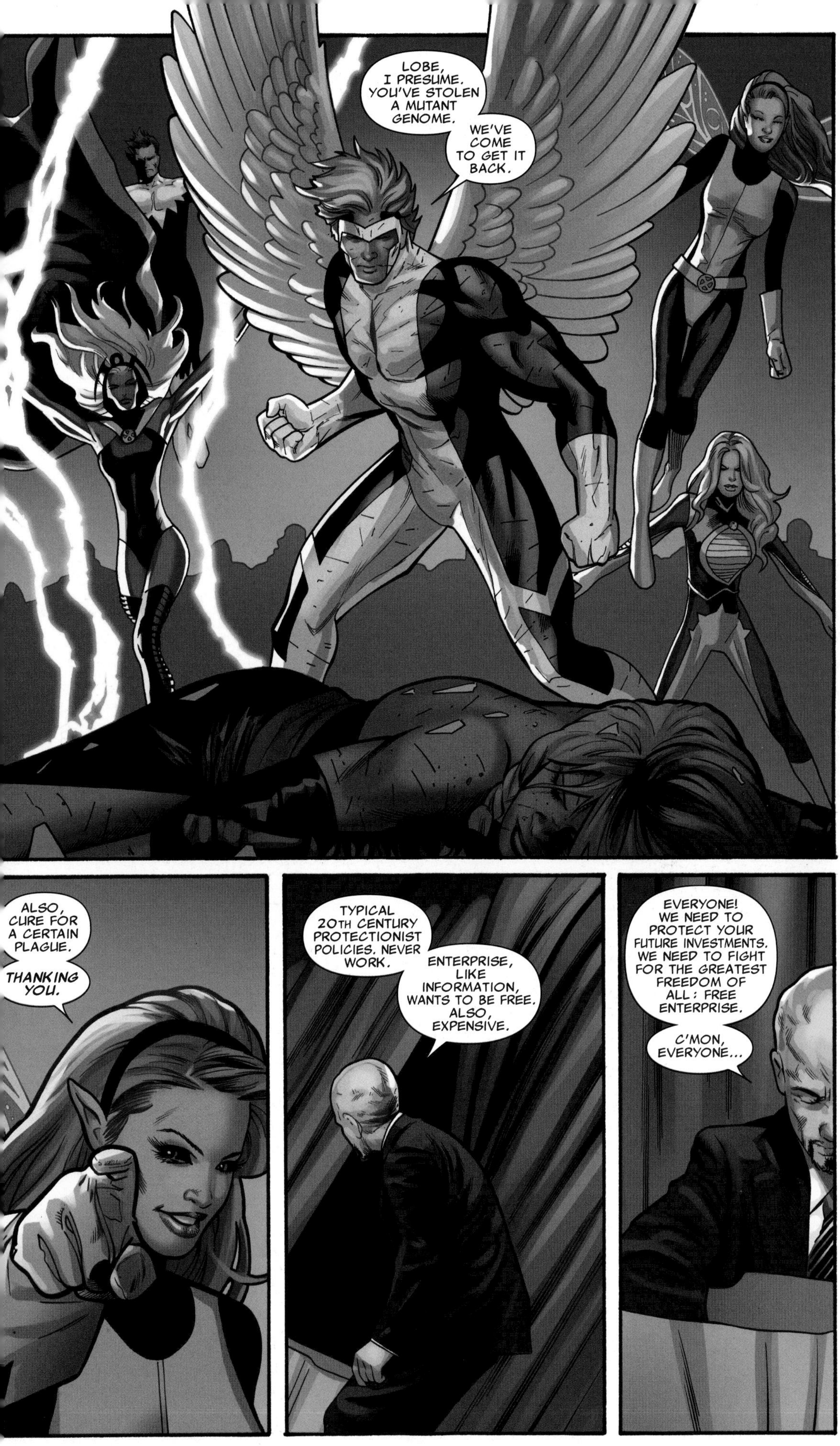
LOBE, I PRESUME. YOU'VE STOLEN A MUTANT GENOME.
WE'VE COME TO GET IT BACK.
ALSO, CURE FOR A CERTAIN PLAGUE.
THANKING YOU.
TYPICAL 20TH CENTURY PROTECTIONIST POLICIES. NEVER WORK.
ENTERPRISE, LIKE INFORMATION, WANTS TO BE FREE. ALSO, EXPENSIVE.
EVERYONE! WE NEED TO PROTECT YOUR FUTURE INVESTMENTS. WE NEED TO FIGHT FOR THE GREATEST FREEDOM OF ALL: FREE ENTERPRISE.
C'MON, EVERYONE...

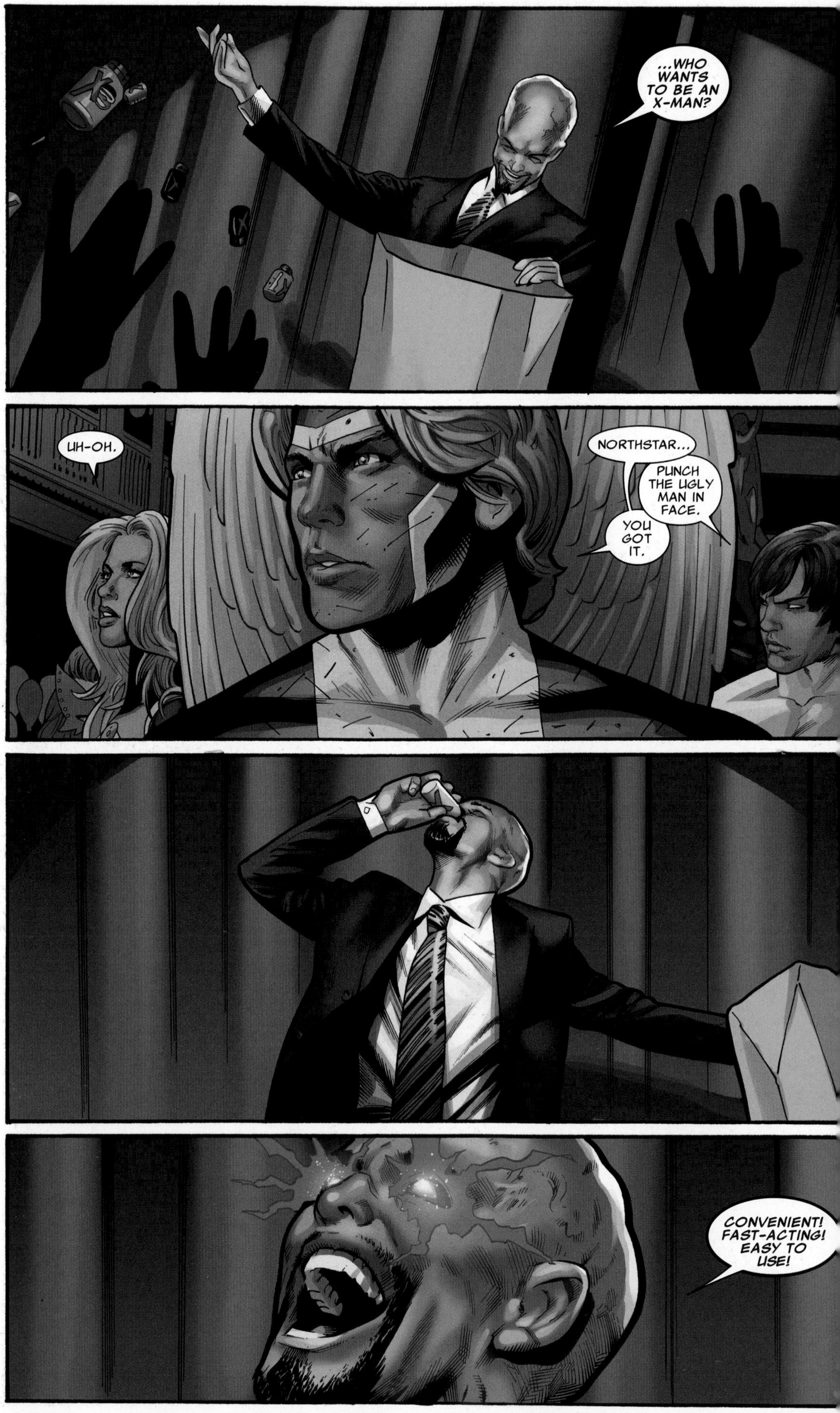
...WHO WANTS TO BE AN X-MAN?
UH-OH.
NORTHSTAR...
PUNCH THE UGLY MAN IN FACE.
YOU GOT IT.
CONVENIENT! FAST-ACTING! EASY TO USE!

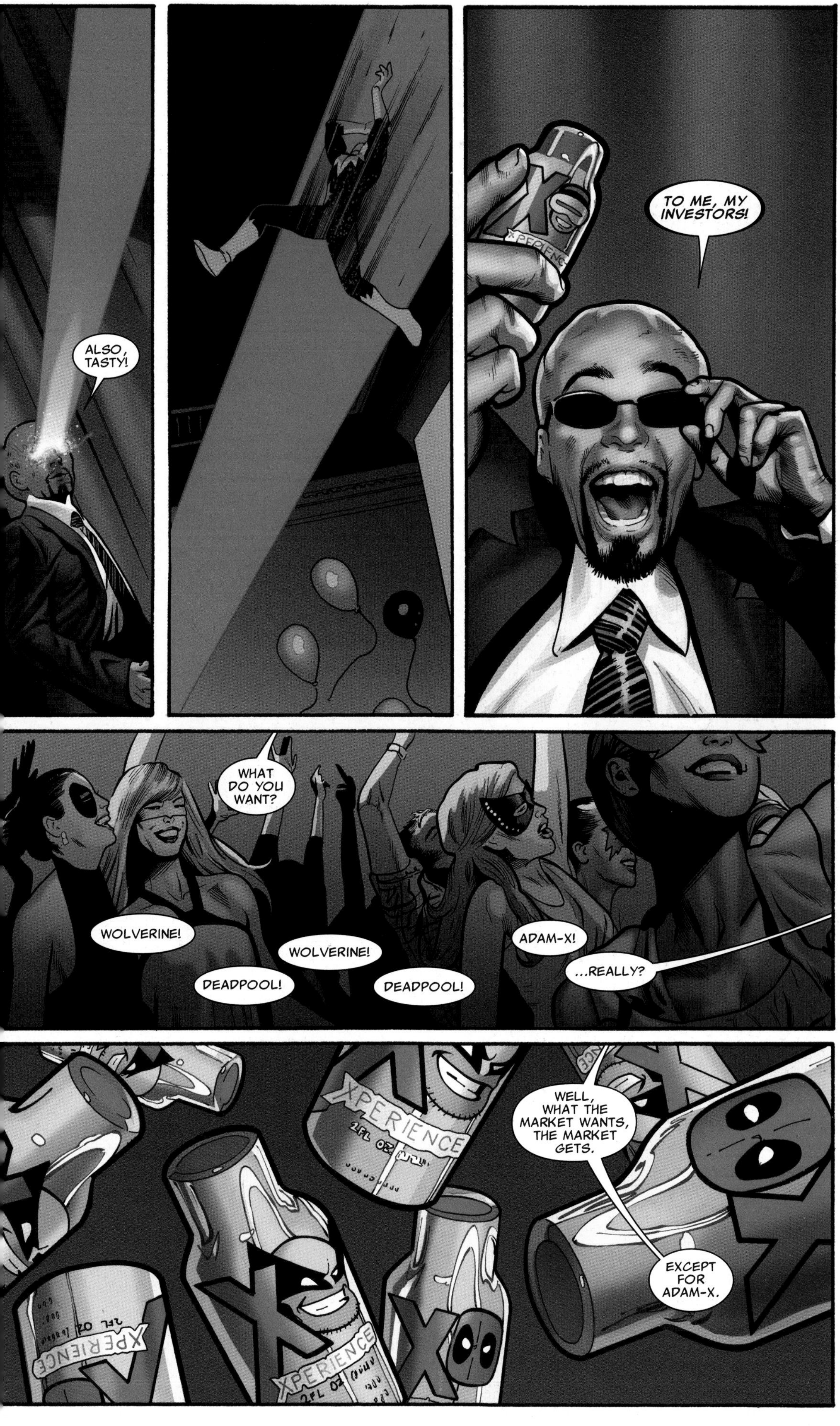
ALSO, TASTY!
XPERIENCE
TO ME, MY INVESTORS!
WHAT DO YOU WANT?
WOLVERINE!
DEADPOOL!
WOLVERINE!
DEADPOOL!
ADAM-X!
...REALLY?
XPERIENCE
2FL OZ
WELL, WHAT THE MARKET WANTS, THE MARKET GETS.
EXCEPT FOR ADAM-X.
XPERIENCE
XPERIENCE

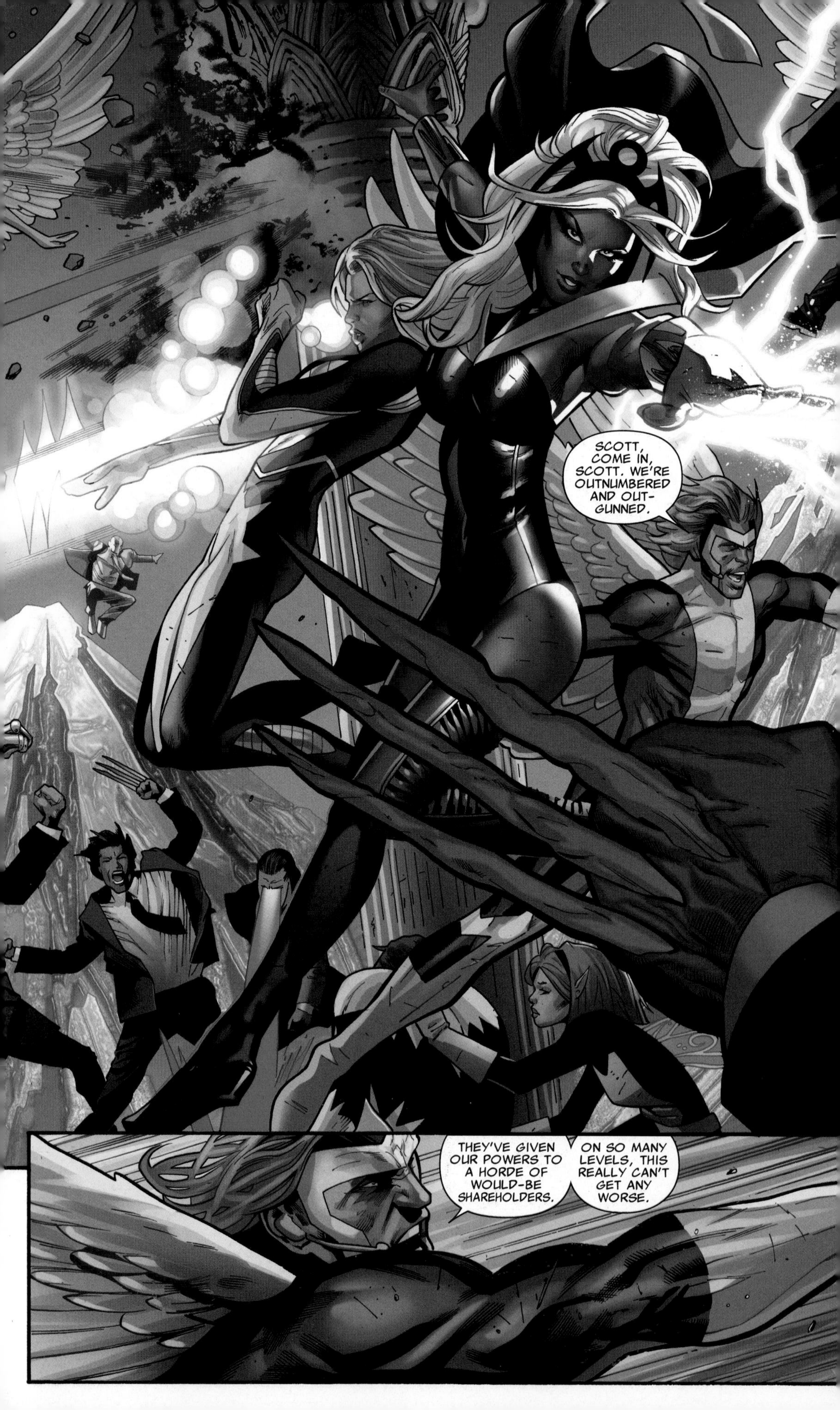
SCOTT, COME IN, SCOTT. WE'RE OUTNUMBERED AND OUT-GUNNED.
THEY'VE GIVEN OUR POWERS TO A HORDE OF WOULD-BE SHAREHOLDERS.
ON SO MANY LEVELS, THIS REALLY CAN'T GET ANY WORSE.

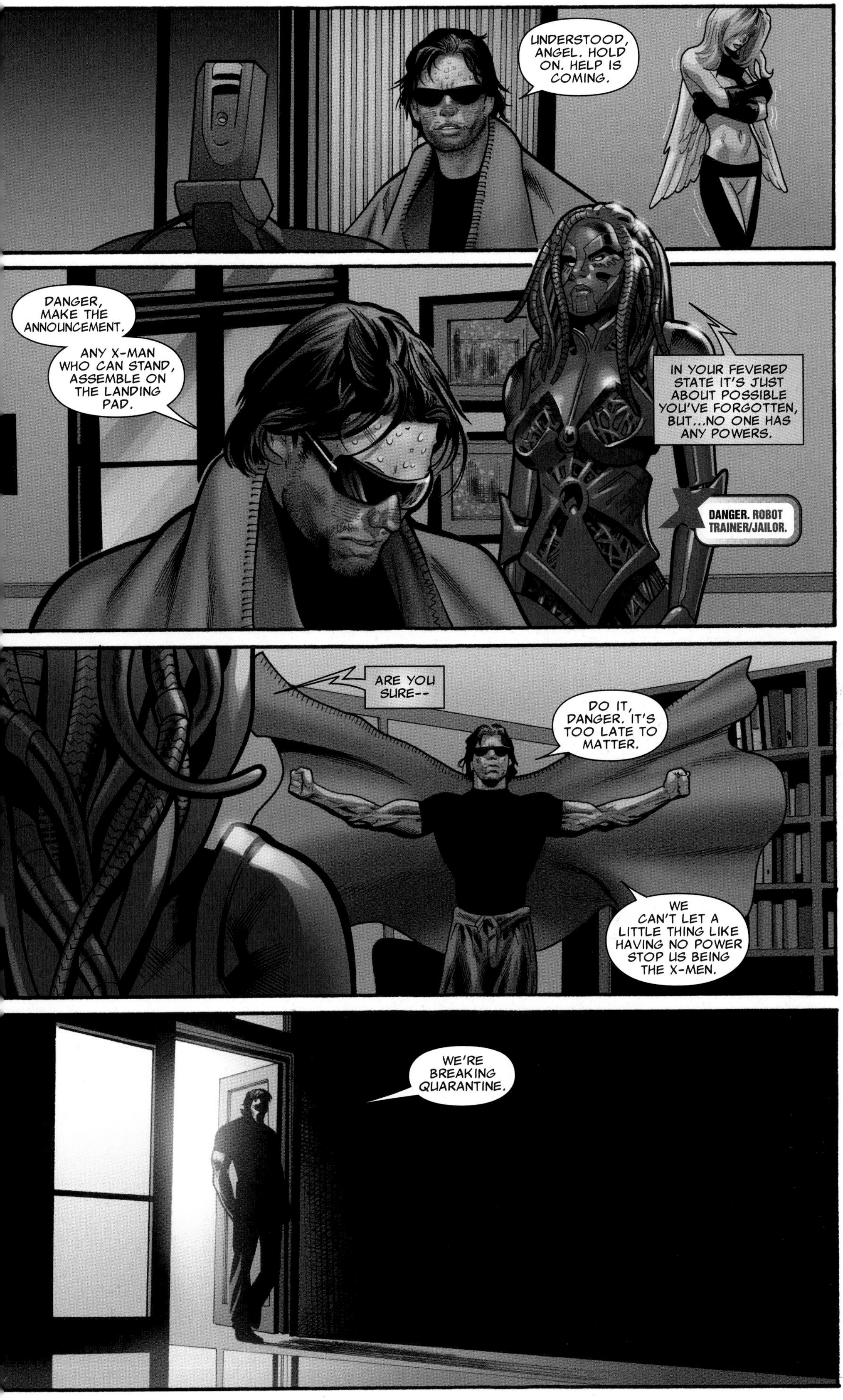
UNDERSTOOD, ANGEL. HOLD ON. HELP IS COMING.
DANGER, MAKE THE ANNOUNCEMENT.
ANY X-MAN WHO CAN STAND, ASSEMBLE ON THE LANDING PAD.
IN YOUR FEVERED STATE IT'S JUST ABOUT POSSIBLE YOU'VE FORGOTTEN, BUT...NO ONE HAS ANY POWERS.
DANGER. ROBOT TRAINER/JAILOR.
ARE YOU SURE--
DO IT, DANGER. IT'S TOO LATE TO MATTER.
WE CAN'T LET A LITTLE THING LIKE HAVING NO POWER STOP US BEING THE X-MEN.
WE'RE BREAKING QUARANTINE.

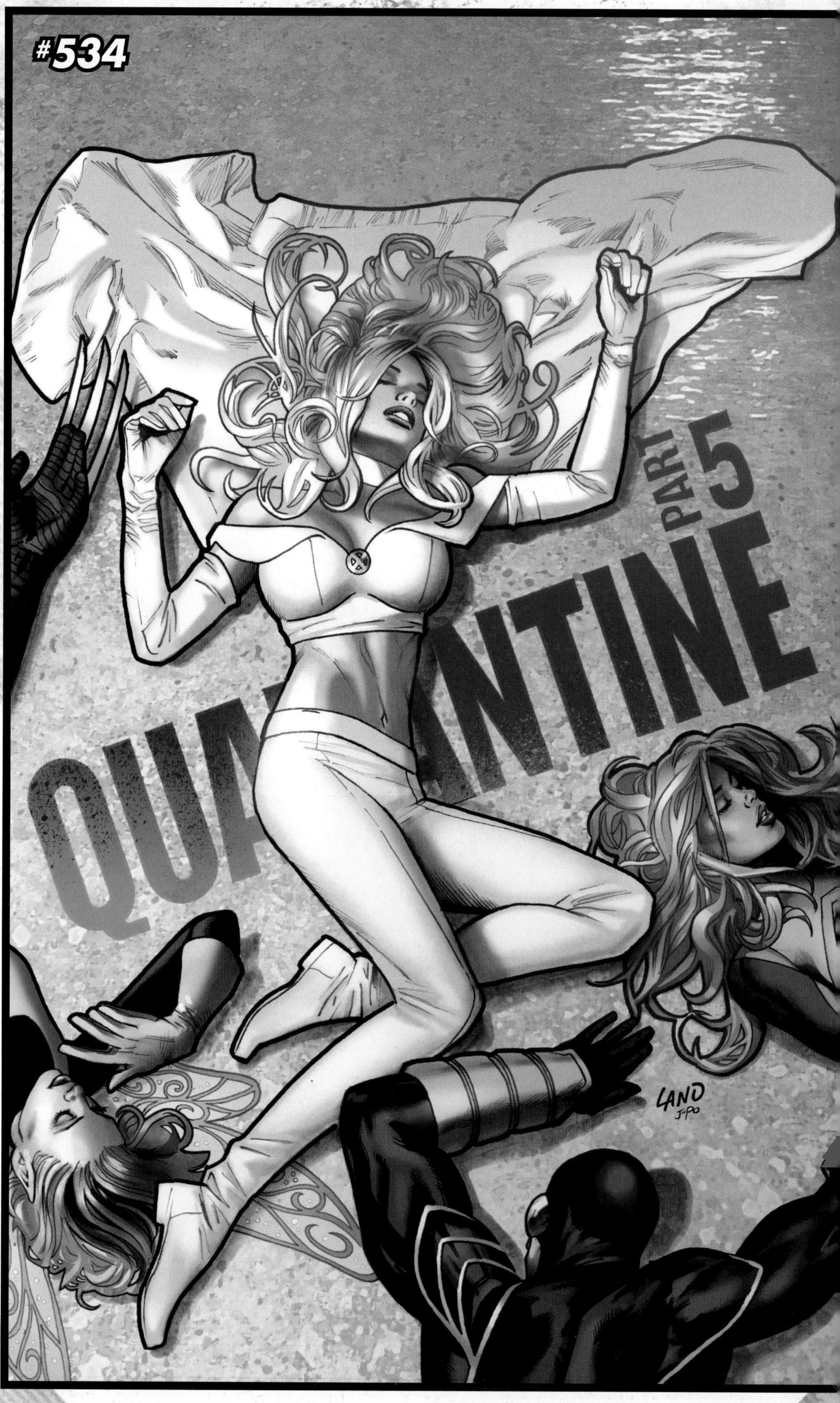

#534
QUARANTINE
PART 5
LAND
J-PO

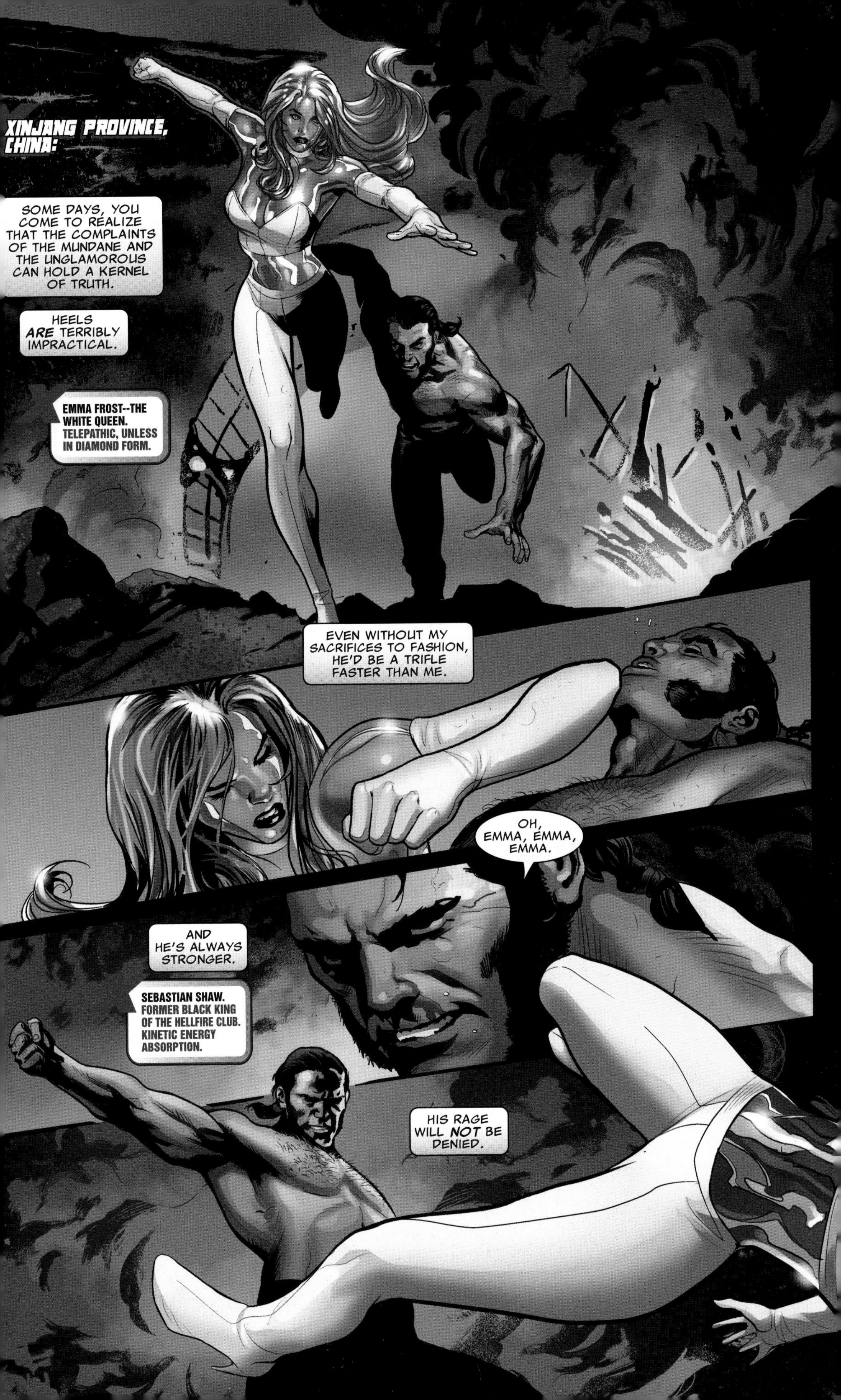

XINJANG PROVINCE, CHINA:
SOME DAYS, YOU COME TO REALIZE THAT THE COMPLAINTS OF THE MUNDANE AND THE UNGLAMOROUS CAN HOLD A KERNEL OF TRUTH.
HEELS ARE TERRIBLY IMPRACTICAL.
EMMA FROST--THE WHITE QUEEN. TELEPATHIC, UNLESS IN DIAMOND FORM.
EVEN WITHOUT MY SACRIFICES TO FASHION, HE'D BE A TRIFLE FASTER THAN ME.
OH, EMMA, EMMA, EMMA.
AND HE'S ALWAYS STRONGER.
SEBASTIAN SHAW. FORMER BLACK KING OF THE HELLFIRE CLUB. KINETIC ENERGY ABSORPTION.
HIS RAGE WILL NOT BE DENIED.

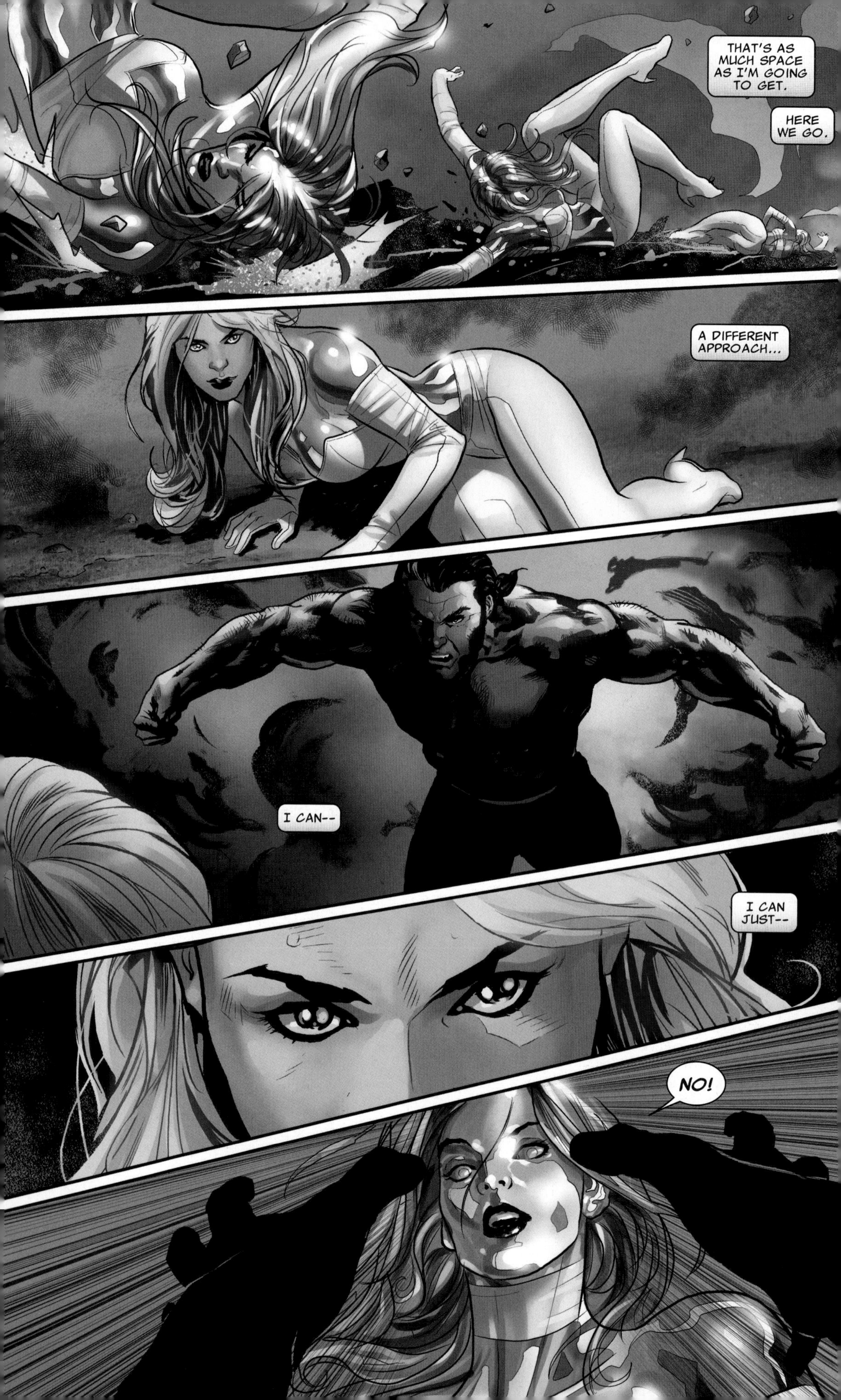
THAT'S AS MUCH SPACE AS I'M GOING TO GET.
HERE WE GO.
A DIFFERENT APPROACH...
I CAN--
I CAN JUST--
NO!

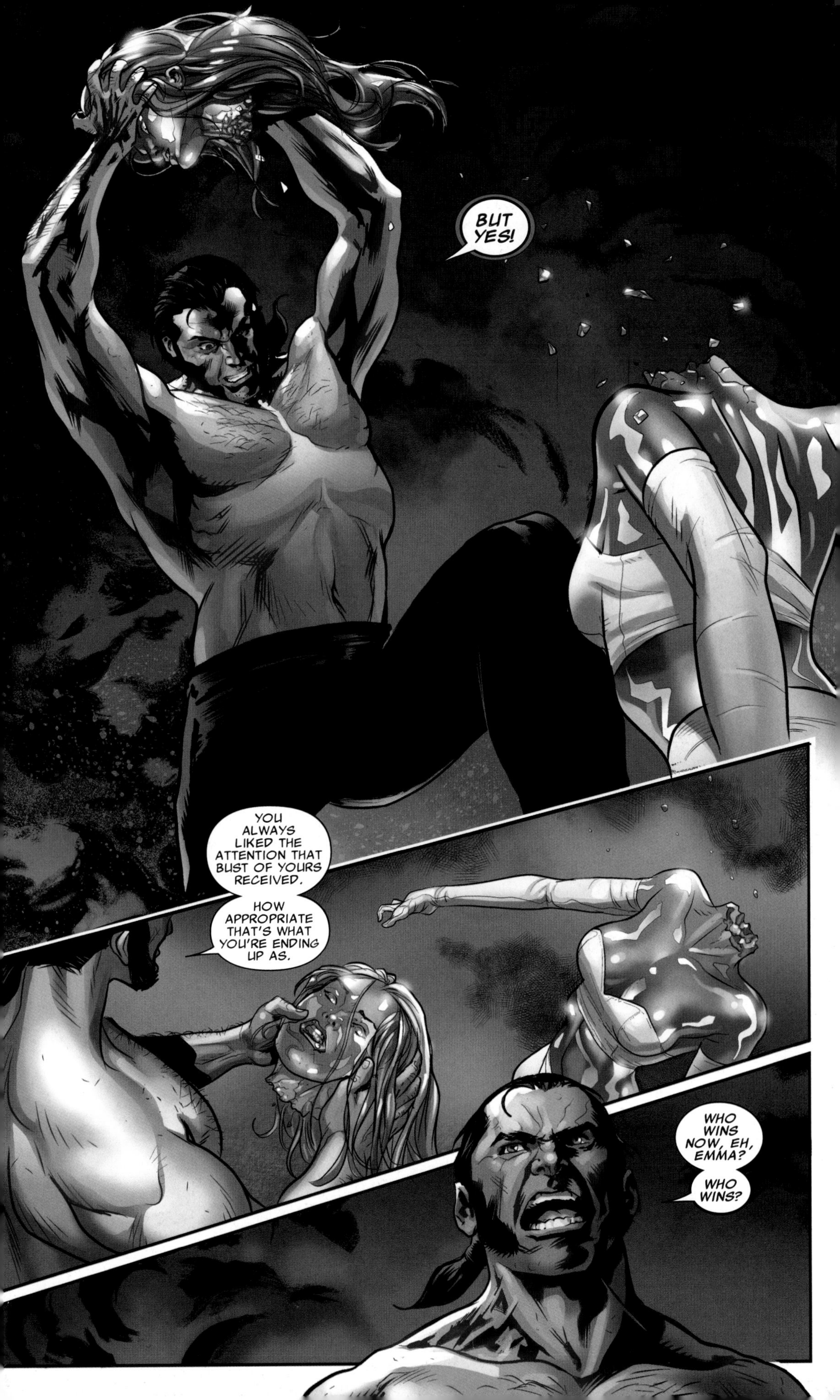
BUT YES!
YOU ALWAYS LIKED THE ATTENTION THAT BUST OF YOURS RECEIVED.
HOW APPROPRIATE THAT'S WHAT YOU'RE ENDING UP AS.
WHO WINS NOW, EH, EMMA?
WHO WINS?

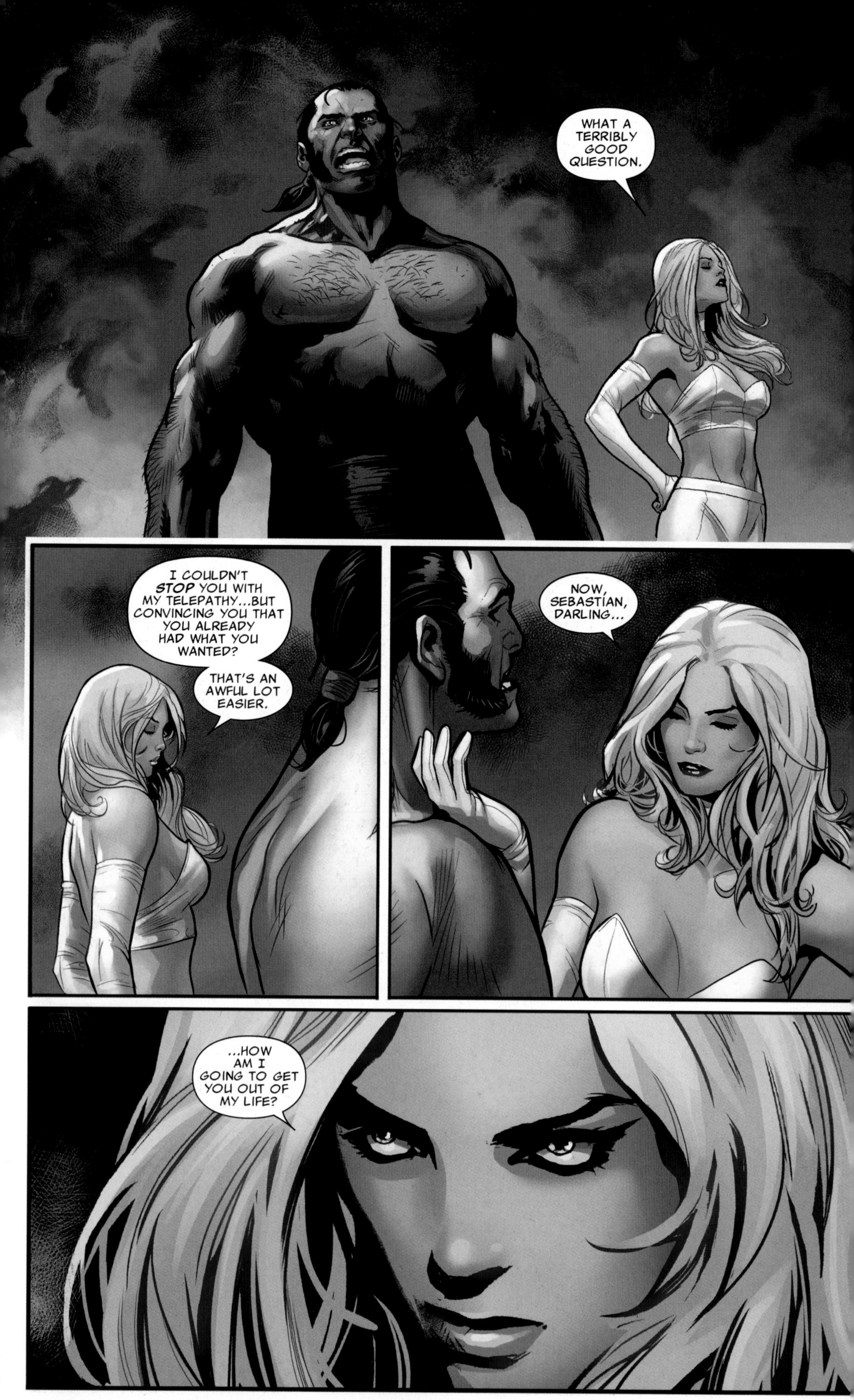
WHAT A TERRIBLY GOOD QUESTION.
I COULDN'T STOP YOU WITH MY TELEPATHY...BUT CONVINCING YOU THAT YOU ALREADY HAD WHAT YOU WANTED?
THAT'S AN AWFUL LOT EASIER.
NOW, SEBASTIAN, DARLING...
...HOW AM I GOING TO GET YOU OUT OF MY LIFE?

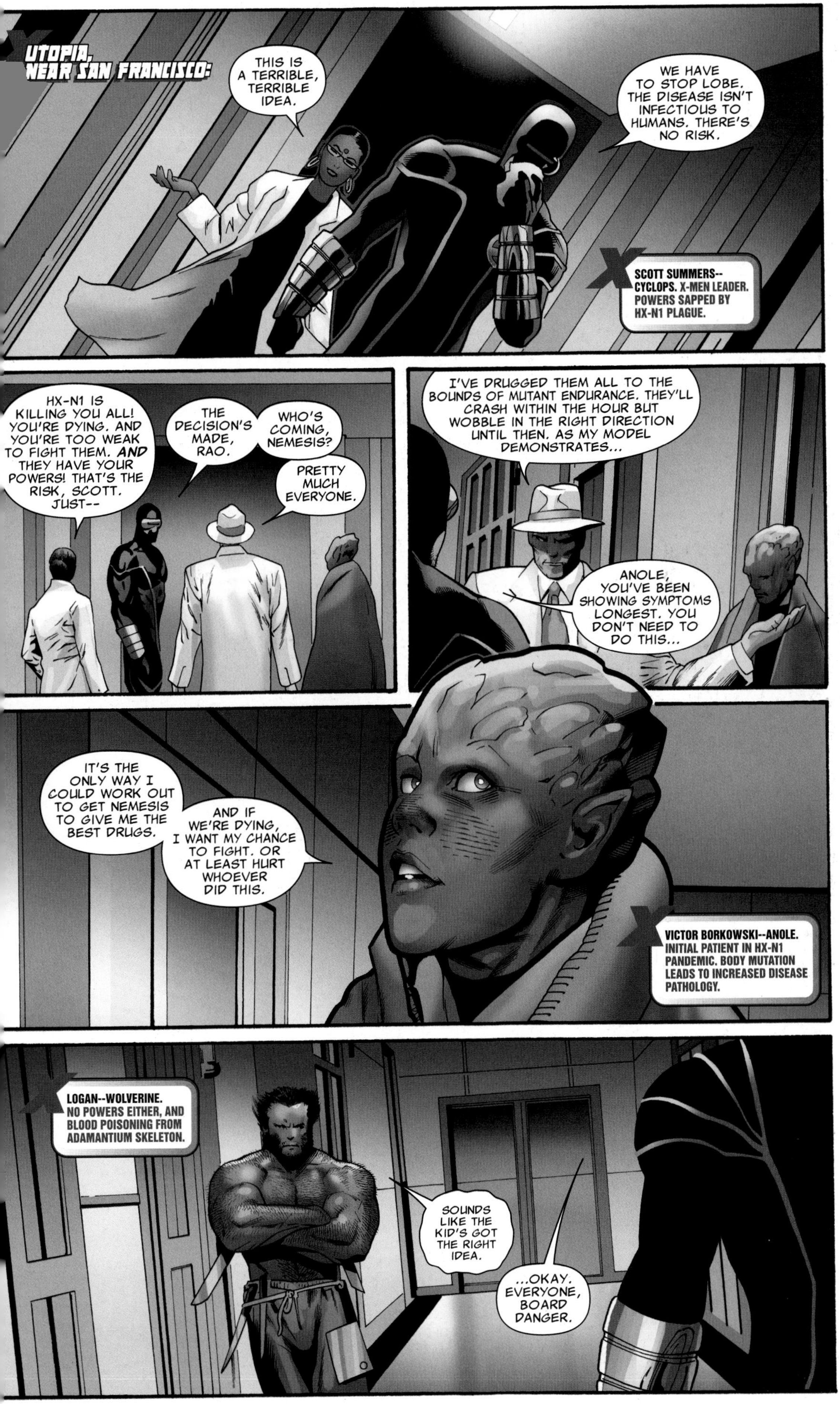
UTOPIA, NEAR SAN FRANCISCO:
THIS IS A TERRIBLE, TERRIBLE IDEA.
WE HAVE TO STOP LOBE. THE DISEASE ISN'T INFECTIOUS TO HUMANS. THERE'S NO RISK.
SCOTT SUMMERS--CYCLOPS. X-MEN LEADER. POWERS SAPPED BY HX-N1 PLAGUE.
HX-N1 IS KILLING YOU ALL! YOU'RE DYING. AND YOU'RE TOO WEAK TO FIGHT THEM. AND THEY HAVE YOUR POWERS! THAT'S THE RISK, SCOTT. JUST--
THE DECISION'S MADE, RAO.
WHO'S COMING, NEMESIS?
PRETTY MUCH EVERYONE.
I'VE DRUGGED THEM ALL TO THE BOUNDS OF MUTANT ENDURANCE. THEY'LL CRASH WITHIN THE HOUR BUT WOBBLE IN THE RIGHT DIRECTION UNTIL THEN. AS MY MODEL DEMONSTRATES...
ANOLE, YOU'VE BEEN SHOWING SYMPTOMS LONGEST. YOU DON'T NEED TO DO THIS...
IT'S THE ONLY WAY I COULD WORK OUT TO GET NEMESIS TO GIVE ME THE BEST DRUGS.
AND IF WE'RE DYING, I WANT MY CHANCE TO FIGHT. OR AT LEAST HURT WHOEVER DID THIS.
VICTOR BORKOWSKI--ANOLE. INITIAL PATIENT IN HX-N1 PANDEMIC. BODY MUTATION LEADS TO INCREASED DISEASE PATHOLOGY.
LOGAN--WOLVERINE. NO POWERS EITHER, AND BLOOD POISONING FROM ADAMANTIUM SKELETON.
SOUNDS LIKE THE KID'S GOT THE RIGHT IDEA.
...OKAY. EVERYONE, BOARD DANGER.

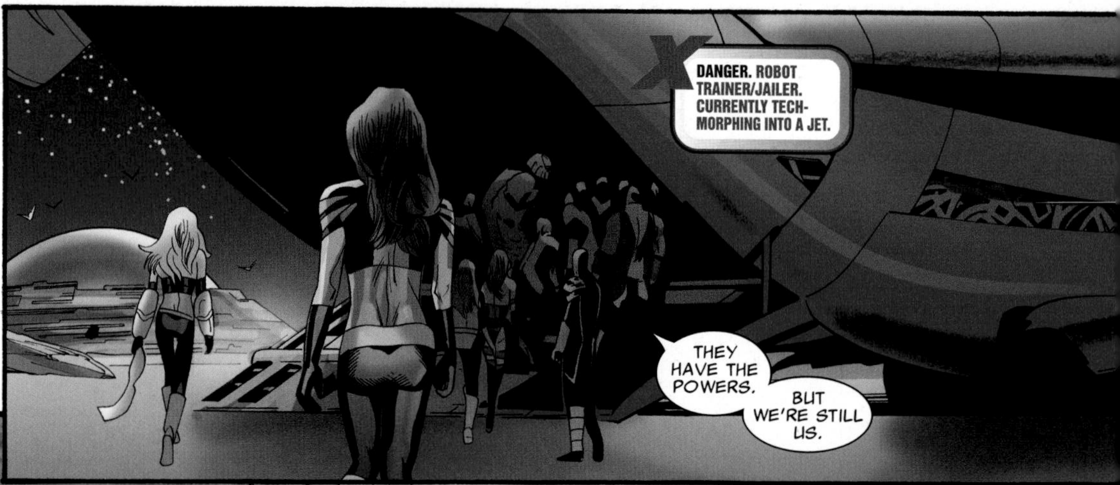
DANGER. ROBOT TRAINER/JAILER. CURRENTLY TECH-MORPHING INTO A JET.
THEY HAVE THE POWERS.
BUT WE'RE STILL US.

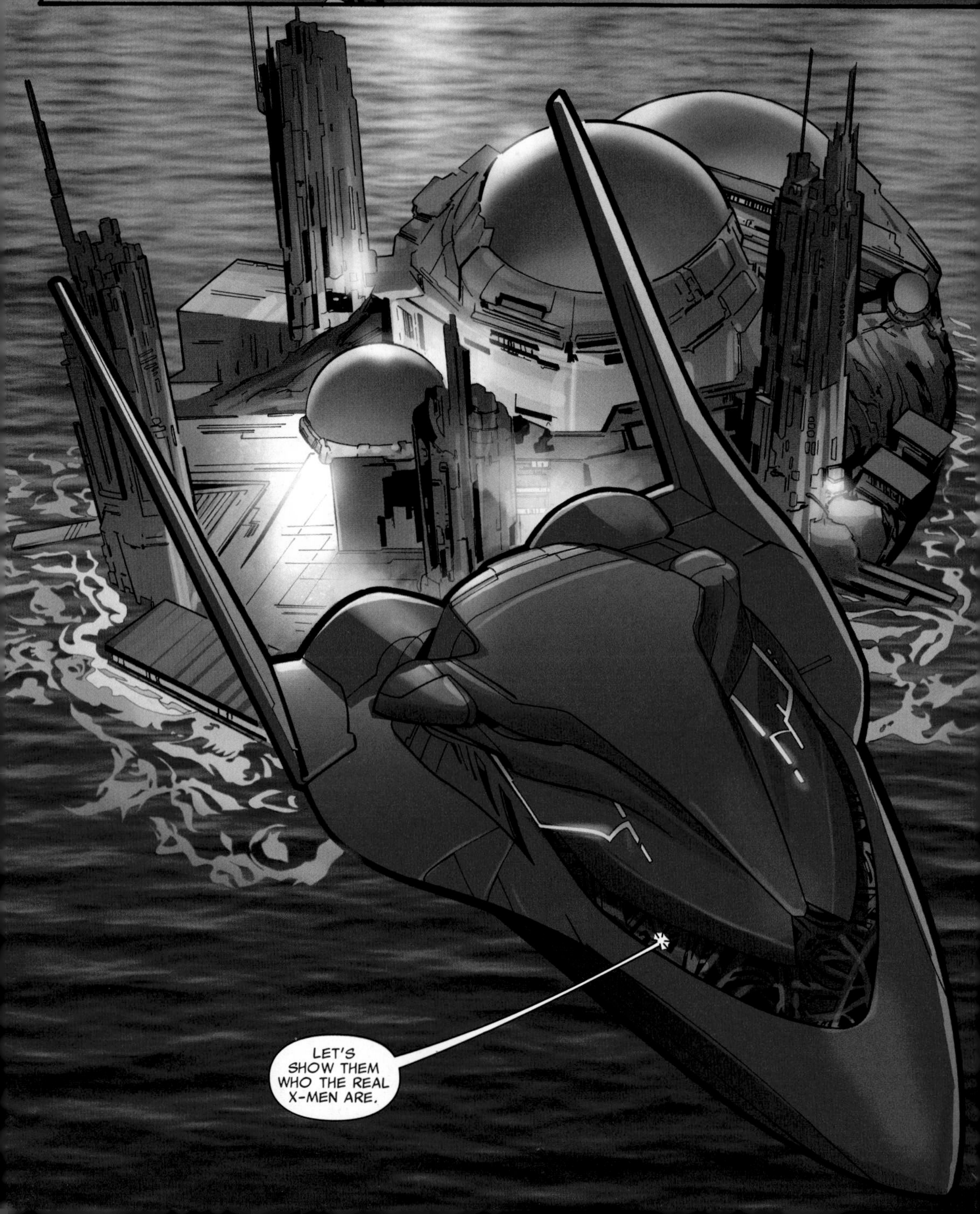
LET'S SHOW THEM WHO THE REAL X-MEN ARE.

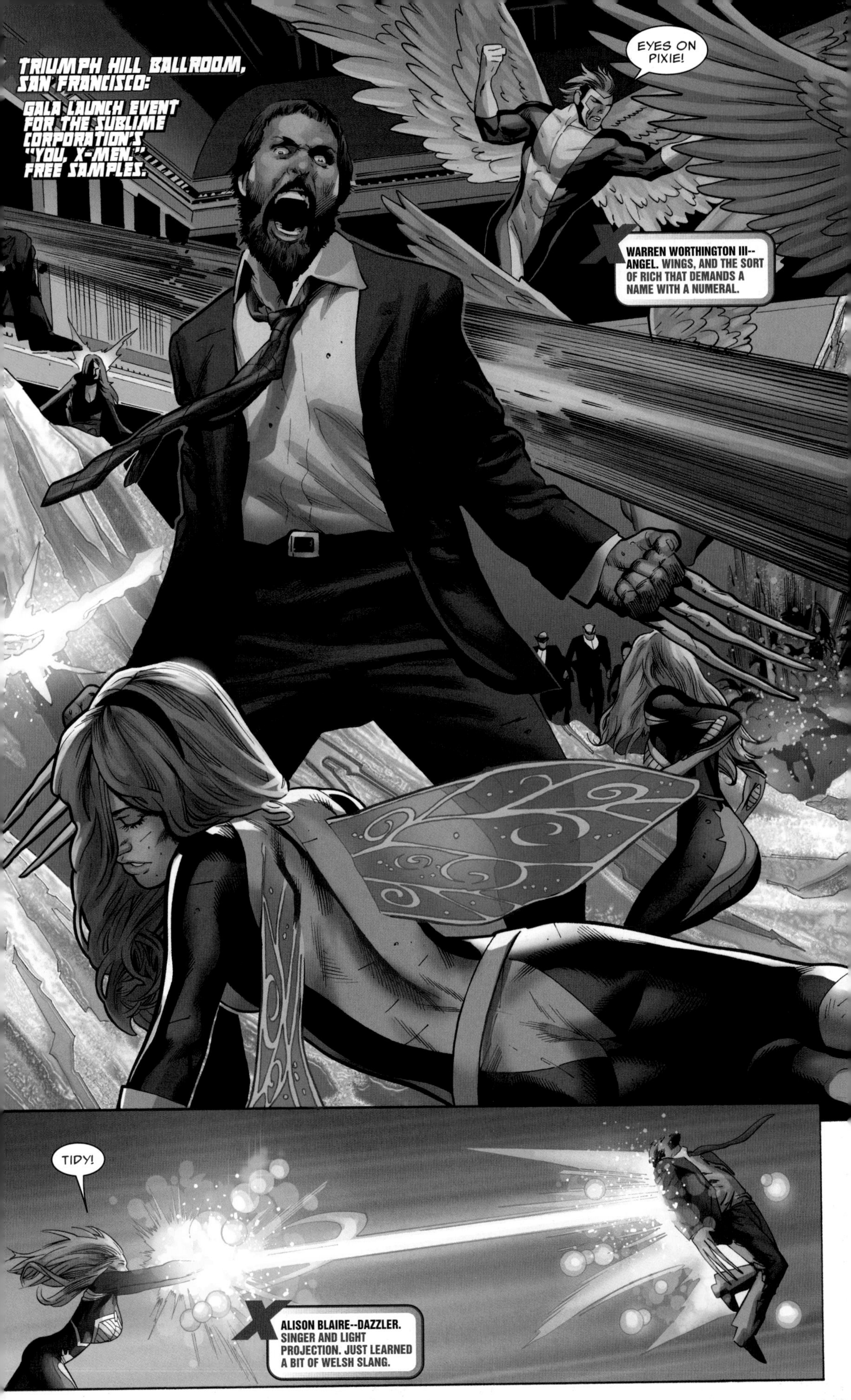
TRIUMPH HILL BALLROOM, SAN FRANCISCO:
GALA LAUNCH EVENT FOR THE SUBLIME CORPORATION'S "YOU, X-MEN." FREE SAMPLES.
EYES ON PIXIE!
WARREN WORTHINGTON III--ANGEL. WINGS, AND THE SORT OF RICH THAT DEMANDS A NAME WITH A NUMERAL.
TIDY!
ALISON BLAIRE--DAZZLER. SINGER AND LIGHT PROJECTION. JUST LEARNED A BIT OF WELSH SLANG.

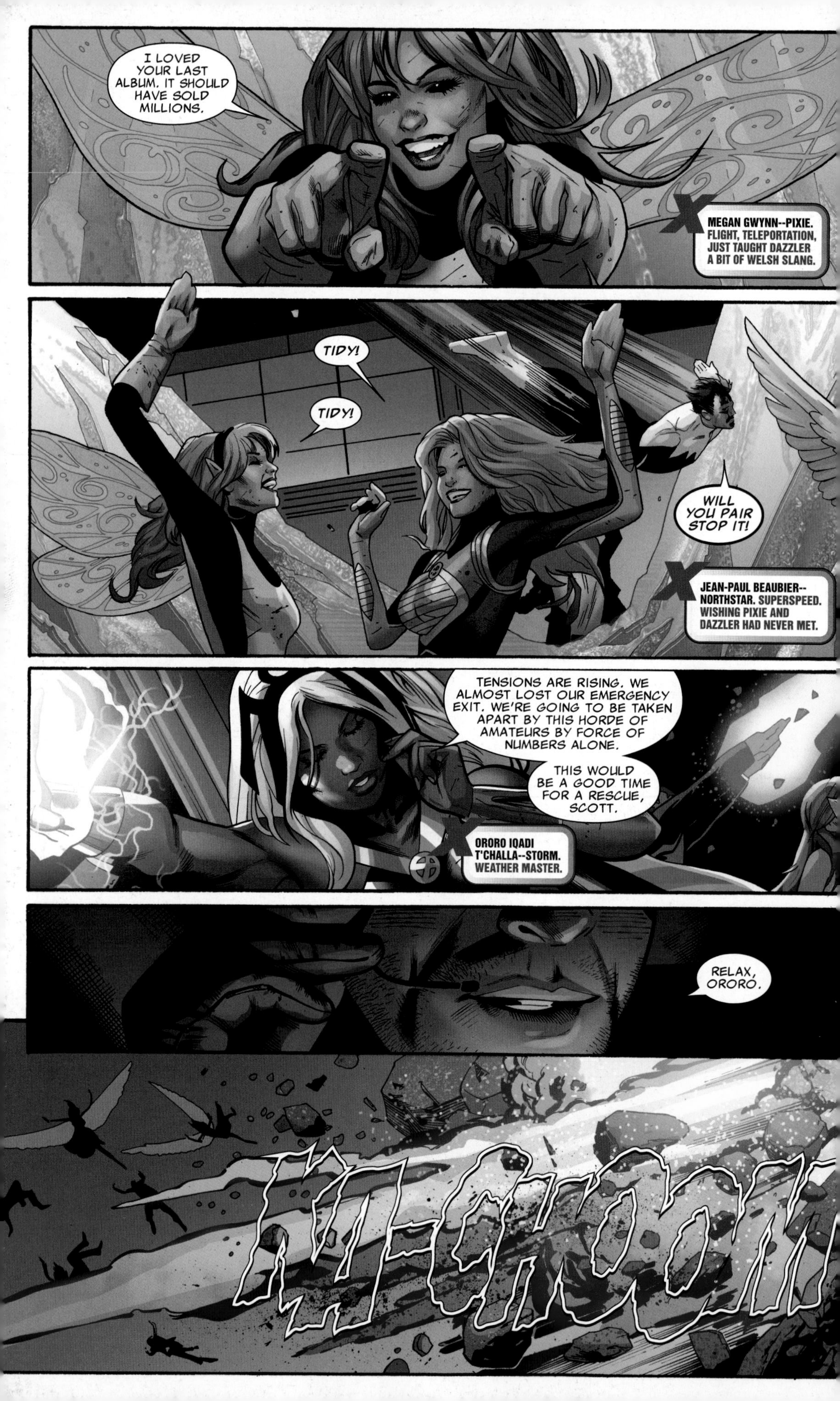
I LOVED YOUR LAST ALBUM. IT SHOULD HAVE SOLD MILLIONS.
MEGAN GWYNN--PIXIE. FLIGHT, TELEPORTATION, JUST TAUGHT DAZZLER A BIT OF WELSH SLANG.
TIDY!
TIDY!
WILL YOU PAIR STOP IT!
JEAN-PAUL BEAUBIER--NORTHSTAR. SUPERSPEED. WISHING PIXIE AND DAZZLER HAD NEVER MET.
TENSIONS ARE RISING. WE ALMOST LOST OUR EMERGENCY EXIT. WE'RE GOING TO BE TAKEN APART BY THIS HORDE OF AMATEURS BY FORCE OF NUMBERS ALONE.
THIS WOULD BE A GOOD TIME FOR A RESCUE, SCOTT.
ORORO IQADI T'CHALLA--STORM. WEATHER MASTER.
RELAX, ORORO.

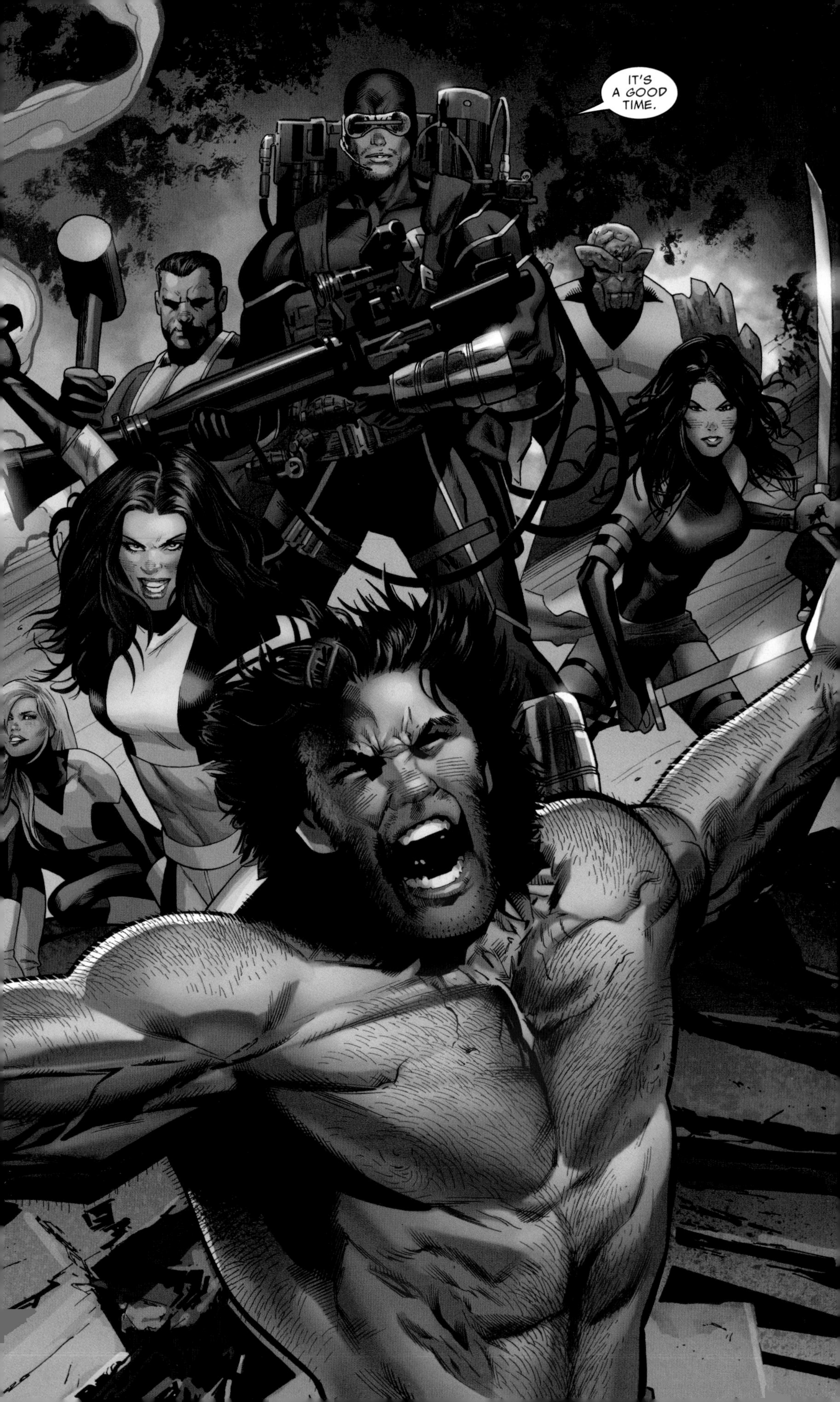
IT'S A GOOD TIME.

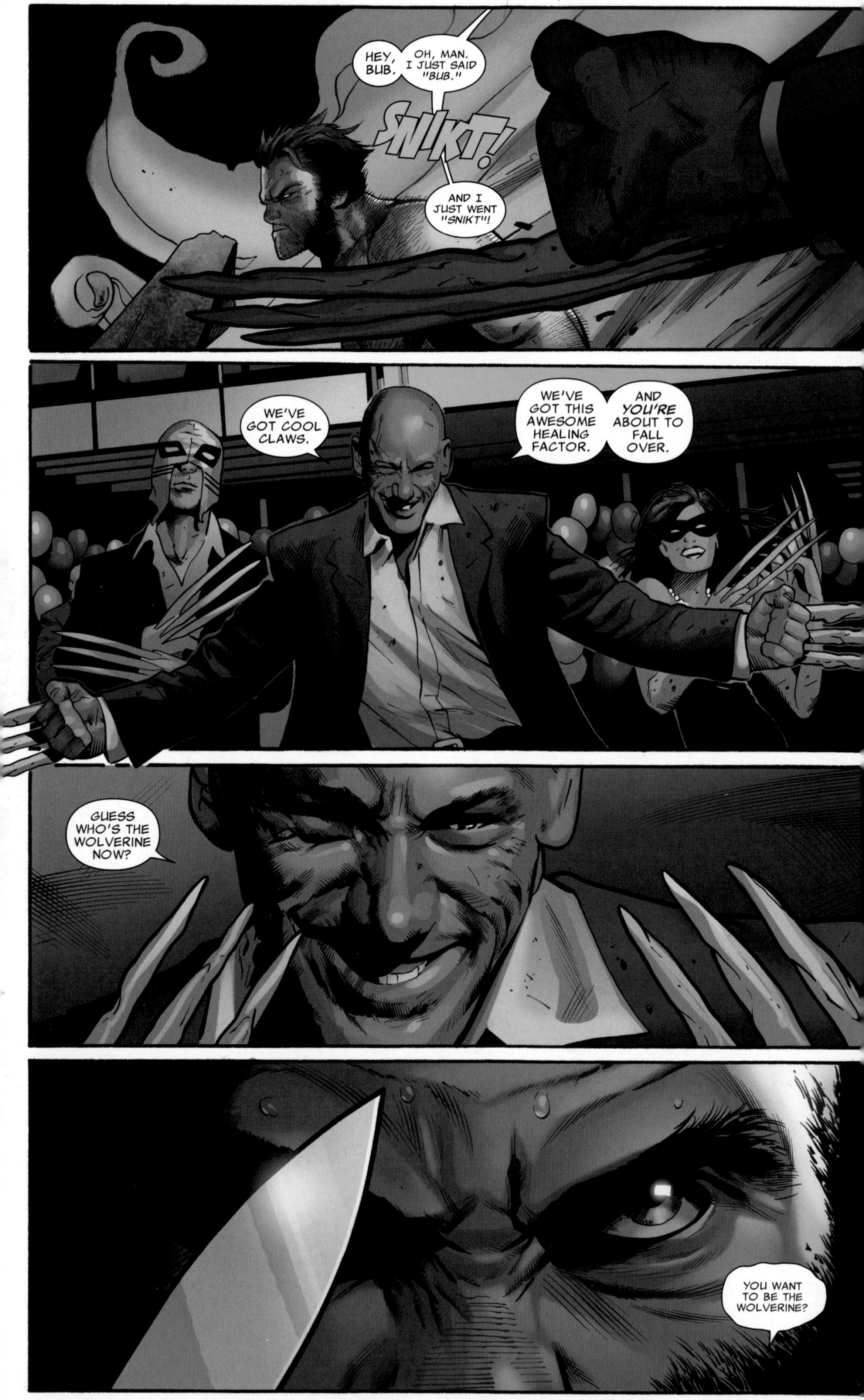
HEY, BUB.
OH, MAN. I JUST SAID "BUB."
SNIKT!
AND I JUST WENT "SNIKT"!
WE'VE GOT COOL CLAWS.
WE'VE GOT THIS AWESOME HEALING FACTOR.
AND YOU'RE ABOUT TO FALL OVER.
GUESS WHO'S THE WOLVERINE NOW?
YOU WANT TO BE THE WOLVERINE?

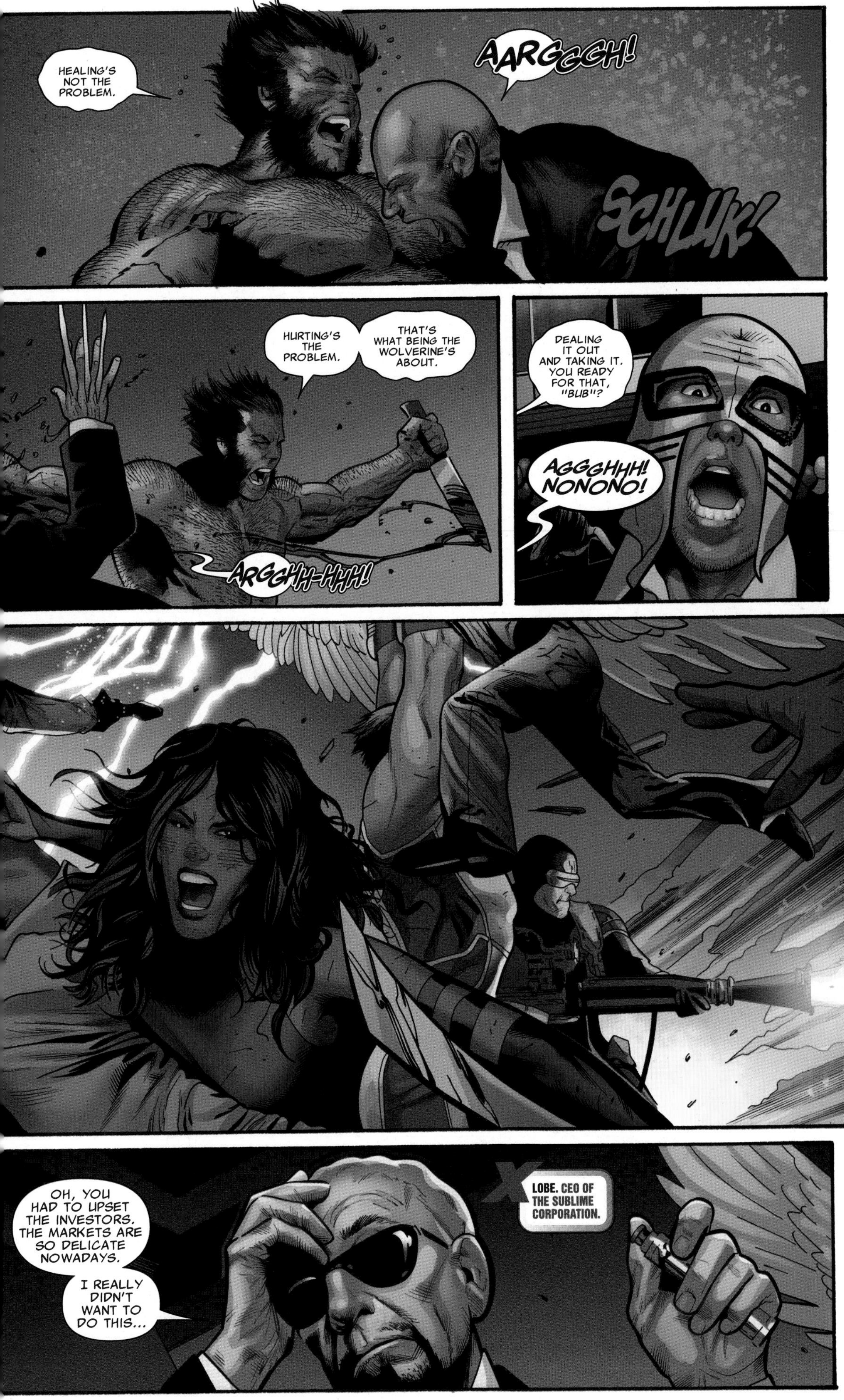
HEALING'S NOT THE PROBLEM.
AARGGGH!
SCHLUK!
HURTING'S THE PROBLEM.
THAT'S WHAT BEING THE WOLVERINE'S ABOUT.
ARGGHH-HHH!
DEALING IT OUT AND TAKING IT. YOU READY FOR THAT, "BUB"?
AGGGHHH! NONONO!
OH, YOU HAD TO UPSET THE INVESTORS. THE MARKETS ARE SO DELICATE NOWADAYS.
I REALLY DIDN'T WANT TO DO THIS...
LOBE. CEO OF THE SUBLIME CORPORATION.

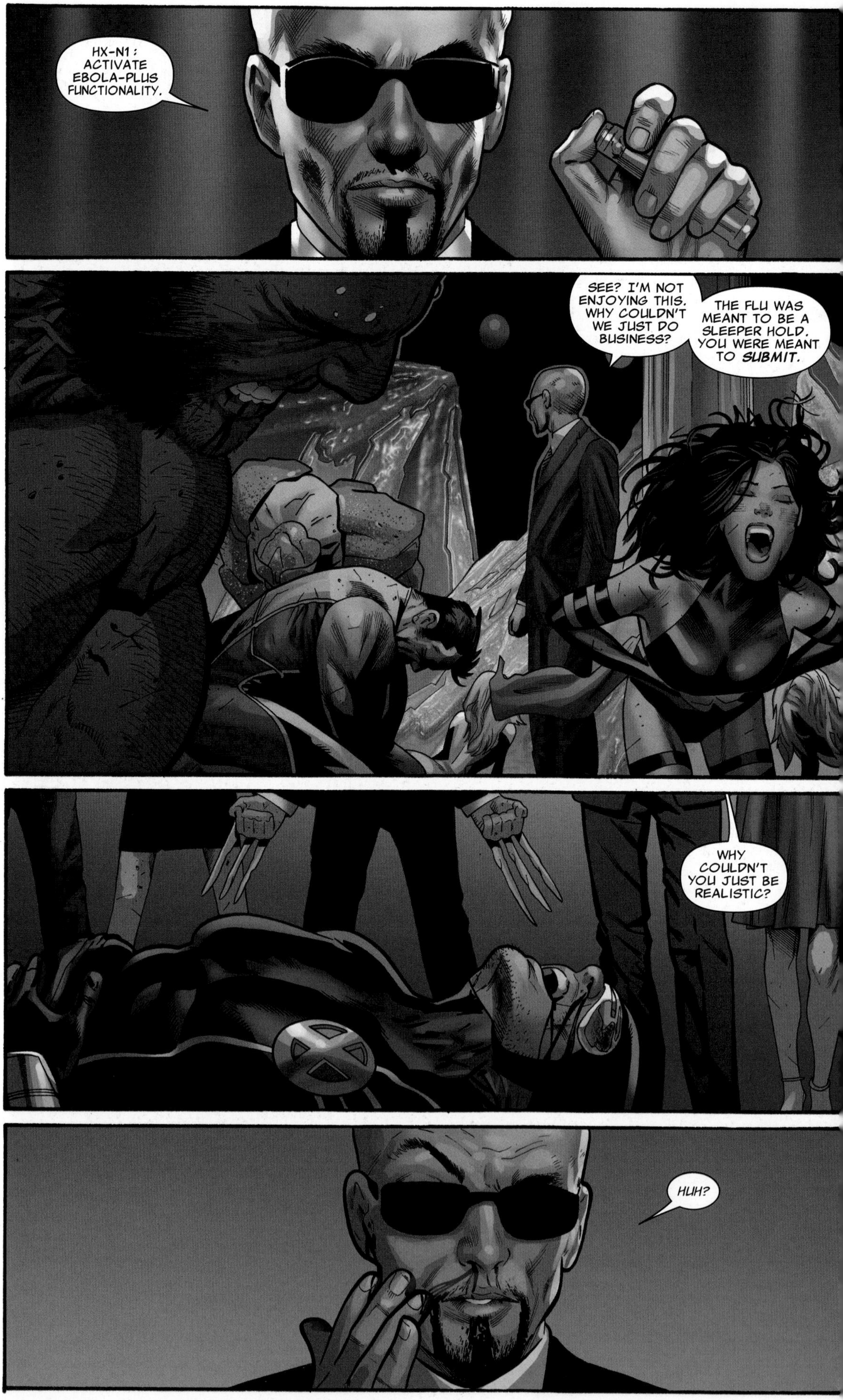
HX-N1: ACTIVATE EBOLA-PLUS FUNCTIONALITY.
SEE? I'M NOT ENJOYING THIS. WHY COULDN'T WE JUST DO BUSINESS?
THE FLU WAS MEANT TO BE A SLEEPER HOLD. YOU WERE MEANT TO SUBMIT.
WHY COULDN'T YOU JUST BE REALISTIC?
HUH?

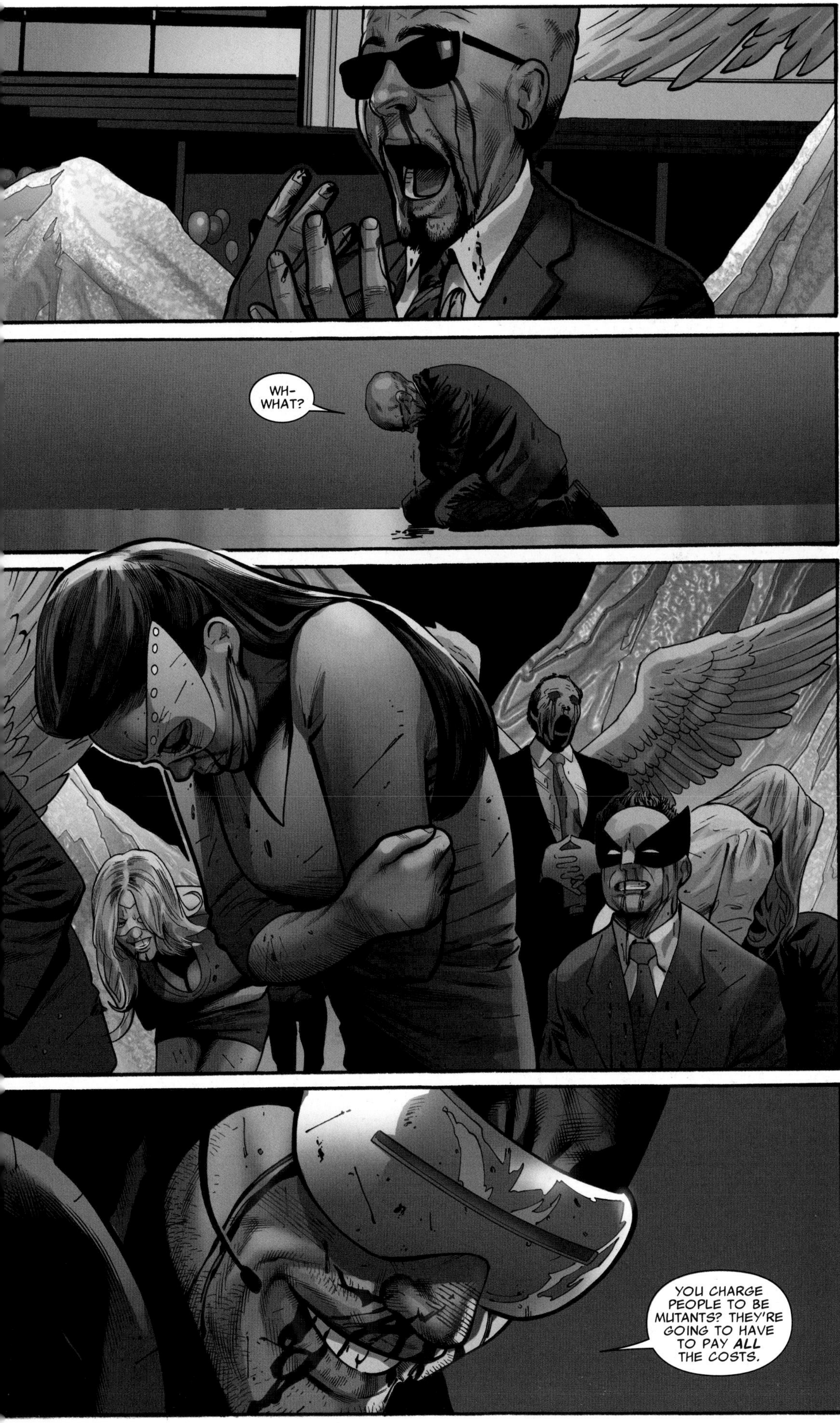
WH-
WHAT?
YOU CHARGE PEOPLE TO BE MUTANTS? THEY'RE GOING TO HAVE TO PAY ALL THE COSTS.

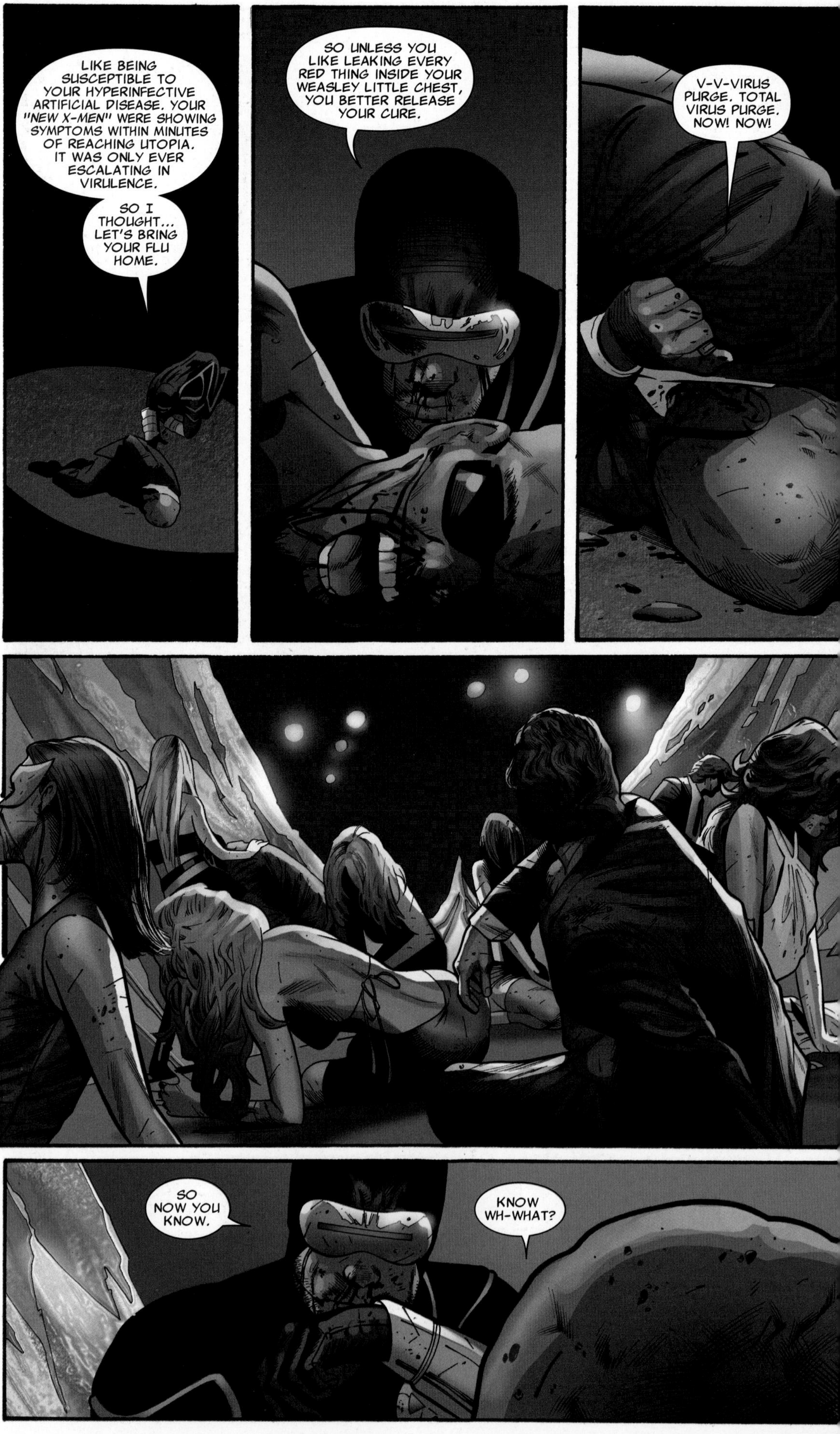

LIKE BEING SUSCEPTIBLE TO YOUR HYPERINFECTIVE ARTIFICIAL DISEASE. YOUR "NEW X-MEN" WERE SHOWING SYMPTOMS WITHIN MINUTES OF REACHING UTOPIA. IT WAS ONLY EVER ESCALATING IN VIRULENCE.
SO I THOUGHT... LET'S BRING YOUR FLU HOME.
SO UNLESS YOU LIKE LEAKING EVERY RED THING INSIDE YOUR WEASLEY LITTLE CHEST, YOU BETTER RELEASE YOUR CURE.
V-V-VIRUS PURGE. TOTAL VIRUS PURGE. NOW! NOW!
SO NOW YOU KNOW.
KNOW WH-WHAT?

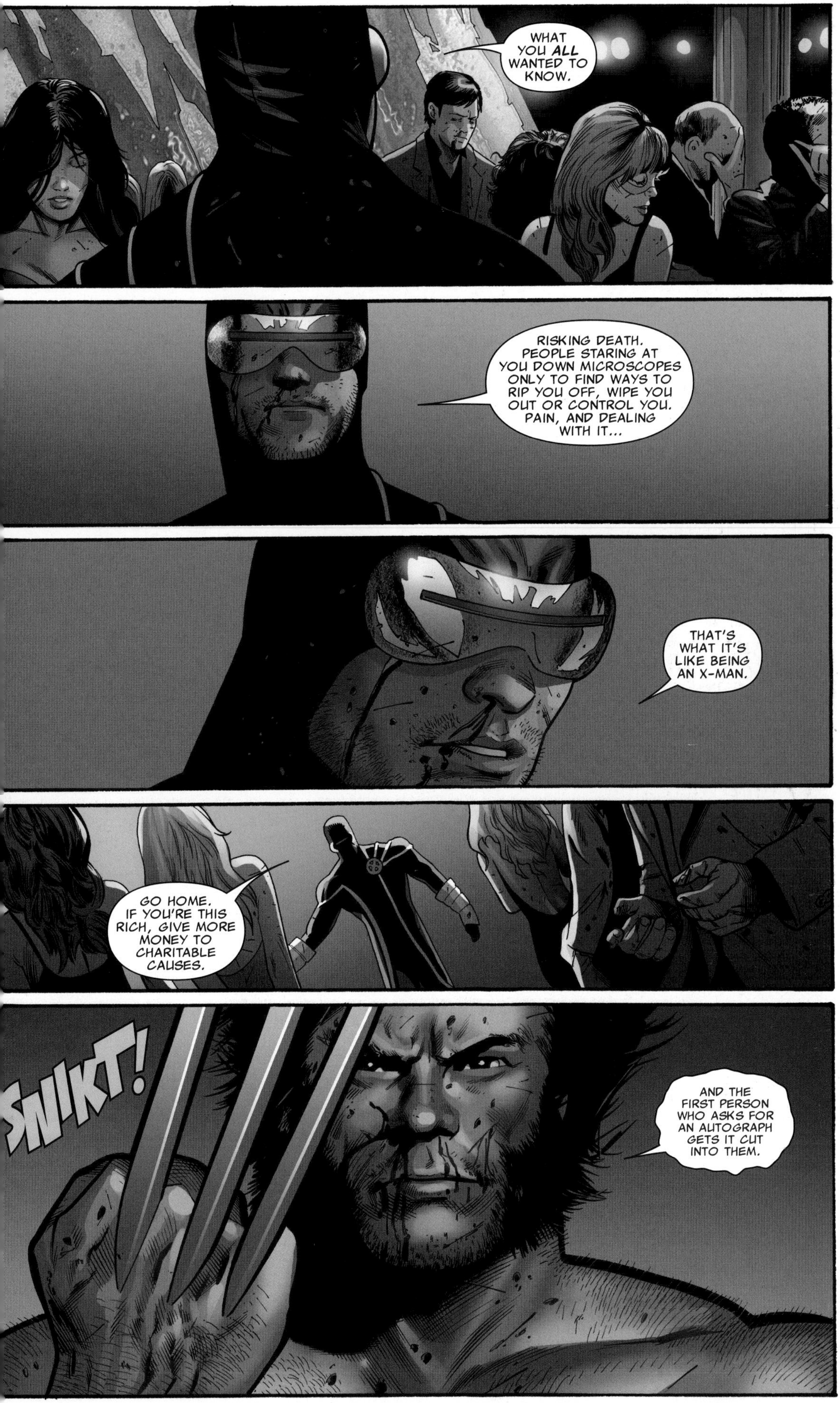
WHAT YOU ALL WANTED TO KNOW.
RISKING DEATH. PEOPLE STARING AT YOU DOWN MICROSCOPES ONLY TO FIND WAYS TO RIP YOU OFF, WIPE YOU OUT OR CONTROL YOU. PAIN, AND DEALING WITH IT...
THAT'S WHAT IT'S LIKE BEING AN X-MAN.
GO HOME. IF YOU'RE THIS RICH, GIVE MORE MONEY TO CHARITABLE CAUSES.
SNIKT!
AND THE FIRST PERSON WHO ASKS FOR AN AUTOGRAPH GETS IT CUT INTO THEM.

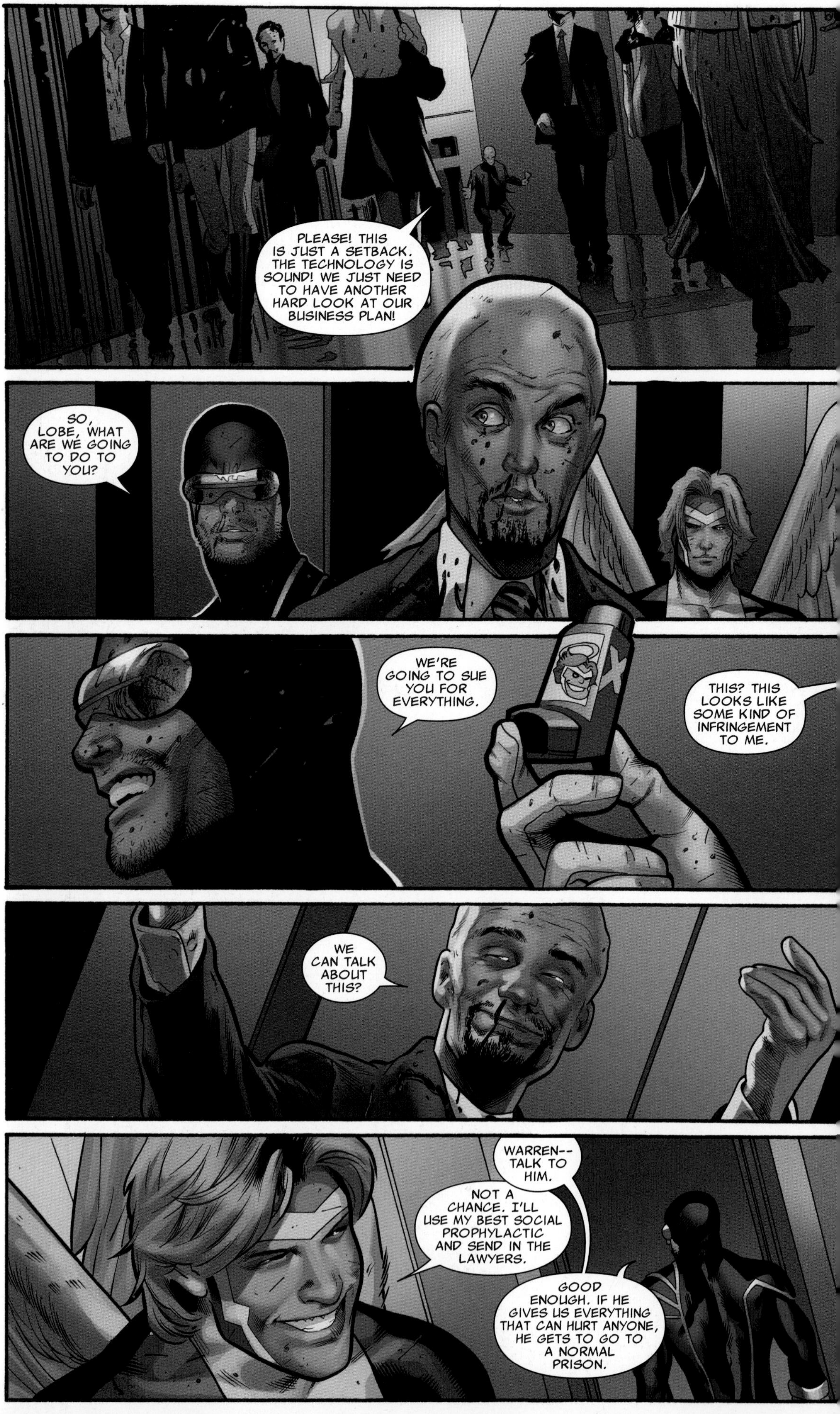
PLEASE! THIS IS JUST A SETBACK. THE TECHNOLOGY IS SOUND! WE JUST NEED TO HAVE ANOTHER HARD LOOK AT OUR BUSINESS PLAN!
SO, LOBE, WHAT ARE WE GOING TO DO TO YOU?
WE'RE GOING TO SUE YOU FOR EVERYTHING.
THIS? THIS LOOKS LIKE SOME KIND OF INFRINGEMENT TO ME.
WE CAN TALK ABOUT THIS?
WARREN-- TALK TO HIM.
NOT A CHANCE. I'LL USE MY BEST SOCIAL PROPHYLACTIC AND SEND IN THE LAWYERS.
GOOD ENOUGH. IF HE GIVES US EVERYTHING THAT CAN HURT ANYONE, HE GETS TO GO TO A NORMAL PRISON.

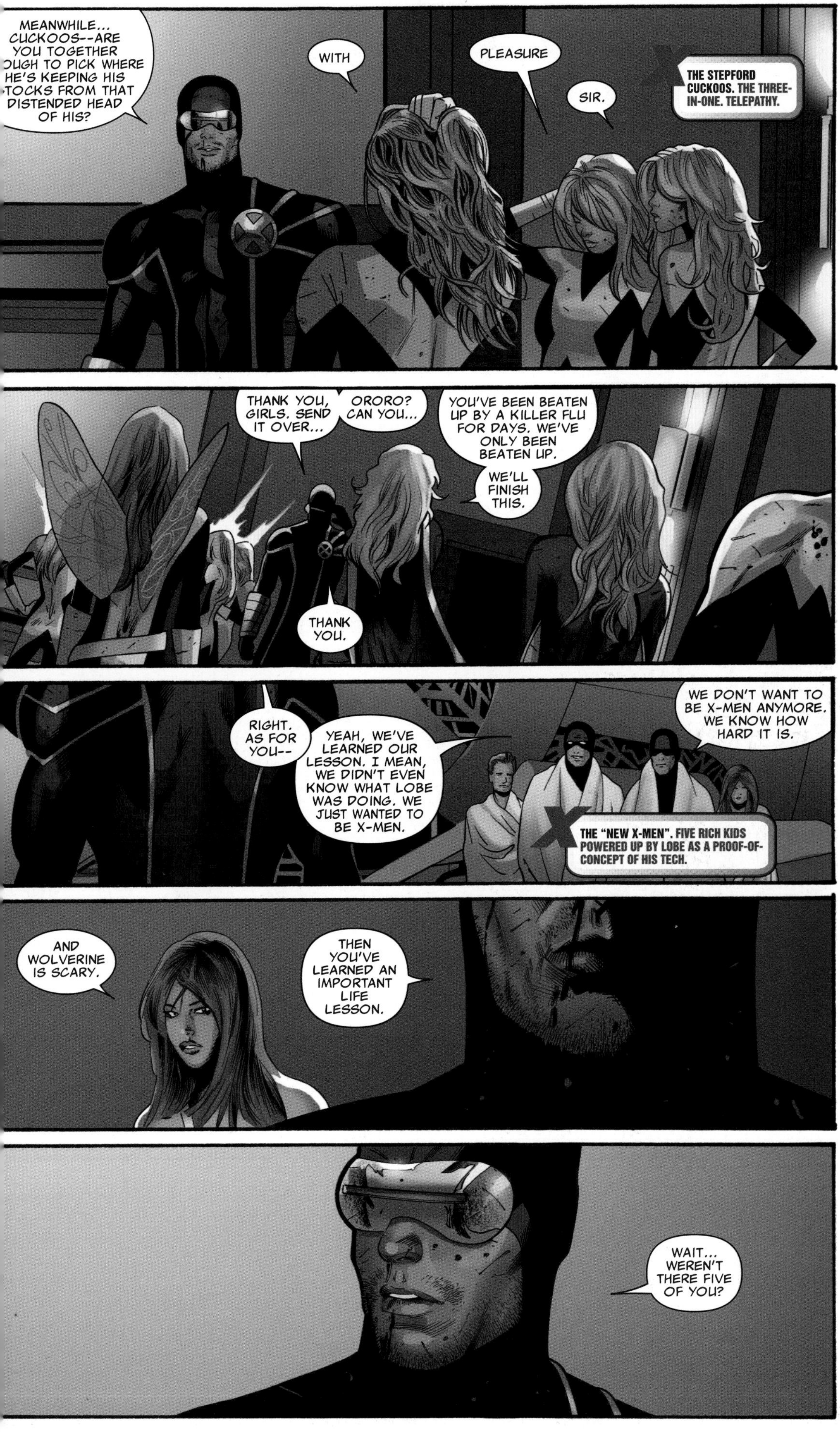

MEANWHILE... CUCKOOS--ARE YOU TOGETHER OUGH TO PICK WHERE HE'S KEEPING HIS TOCKS FROM THAT DISTENDED HEAD OF HIS?
WITH
PLEASURE
SIR.
THE STEPFORD CUCKOOS. THE THREE-IN-ONE. TELEPATHY.
THANK YOU, GIRLS. SEND IT OVER...
ORORO? CAN YOU...
YOU'VE BEEN BEATEN UP BY A KILLER FLU FOR DAYS. WE'VE ONLY BEEN BEATEN UP.
WE'LL FINISH THIS.
THANK YOU.
RIGHT. AS FOR YOU--
YEAH, WE'VE LEARNED OUR LESSON. I MEAN, WE DIDN'T EVEN KNOW WHAT LOBE WAS DOING. WE JUST WANTED TO BE X-MEN.
WE DON'T WANT TO BE X-MEN ANYMORE. WE KNOW HOW HARD IT IS.
THE "NEW X-MEN". FIVE RICH KIDS POWERED UP BY LOBE AS A PROOF-OF-CONCEPT OF HIS TECH.
AND WOLVERINE IS SCARY.
THEN YOU'VE LEARNED AN IMPORTANT LIFE LESSON.
WAIT... WEREN'T THERE FIVE OF YOU?

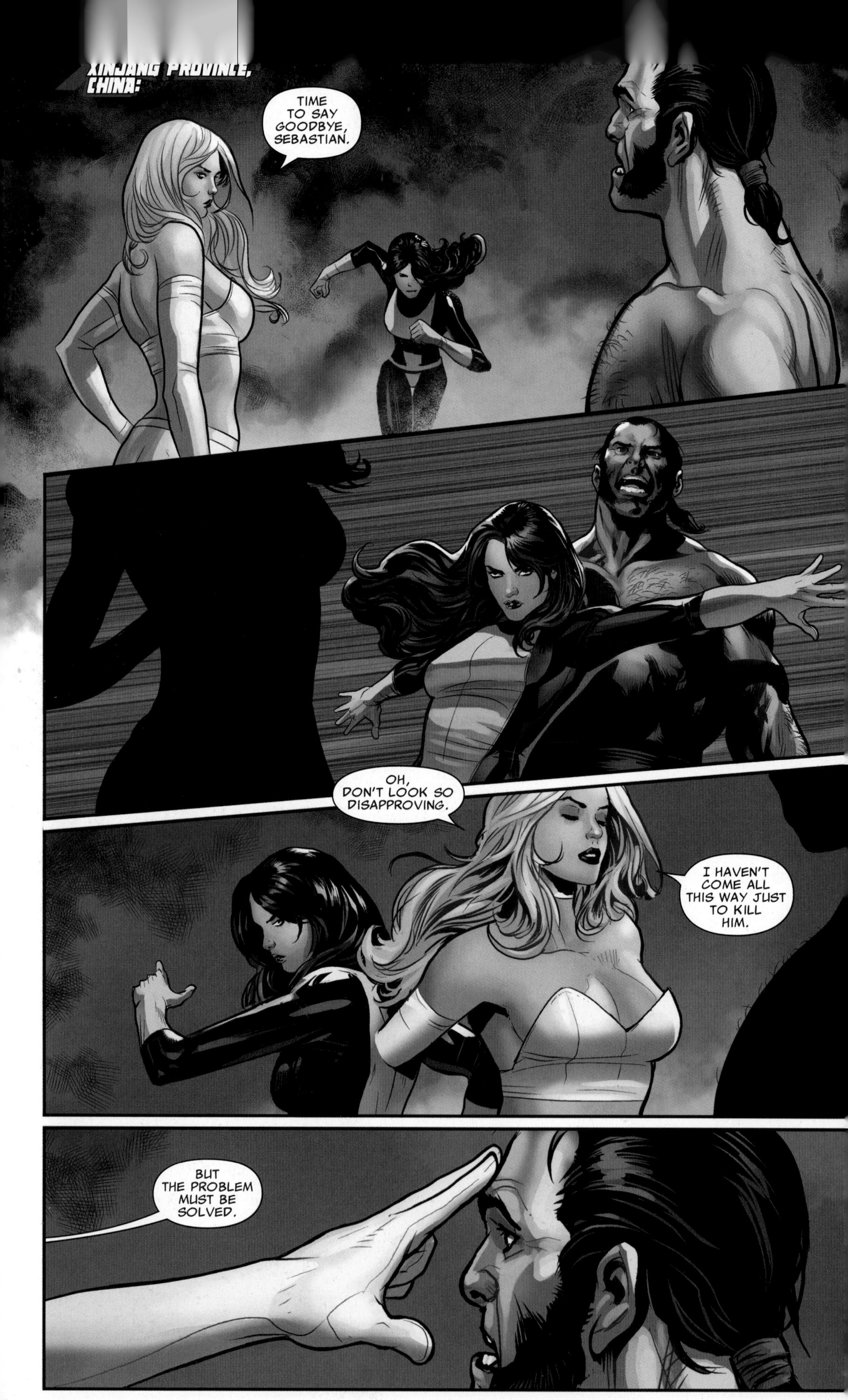
XINJANG PROVINCE, CHINA:
TIME TO SAY GOODBYE, SEBASTIAN.
OH, DON'T LOOK SO DISAPPROVING.
I HAVEN'T COME ALL THIS WAY JUST TO KILL HIM.
BUT THE PROBLEM MUST BE SOLVED.

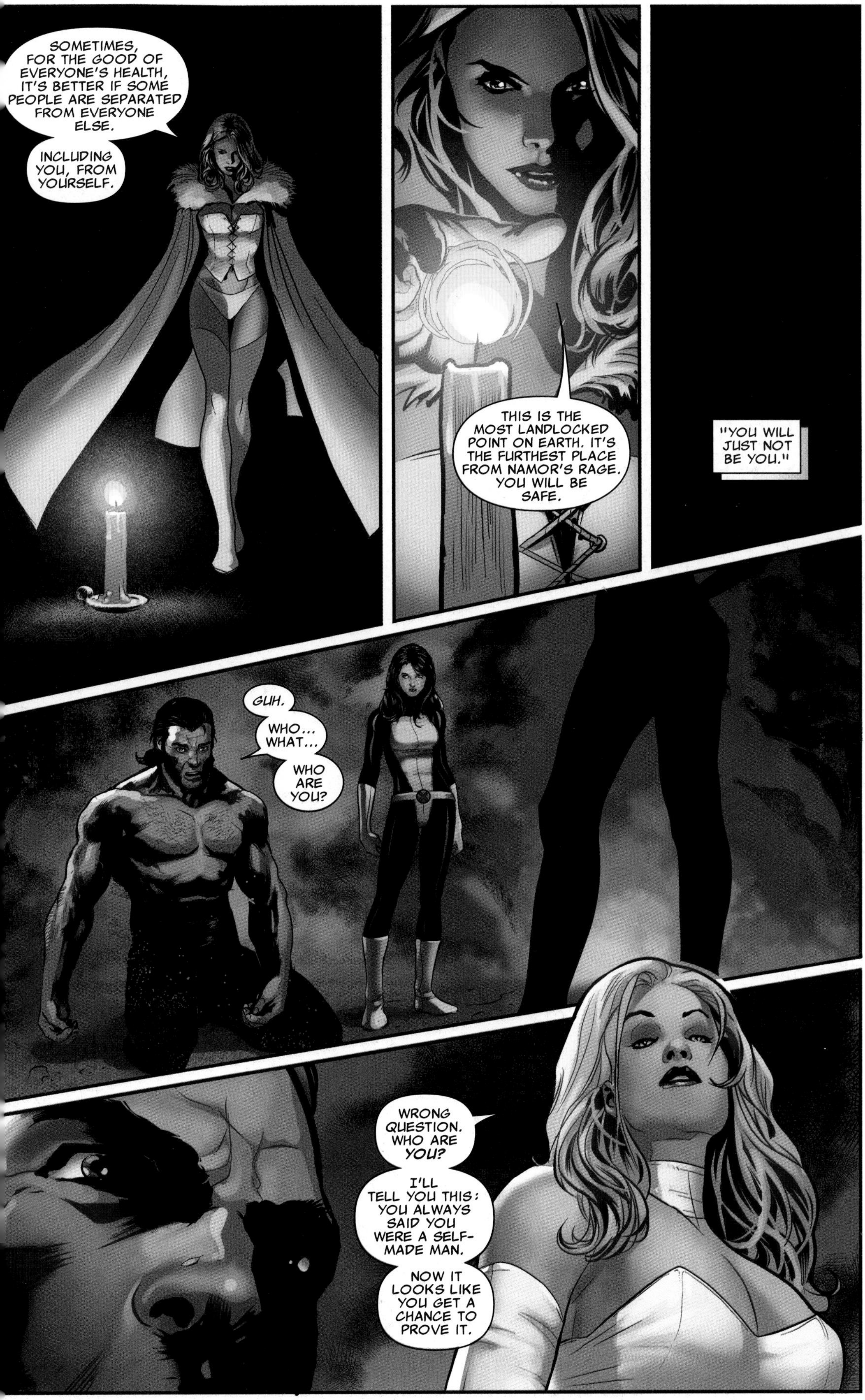
SOMETIMES, FOR THE GOOD OF EVERYONE'S HEALTH, IT'S BETTER IF SOME PEOPLE ARE SEPARATED FROM EVERYONE ELSE.
INCLUDING YOU, FROM YOURSELF.
THIS IS THE MOST LANDLOCKED POINT ON EARTH. IT'S THE FURTHEST PLACE FROM NAMOR'S RAGE. YOU WILL BE SAFE.
"YOU WILL JUST NOT BE YOU."
GUH.
WHO... WHAT...
WHO ARE YOU?
WRONG QUESTION. WHO ARE *YOU?*
I'LL TELL YOU THIS: YOU ALWAYS SAID YOU WERE A SELF-MADE MAN.
NOW IT LOOKS LIKE YOU GET A CHANCE TO PROVE IT.

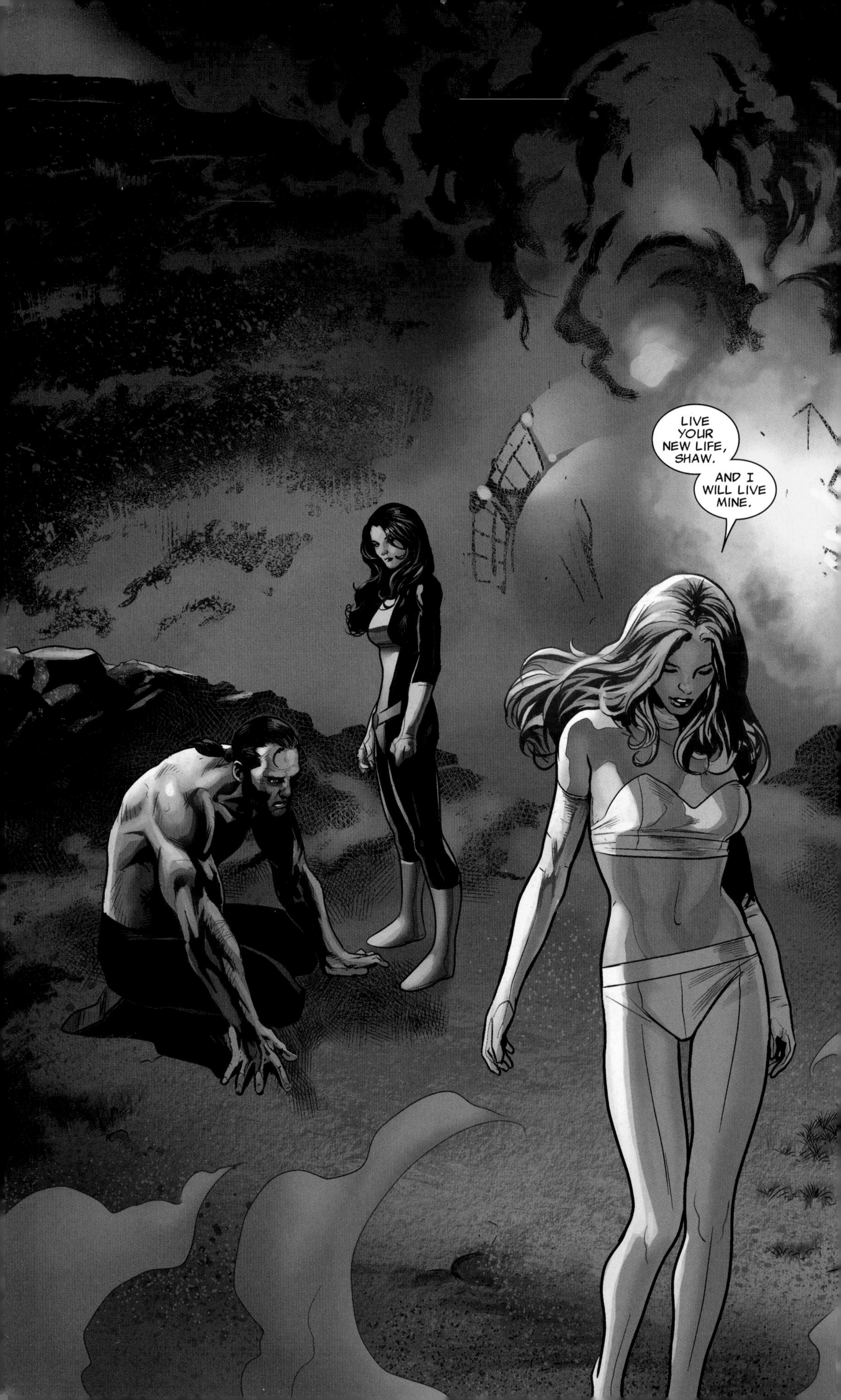
LIVE YOUR NEW LIFE, SHAW.
AND I WILL LIVE MINE.

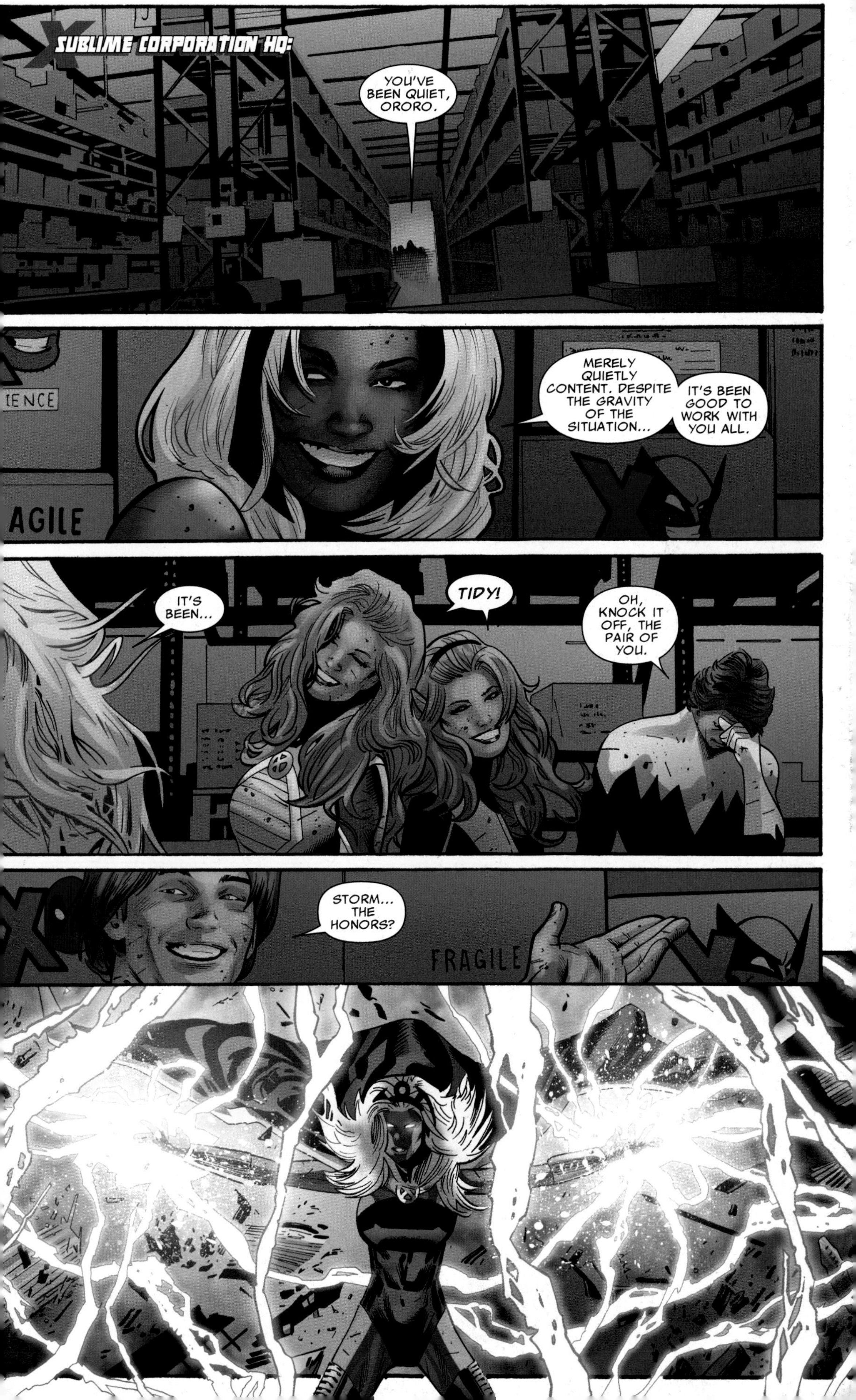
SUBLIME CORPORATION HQ:
YOU'VE BEEN QUIET, ORORO.
MERELY QUIETLY CONTENT. DESPITE THE GRAVITY OF THE SITUATION...
IT'S BEEN GOOD TO WORK WITH YOU ALL.
IENCE
AGILE
IT'S BEEN...
TIDY!
OH, KNOCK IT OFF, THE PAIR OF YOU.
STORM... THE HONORS?
FRAGILE

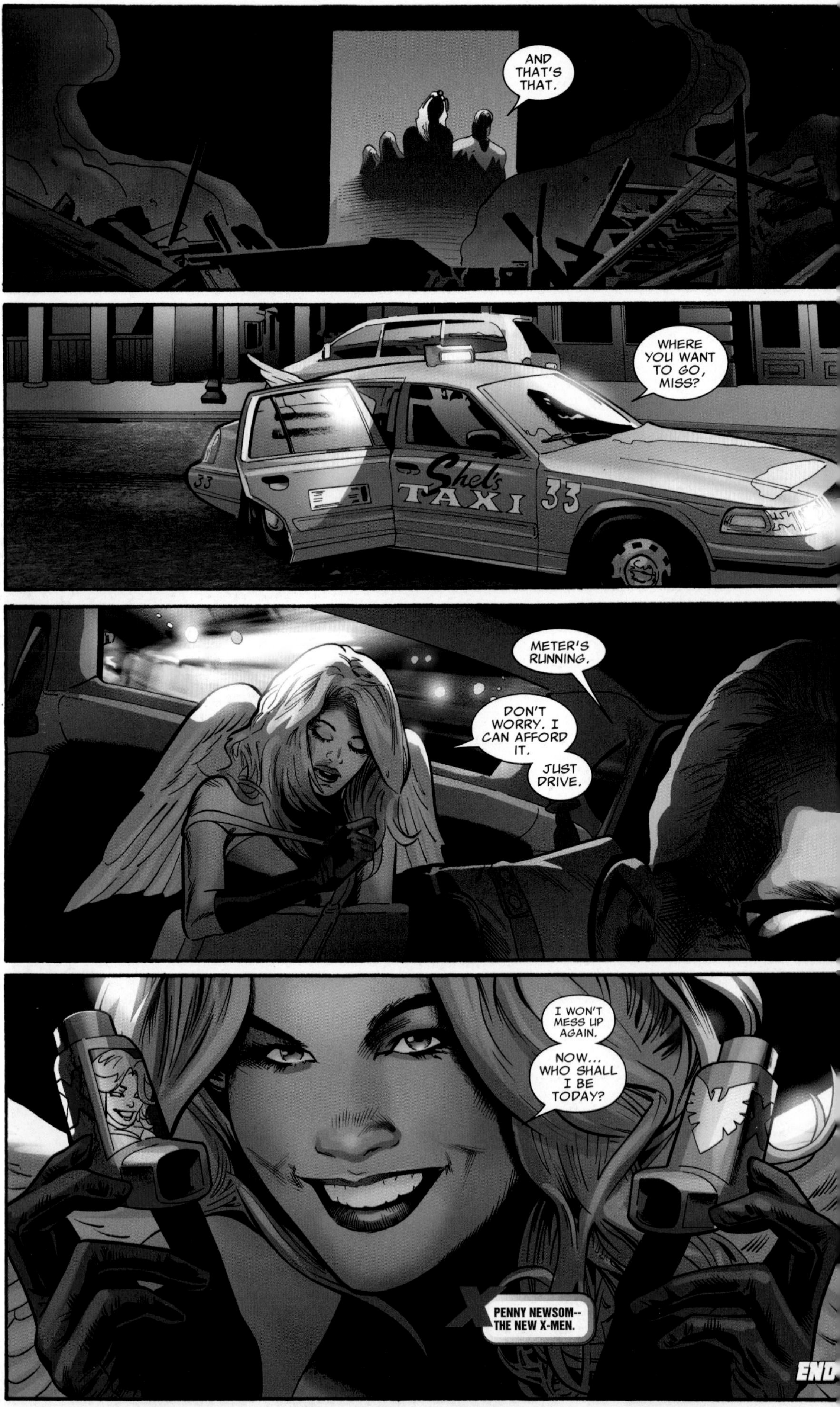

AND THAT'S THAT.
WHERE YOU WANT TO GO, MISS?
METER'S RUNNING.
DON'T WORRY. I CAN AFFORD IT.
JUST DRIVE.
I WON'T MESS UP AGAIN.
NOW... WHO SHALL I BE TODAY?
PENNY NEWSOM-- THE NEW X-MEN.
END

#534 Variant by Janet Lee

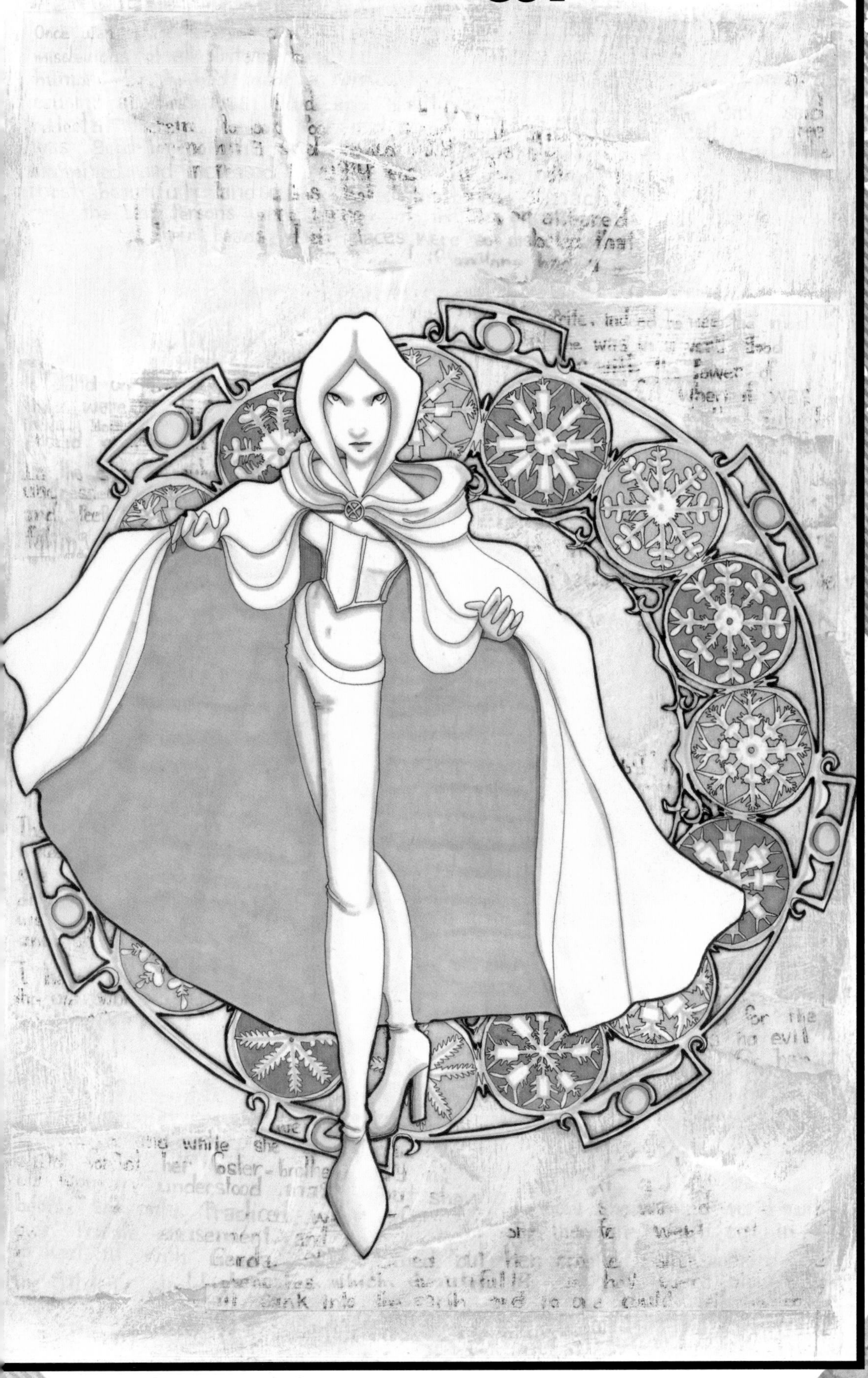

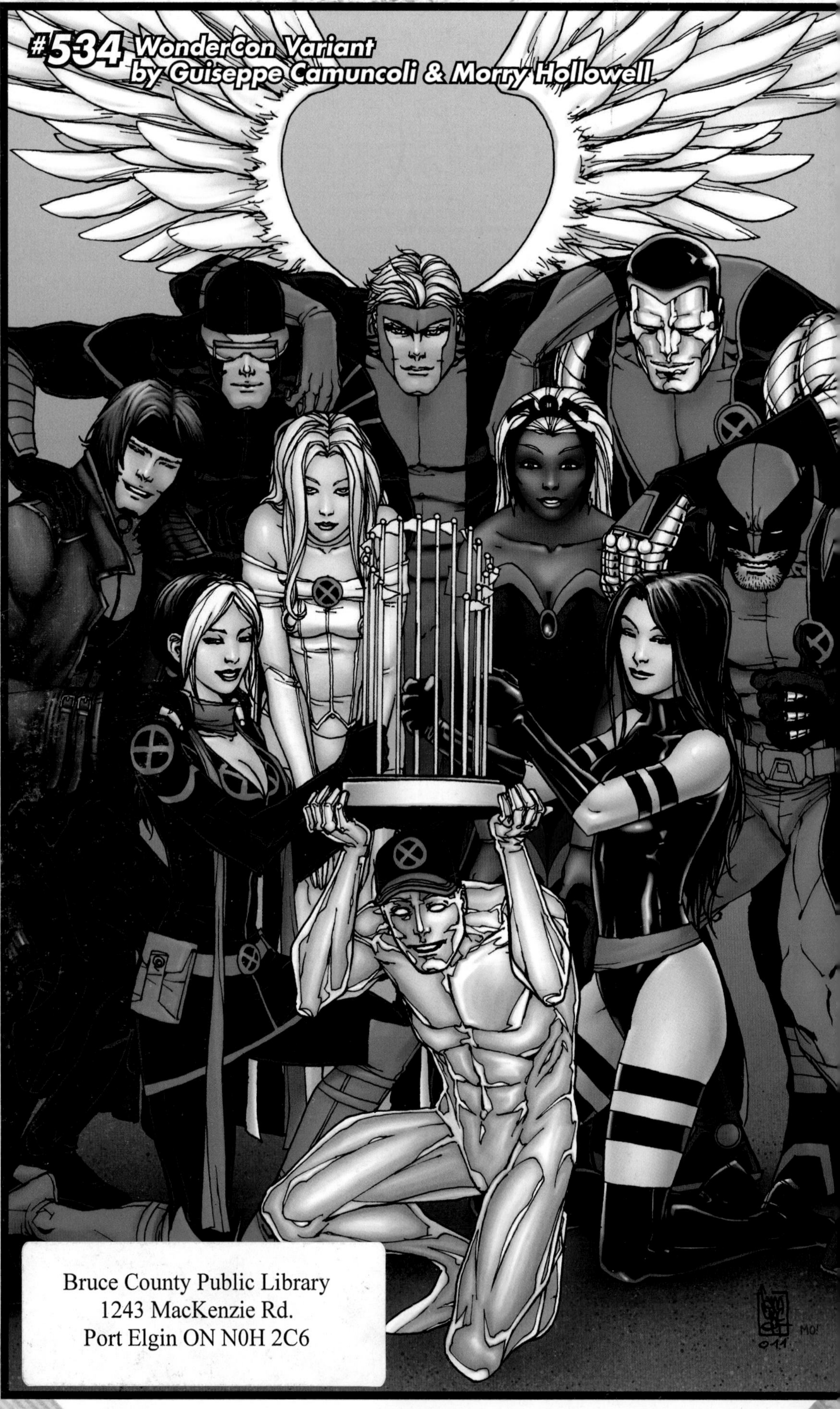
#534 WonderCon Variant
by Guiseppe Camuncoli & Morry Hollowell